Elizabeth Bishop at Work

Elizabeth Bishop at Work

Eleanor Cook

Harvard University Press

CAMBRIDGE, MASSACHUSETTS
LONDON, ENGLAND
2016

First printing

Library of Congress Cataloging-in-Publication Data

Names: Cook, Eleanor, author.
Title: Elizabeth Bishop at work / Eleanor Cook.
Description: Cambridge, Massachusetts : Harvard University Press, 2016. |
    Includes bibliographical references and index.
Identifiers: LCCN 2016023341 | ISBN 9780674660175 (hardcover : alk. paper)
Subjects: LCSH: Bishop, Elizabeth, 1911–1979—Criticism and interpretation. |
    American poetry—20th century—Criticism and interpretation.
Classification: LCC PS3503.I785 Z624 2016 | DDC 811/.54—dc23 LC record
    available at https://lccn.loc.gov/2016023341

Book design by Dean Bornstein

For Katherine and Joshua
one of these days . . .

Contents

Abbreviations

All quotations from Bishop's poetry, unless otherwise indicated, are from Elizabeth Bishop, *Poems* (New York: Farrar, Straus and Giroux, 2011).

Barker letters: Elizabeth Bishop Letters to Ilse and Kit Barker, Manuscripts Division (C0270), Princeton University Library, Princeton, NJ.

Concordance: *A Concordance to Elizabeth Bishop's Poetry,* comp. Anne Merrill Greenhalgh (New York: Garland, 1985).

CProse: Elizabeth Bishop, *The Collected Prose* (New York: Farrar, Straus and Giroux, 1984).

EAP: *Edgar Allan Poe & the Juke-Box: Uncollected Poems, Drafts, and Fragments,* ed. Alice Quinn (New York: Farrar, Straus and Giroux, 2006).

L: *One Art: Letters,* ed. Robert Giroux (New York: Farrar, Straus and Giroux, 1994).

LEBNY: *Elizabeth Bishop and the New Yorker: The Complete Correspondence,* ed. Joelle Biele (New York: Farrar, Straus and Giroux), 2011.

LEBRL: *Words in Air: The Complete Correspondence between Elizabeth Bishop and Robert Lowell,* ed. Thomas Travisano with Saskia Hamilton (New York: Farrar, Straus and Giroux, 2008).

LOA: *Elizabeth Bishop: Poems, Prose, and Letters,* ed. Robert Giroux and Lloyd Schwartz (New York: Library of America, 2008).

MacMahon: Candace W. MacMahon, *Elizabeth Bishop: A Bibliography, 1927–1979* (Charlottesville: University of Virginia Press, 1980).

NYPL: New York Public Library; Berg: Henry W. and Albert A. Berg Collection of English and American Literature; FSG: Farrar, Straus and Giroux, Inc., Records, 1885–1997.

OED: *Oxford English Dictionary*, 2nd ed. (Oxford, UK: Clarendon, 1989); also available online, updated at www.oed.com.

Schwarz and Estess: Lloyd Schwartz and Sybil P. Estess, ed., *Elizabeth Bishop and Her Art* (Ann Arbor: University of Michigan Press, 1984).

Swenson-Bishop letters: May Swenson Papers, Olin Library, Washington University, St. Louis, MO.

Vassar: Elizabeth Bishop Papers, Archives and Special Collections, Vassar College Libraries, Poughkeepsie, NY.

Elizabeth Bishop at Work

Introduction

You might say that this book began years ago when I tore Elizabeth Bishop's poem "North Haven" out of the *New Yorker*. It is an elegy for her close friend and fellow poet Robert Lowell, and I found it immensely moving: intimate and grave and sorrowing all at once. I found its art breathtaking. Here was a writer who knew the fountainhead of all English elegy, Milton's *Lycidas*, and who had absorbed it as well as the tradition descending from it, including Walt Whitman's elegy for Lincoln, "When Lilacs Last in the Dooryard Bloom'd." Here was a writer who had just added a noteworthy elegy to that tradition. Since then, my sense of her breathtaking art has only grown, along with curiosity about exactly how she did it, this master poet of the twentieth century.

Or you might say that this book began when I was able to read some of Bishop's other poems much more fully: "The Map," "Paris, 7 A.M.," "Brazil, January 1, 1502," and more. Here were poems that were small worlds, evoking a time, a place, an ambience. They were packed with implication and intimation, packed so easily and quietly that their richness could be overlooked.

I myself would say that this book began when I broke my leg and was confined. I decided to use the occasion to look closely at all Bishop's collected poems, starting from the basics of her art: diction (the most obvious, at least nowadays), rhythm and meter ("I fought the battle of the iambic pentameter," she once said), and so on.[1] A general reader may suppose that this kind of close work has already been done with Bishop's poems. After all, she was well known for her perfectionism, for years spent on one poem until it finally satisfied her. ("Do you still hang your words in air, ten years / unfinished?" Lowell once wrote.)[2] But close reading fell out of fashion in the academy, even close reading of such rich and packed work as Bishop's. She paid close attention to details, and surely we should too. (And since when did we not pay attention to details in anything that really matters to us?)

Along the way, the shape of her collections began to emerge, putting paid to any idea that her collections are a random miscellany with little sense of shaping.

So I have arranged this book chronologically, mapping Bishop's development and treating the poems she approved for publication over her lifetime, fewer than ninety.[3] Critics have recently lavished attention on her many drafts, published in 2006 as *Edgar Allan Poe & the Jukebox: Uncollected Poems, Drafts, and Fragments.* These drafts have their own interest, but they are mostly unfinished; and meantime, her well-known poems repay more attention.

The first few chapters alternate between overviews of Bishop's collections and explorations of one aspect of her art. After an initial chapter on two case studies, I have started with diction because that is what people usually associate first and foremost with poetry. And everyone uses some diction, some vocabulary. Chapter 2 is titled "Elizabeth Bishop's Ordinary Diction — Yes, *But* . . ." and is meant for all readers and writers. Experienced ones will not need it but may find some of Bishop's working methods suggestive. I have included in this chapter a few short exercises for student writers. Similar exercises on other topics treated in this book should be easy to devise. Chapter 4, "Diction on the Move," is centered on rhythm, prosody, and meter. It is of special interest to poets but hardly only to poets, for there is rhythm in all writing and speaking. Critics might observe that some of Bishop's effects have been there on the page for decades but are so quiet that they have apparently missed attention, for example, *terza rima* snaking its way down a longish poem. The effects of Old English (Anglo-Saxon) poetry in one short poem take us back to the astonishing ending of "At the Fishhouses," displaying its language in a new way.

By curiosity about Bishop's art, I don't mean the initial germ of a poem, because that is a mystery even for writers themselves. It may begin with an image or a rhythm or a dream or any number of unpredictable beginnings. Take rhythm. "Searching my soul, I find a fell —, fierce —, fearsome —/Yen to write sapphics": thus in the opening poem to a fifteen-poem section of Jay Macpherson's *Welcoming Disaster*.[4] All fifteen poems are written in expertly crafted sapphics —a handbook for poets wanting to study the form. Similarly, the initial germ of good metaphor, the sine qua non of poetry since Aristotle, remains a mystery.

Nor by curiosity about Bishop's art do I mean the biographical or psychological factors that go into making a poem. In fact, I found myself frustrated by those who were fascinated by her biography but not by her work. Of course biography matters for any artist, but only indirectly. It's what Aristotle called the efficient cause of an art, the agency. For Bishop, art was a sufficient end in itself — not an absolute end, a sufficient end, just as the art of medicine is a sufficient end in itself for the surgeon while working over the operating table. As illustration, see Bishop's note late in life about refusing to appear in an anthology of women poets, a note not widely known. She offered it to the anthologist for possible publication:

Undoubtedly gender does play an important part in the making of any art, but art is art and to separate writings, paintings, musical compositions, etc., into two sexes is to emphasize values in them that are *not* art.[5]

In biographical criticism, there is sometimes exclusive emphasis on Bishop's memories of her tragic childhood. (Her father died in 1911 when she was a few months old, and her mother, after several breakdowns, was confined permanently to a mental hospital in 1916. Bishop never saw her again.) Of course Bishop's memories of her difficult childhood enter into her art. Art is a way of ordering things, especially painful memories, as David Kalstone says in his *Becoming a Poet*.[6] Herbert Marks in "Elizabeth Bishop's Art of Memory," by means of subtle and persuasive readings of Bishop's poems, shows how she "controls the past more cunningly than any other modern poet."[7] What I want to emphasize is something different. By Bishop's own testimony, other early memories were vital too, for example, early nursery rhymes and hymns. "One of my grandmothers was great at reading old English ballads, nursery rhymes, riddles and so on, and I think I took to it [poetry] in that way very easily, without thinking much about it."[8] "I'm full of hymns, by the way — after church-going in Nova Scotia, boarding school, and singing in the college choir — and I often catch echoes of them in my own poems" (to Anne Stephenson, 8 Jan. 1964, LOA 862). In her story "Gwendolyn," the child who is her persona loves the sound of the name "Gwendolyn": "Its dactyl trisyllables could have gone on forever as far as I was concerned" (*CProse* 216). The art of poetry is also, in itself, a pleasure.

My curiosity about Bishop's art was only whetted by admirers who talked about her quiet art but didn't demonstrate it. The best comparison is to a quiet perfection in someone like Vermeer, another artist whose output was small. Randall Jarrell made the comparison in 1955: "her best poems . . . remind one of Vuillard or even, sometimes, of Vermeer" — and this was before her masterly collections, *Questions of Travel* (1965) and *Geography III* (1976).[9] Bishop was immensely pleased: "it has been one of my dreams that someday someone would think of Vermeer, without my saying it first, so now I think I can die in a fairly peaceful frame of mind, any old time, having struck the best critic of poetry going that way" (26 Dec. 1955, L 312). She went on to say that she had Vuillard in mind in connection with a long poem she'd been working on about an aunt, probably "In the Waiting Room."[10]

Art critics and art historians have looked hard at Vermeer and have helped viewers see just how he worked and thereby the richness of his effects. They have shown how some of his paintings are little worlds, personal and public both. So are some of Bishop's poems, for example, the two with which I have started, two early and very different poems, two case studies: "The Map" and "Casabianca." Sometimes, as with "The Map" and "Paris, 7 A.M." and more, a historical time and place is re-created. Take for example one small detail, the first line of "Paris, 7 A.M.," a 1937 poem: "I make a trip to each clock in the apartment." I simply assumed as a given that you might just check the clocks in what must be a sizable apartment. Other explanations sounded far-fetched, and for years things stayed that way until something — what? — triggered the obvious historical answer. (See Chapter 3.)

Again and again, as with Vermeer, details matter. We need to slow down when reading most poems, and all the more with Bishop's poems. As with reading a map or a painting, so with reading these poems. As the painter Fairfield Porter saw, "I think my admiration for Elizabeth Bishop's poems, aside from the fact that she has a descriptive visual mind, and aside from the fact that she has humor and is not sentimental, comes from an admiration of her relaxed line which allows each word enough space to be savored properly for what it is."[11]

Bishop is renowned for her "descriptive visual mind," her "famous eye." Like others, she noted the difficulty of seeing what is in front of us. "Some students even SEE flowers still, although I know only too well that TV has weakened the sense of reality so that very few students see anything the way it is in real life" (to John Frederick Nims, 6 Oct. 1979, L 638). One student wrote a story in which a character could see his face in a dinner plate. When Bishop said this was impossible, the "whole class, in unison, said 'Joy!'" — referring to an ad for soap. "I found this very disturbing," Bishop commented. "TV was real and no one had observed that it wasn't. Like when Aristotle was right and no one pointed out, for centuries, that women *don't* have fewer teeth than men."[12] She admired Darwin among other reasons because of the quality of his attention ("his endless heroic *observations*"), and she felt strongly about its lack in some writers: "I'm often thunderstruck by the helplessness, ignorance, ghastly taste, lack of worldly knowledge, and lack of observation of writers who are much more talented than I am. . . . Lack of observation seems to me one of the cardinal sins, responsible for so much cruelty, ugliness, dullness, bad manners — and general unhappiness, too" (to Anne Stevenson, 8 Jan. 1964, LOA 861, 860).[13] She played with the theory that women notice more than men on the whole: "But it is my chief complaint against the opposite sex, anyway — with the exception of poets and painters — they don't *see* things. They're always having ideas and theories, and not noticing the detail at hand. . . . I have a small theory of my own about this — that women have been *confined*, mostly — and in confinement details count. — They have to see the baby's ear; sewing makes you look closely. — They've had to do so much appeasing they do feel moods quickly, etc." (to Kit and Ilse Barker, 6 Feb. 1965, Barker letters; ellipsis in original).

Jerry Brotton has recently summarized the argument of Svetlana Alpers's influential 1983 book *The Art of Describing: Dutch Art in the Seventeenth Century:* that there was "a specifically Dutch visual tradition that Svetlana Alpers has called 'the art of describing' — the impulse to observe, record and define individuals, objects and places as real, without the kind of moral or symbolic associations which shaped Italian Renaissance art."[4] "Bishop was Dutch in her love of curiosities locatable in time and place," as James Merrill writes — and of more than curiosities (afterword to Kalstone, *Becoming a Poet*, 258). But as with Italian Renaissance art, and as with Lowell's poetry, moral or symbolic associations made such art appear more important, the standard to be imitated. Dutch painting was routinely judged inferior to this tradition. David Kalstone saw that the contrast between Italian Renaissance painters and Dutch painters was analogous to the perceived contrast between Lowell's poems and Bishop's (ibid., 258–259). Alpers's fine book demonstrated that the Italian tradition was not innately superior. Dutch painters were following a different and equally valid tradition. So also with Bishop's poems.

This book is about Elizabeth Bishop at work, at work at her desk, so to speak, reflecting, choosing. It is a study of development, of Bishop working *at* something, challenging herself to try new things, to expand in some area, to push boundaries, all the while keeping that natural tone she loved in Herbert and knew about from Coleridge's *Biographia Literaria*. It is also about what subjects Bishop worked at, what engaged her passionate attention, what her great skill focused on. It could be anything, of course, as with the oddities and beauties of experience. The natural world including its creatures always drew her, with an attention like Darwin's. She could not bear suffering or cruelty toward creatures ("The Armadillo," the cattle in "From Trollope's Journal," "Pink Dog") or toward the humans that creatures sometimes represented (victims of bombs, the beggars in "Pink Dog"). She knew that it is all too easy to disregard suffering at a distance ("The Armadillo"). Her social conscience bore on this kind of subject, especially after *North & South*.

Bishop had an acute sense of place throughout her work, which is a model for awareness of just where and how we inhabit the earth. Geography is at the core of her poems, a geography always rooted in history. Only with such roots can she write poems that are little worlds in themselves, poems like Vermeer's paintings. Some poems are not so much Vermeer paintings as they are Breughel or Orozco paintings: the counterpoint poems, the dream or nightmare material, the reverse side of the tapestry, the underside of outward life. Place includes that too. Any sense of place depends not only on what we see and hear and touch and smell and taste. It depends as much on what eyes we see through.

Sometimes Bishop is described as having a fresh eye that looked at things directly in a new way, what John Ruskin called an "innocent eye." But there is no such thing as Ruskin's "innocent eye," as E. H. Gombrich demonstrated apropos of mimesis in his classic study *Art and Illusion*.[15] "And have you read *Art &*

Illusion? by one Gombrich? — it is fascinating," Bishop wrote to Robert Lowell in July 1960 (L 388). Lowell replied, "Gombrich, funny, just after your [letter] I had dinner with Spender and he brought up Gombrich. I must read him" (9 Aug. 1960, LEBRL 338).

Gombrich showed conclusively that we cannot physically look at things "as they are," purging our eyes of all previous knowledge. We see through patterns that we learn very early, what he called *schemata* — not ideas or biases or conceptual viewpoints but the actual seeing of physical objects out there. The brain receives so many visual stimuli that it must filter out what is important, and the filtering starts when we are infants. When we grow older, paintings, drawings, photographs, and more give us patterns for seeing. We perforce use some filter, and artists paint what they see. One of Gombrich's most telling examples is a Chinese artist who painted a landscape from the Lake District in England (84–85). It came out looking like a Chinese wall hanging. The Chinese painter was not being perverse. That is what he saw, through an eye accustomed to find and highlight a few striking trees and animals in the foreground, a muted indistinct background, a soft light. When describing actual objects or landscapes in words, the same applies. Artists inherit such *schemata,* and good ones modify or extend or play with them. Only great artists will change the *schemata* themselves, as a Picasso or a Matisse or a Wordsworth or an Eliot will.

To this day, literary critics can speak of Bishop's famous eye as if it looked directly and freshly at the outside world, as if such a thing were possible. Randall Jarrell is frequently quoted: "all her poems have written underneath, *I have seen it.*"[16] How many people assume that this is easy? She knew better. It is the reordering of a given verbal *schema* that marks Bishop's mastery.

This book tries to demonstrate how a little of that mastery is achieved. It is designed to enhance our pleasure in her work, to increase what we learn from it, and just possibly to improve our own work a bit.

CHAPTER ONE

Land, Water, Fire, Air: Two Poems

Playing Detective

It was pure serendipity. I had walked over to the main library at
Vassar College, which I was visiting for the first time. The June
morning was bright and fresh, and the campus with its huge old
trees was inviting. So when I discovered that Archives and Special Collections did not open until ten A.M., I was tempted to
stroll around campus. Instead, being a little tired from traveling,
I opted for a quick exploration of the library and a glance over
some new books, shelved in a corner in the main foyer. Alan
Gurney's *Compass: A Story of Exploration and Innovation* was
one, and I pulled it down because I have always been interested
in exactly where I am located in the world — not just the name
of my home city, Toronto, but its latitude, its relation to the great
lake that it borders, and more. Similarly when I was traveling
up the Hudson Valley the day before. It was my first trip at
ground level, though I'd seen it often enough from the air, and
I followed it on a map, being fond of reading maps, both modern
and ancient. In that, I have a temperamental affinity with Elizabeth Bishop, the writer whose papers I had come to read. I
remember reading sections of Gurney's book with interest and
then rather idly looking in the index for the place-names from
"The Map," the first poem of her first collection: "Norway,"
"Newfoundland," "Labrador." This in turn led to a section on
the magnetic north and to several pages with illustrations of

the compass rose. At that sight, I sat up abruptly, because I knew what Bishop had chosen for a cover design for her first book, *North & South* (1946): a compass rose. I sat up for another reason too. Directions in "The Map" are highlighted, and "North" is one of them. I needed to think a bit more about that compass rose and also about the magnetic north and what part it played, if any, in Bishop's work.

A compass rose is a navigational device, familiar from some old maps or from modern charts. It consists of four main petal-like extensions from a central point, indicating north at the top, south at the bottom, east to the right, and west to the left. In the spaces between the main petals of a compass rose are four shorter petals, marking the forty-five-degree angles of northeast, southeast, southwest, and northwest. In the form that Bishop chose, there are eight, yet shorter petals indicating north-northeast and so on. She also chose straight-line petals in a diamond shape rather than curved ones. All the petals are shaded down one half of their length, so that adjacent half petals are always contrasted, making the directions easier to read. A circle encloses the entire compass rose, whose four large petals touch the perimeter. The device is repeated on the title page of *North & South* and also on Bishop's half-title page, but with a difference. Here, the letter *N* appears in large script at the center top above the compass rose, the letter *S* similarly at the center bottom, and the ampersand is centered on the right-hand side.

The compass rose is an essential device on any navigational chart, whether for mariners, fliers, or others. When navigating, you plot your course from point A to point B. Then by means of parallel rulers, you transfer it to the compass rose so that it passes through zero degrees. After that, you must make two simple mathematical calculations because of the magnetic north. You must take into account the angle of deviation between the true north and the magnetic north. You must also take into account the variation of the magnetic north, because it moves around, changing over many years.[1] Local magnetic forces, such as the strong magnetic force at the northernmost tip of Labrador, may or may not be pertinent. Without these calculations, you will be following a "false north." In the first draft of Bishop's last published poem, "Sonnet," the phrase "the false north" is attached to lines about the compass needle.[2] The metaphorical possibilities of a true north and a magnetic north are obvious.

It is a pity that the device was not reprinted in Bishop's 1969 *Complete Poems* or her *Complete Poems, 1927–1979* (1984) or her *Poems* (2011). Bishop cared about book design, and a thrice-repeated device calls attention to itself. (She even cared about the ampersand: "Don't you think the title would look well as *North & South*, using the '&' sign? It seems more forceful that way to me" [22 Jan. 1945, L 125].) The compass rose suggests something more than a collection of northerly and southerly poems. It suggests voyaging, sailing, and above all navigating — all the more if we happen to know that Bishop came from a seafaring family on her mother's side and was an ardent sailor herself. She told friends about her great-grandfather, who sailed the North and South American coasts and maybe more in the nineteenth century and who went down with his ship and all hands off Sable Island in 1866.[3] In her teens, she went to a camp at Wellfleet, Massachusetts, for the summers of 1924 through 1929, where she excelled at swimming and sailing and performing sea shanteys too ("Chronology," L xxiii). She was good enough at age eighteen to sail a fifteen-foot sailboat, along with two young friends, from Plymouth to York Harbor in Maine, arriving to the shock of one friend's parents.[4] Bishop was a water person. All her life,

Title page of *North & South*, showing compass rose

she lived on or near the ocean, and she loved to fish and to swim. "I love to go fishing, you know — any kind of fishing," she wrote to her Aunt Grace in 1963 when planning a visit to Nova Scotia (to Grace Bowers, 28 Oct. 1963, Vassar 25.11). Her 1932 Newfoundland travel diary mentions a sudden high dive into a gorge "amid loud cries," when a schooner sailed into sight of a swimmer clad as nature intended.[5] A friend recalled "very clearly" from a student summer on Cape Cod that Bishop said, "If anything ever happens to me, take me to the ocean."[6]

Over a year later, there was another bit of serendipity. In my mail, there arrived an issue of the Elizabeth Bishop Society of Nova Scotia newsletter with a poem by Keith Ekiss about his trip to Vassar to read Bishop's papers. When I read the last two lines, I once more sat up abruptly:

the compass rose painted on the library floor
predicted all the ways she would travel.

Within minutes, I was on e-mail to Dean Rogers at Vassar. What I needed to know was whether this was a figure of speech — very apt, if it was — or literal. Was there somewhere in Vassar's library system a compass rose in the floor? I had not seen one. But in fact, I had stepped on that compass rose every time I descended the main stairs to the Archives and Special Collections. It is at the foot of the stairs but has been covered with carpeting since a fairly recent renovation. The architect and the Vassar authorities clearly had little notion that they were covering up an important device of one of their most famous graduates, a graduate who is the reason for many visitors to their library.[7]

I tried to imagine Bishop's own reaction, coming to Vassar, descending the stairs, and finding at the bottom a navigational device very familiar to her. She was on her own far more than most of her fellow students. Her father had died when she was eight months old, and her mother had been confined to a mental hospital when she was five; she had not seen her mother since. Vassar became her home for four years in a special way. The compass rose on *North & South* harkens back not only to Bishop's family but also to her time in college.

"The Map" was written in early 1935, within a year of Bishop's graduation from Vassar and probably before her twenty-fourth birthday on February 8.[8] In her hands, the poem becomes a little world. All her life, Bishop would write this kind of poem, focusing on one place or one area and quietly, slowly, indirectly showing us an entire world as surely as Vermeer shows us an entire world in some of his paintings. To continue Fairfield Porter's tribute, "her relaxed line . . . allows each word enough space to be savored properly for what it is; and this comes from knowing when to change as well as when to repeat, how to keep such a distance that you pay attention and can go on, as you might go over the surface of a canvas."[9]

Poems as Little Worlds

"The Map"
> Land lies in water; it is shadowed green.
> Shadows, or are they shallows, at its edges.

The first time that the singer Suzie Leblanc read these lines, she found that she had to stop and go out for a walk. She too is a Maritimer, and these words about land and water affected her intensely. Bishop, looking intently at a map, has translated some of her own intensity into her lines. A map with shaded areas along the coastline in a narrow strip causes the adjoining land to look as if it casts a shadow. The effect makes the map look three-dimensional, alive.

The question — shadows or shallows? — has sounded whimsical to some readers. It is not. In fact, it is crucial in one context. If you are a sailor, you need to know whether you are seeing shadows or shallows on a coastline. Otherwise you are in danger of foundering. That is why navigational charts that I've seen indicate the depth of the water along the shoreline up to six fathoms. If you are a writer, it is just as well to know about shallows too.

The perspective changes with lines 4 to 8.

> Or does the land lean down to lift the sea from under,
> drawing it unperturbed around itself?
> Along the fine tan sandy shelf
> is the land tugging at the sea from under?

The sea is now a garment or covering, with the land pulling it up around itself. The two questions again sound fanciful or maybe touched with allegory and not descriptive. But in fact, they are descriptive, more obviously for a seacoast, descriptive in figurative terms.

The question to ask is much the same as for shadows and shallows in line 2. When might these lines be accurate or significant? Surely, during the flowing of the tide. Again, Bishop is drawing on a sailor's knowledge and here childhood knowledge. Her Nova Scotia home was Great Village, which lies close to the innermost point of the Bay of Fundy, famous for its phenomenal tides, the highest in the world: "My aunt lives on an enormous (for that part of the country) farm . . . always described as the most beautiful farm on the Bay of Fundy. You know about the Bay of Fundy and its tides, I imagine, that go out for a hundred miles or so and then come in with a rise of 80 feet" (to Marianne Moore, 29 Aug. 1946, L 139). When the tide is flowing, the land gives the effect of lifting or drawing or "tugging at the sea from under." It doesn't, of course. But on the Bay of Fundy, as on other long tidal stretches, things can look different. (Bishop wants the verbs here for other reasons as well, I think, but reasons that emerge only gradually from the poem.) Even on some freshwater coasts, there is a similar effect — not from tides but from pressure. On the coastlines of any large body of water, rising pressure will cause the water to drop, while a low-pressure system will cause the water to rise, as in an old storm glass. Of course, the land does not literally lift or draw or tug the water; it is the atmosphere above that does so. But the effect can look that way.

Later, I came to realize that one test for some of Bishop's lines or phrases is whether simple accuracy accounts for them. Sometimes there is not the slightest need to assume whimsy or fantasy or imaginary worlds.

An anecdote: I flew into Halifax in June 2011, and as the plane descended, I saw a very large riverbed, huge in fact. Then I saw that it was dry, then, further down, that it was damp and that the soil was reddish. And I suddenly exclaimed, partly aloud, "Heavens, I recognize the place. I know it!" I told my seat partner that it must be the Bay of Fundy, and she smiled indulgently, being a Haligonian. In fact, I had seen the bay but had not realized it, as Elizabeth Peabody said when she walked into a tree. Its shape on a map was very familiar, and I knew that Bishop said the tides went out about one hundred miles before returning. Why had I not imagined what this process looked like on the ground? I had not seen it that way since my teens, but still — a salutary lesson in realizing, imagining.

The word "unperturbed" in line 6 can modify "land" or "sea," but why should either land or sea be perturbed or unperturbed? Once again, a sailor's knowledge is in play. The word "unperturbed" is a benchmark for measuring the sea; calculations are made on the basis of "the unperturbed sea level" or "the unperturbed sea depth" or floor and the like. That is, measurements are taken "in the absence of tides, winds, currents and other factors," as the online *Proceedings of Estuarine and Coastal Modeling* puts it. A geographer may speak of Labrador's "perturbed sea-ice border," say, for January. The double meaning of "perturbed" suggests two different kinds of writing that quietly interweave: both ordinary descriptive writing and a kind of fable in which impossible things can happen in the most ordinary way. The young writer who is also a sailor has noted this word and its possibilities, part of her early self-training in diction and syntax.

The second stanza returns to boundaries, the place where the poem started.

> The names of seashore towns run out to sea,
> the names of cities cross the neighboring mountains
> — the printer here experiencing the same excitement
> as when emotion too far exceeds its cause.

The change in tone is palpable. So is the heightening of the affective language: "unperturbed," "lovely bays," and now "excitement," a putative excitement playfully assigned to the printer. Helen Vendler first heard the allusion to T. S. Eliot: "Eliot's famous criticism of *Hamlet* — that it did not work as an 'objective correlative' of its author's presumed feelings because Shakespeare's emotions had been too intense for the invention constructed to contain them — hovers behind Bishop's remark here."[10]

To follow Eliot, the printer here has failed as artist. In a work of art (or so Eliot argues), an emotion that exceeds its cause indicates that the artist has failed, even Shakespeare. Hamlet's emotion toward his mother is Eliot's case in point. Shakespeare has not found an objective correlative, a way to correlate emotion and story, "a set of objects, a situation, a chain of events which shall be the formula for that *particular* emotion."[11] Bishop, on the other hand, has done so. A possible artistic failure in a printer provides an exact objective correlative for some "emotion that too far exceeds its cause." (The qualification of "too far" is Bishop's.) Here is a metaphor that exactly indicates this condition, this excess, this odd state that most of us experience at some point in our lives: some perturbation, some excitement, some agitation beyond an obvious cause, as Eliot put it. What the emotion might be here Bishop does not say.

In the printer's world, there are conventions for writing down such apparently excessive emotions, conventions that we all accept as we read maps on which names of towns and cities sprawl far beyond their boundaries. Conventions in writing poems are similar; they too find ways of ordering excessive emotions. A cartographic convention may also stand as a warning to Bishop's young self about possible hazards in writing, especially when treating excess emotion. Her touch of humor (usually ignored) speaks to Eliot's occasional solemnity. Even more, it indicates Bishop's writerly confidence, young as she was and painfully shy as she was in public.

The next sentence, which closes the second stanza, confirms this:

These peninsulas take the water between thumb and finger
like women feeling for the smoothness of yard-goods.

This apparently simple sentence suggests three different contexts, all related by one word. First, the women, and the craft of
a seamstress, a home craft that women in charge of a household
commonly possessed or knew where to find in Bishop's day.
Here, the sense of boundaries is very different from what just
precedes it. This is another example of correlation, finding the
correlation between the look of a fabric and the feel of it. If the
simile does suggest an emotion, it is an everyday emotion, a measured, considered, experienced, perhaps pleasurable emotion in
reading fabric. There may be very little of what we commonly
call emotion when cloth is so felt. These are feelings involved in
ordinary work, feelings we surmise in the look of the eye, the
gestures, of a woman making decisions about cloth or food or
any one of those elementary matters over which women traditionally presided and which we so easily take for granted. These
women are reading texture through their fingertips in order to
make something. This is an objective correlative that works.

As with the metaphor of the printer, so with the metaphor
of the women. Here, it is as if these women can measure out
the sea — an activity usually reserved for the Almighty, "who
hath measured the waters in the hollow of his hand," the *deus
artifex* — measure it out like yard-goods.[12] Bishop is once more
turning all those metaphors of the sea as a garment, some of them
very familiar: the "sea-girt isles"; "and round it hath cast like a
mantle the sea"; "The Sea of Faith / Was once, too, at the full,
and round earth's shore / Lay like the folds of a bright girdle
furled"; "then all collapsed, and the great shroud of the sea
rolled on as it rolled five thousand years ago"; "The water . . . /
Like a body wholly body, fluttering / Its empty sleeves" — this
last from a poem published a few months before Bishop wrote
hers.[13]

These peninsulas take water between thumb and finger. To go back to my earlier question for Bishop's work: in what other context might these words work? Who else feels water for smoothness? Who else but sailors? Not by taking water between thumb and finger but by feeling for smoothness of the water through the skin and the eyes and the ears. Sailors read the water much as the women read cloth. Against the look of it, they test the feel and smell of the air above it, the sound of it ("the distant rote in the granite teeth"), and more.[14] As with the women, such judgment may be called intuitive, but only if we define "intuitive" as that combination of knowledge, experience, and instinct that mysteriously issues in an art or craft: sewing, sailing, sculpture, medicine.

When the peninsulas take the water between thumb and finger, it is as if they could also take a pen between thumb and finger, as if the peninsulas could write down themselves. The prefix "pen-" means "almost" (from Latin *paene*), almost an island or *insula*. Our word "pen" as a writing implement derives from Latin *penna* or "feather," the original quill pen. A *paene insula* is like a thumb and finger, which can take between them a *penna* — and Bishop knew Latin well enough to make this hidden pun. These lines suggest a third occupation beyond the sailor's, an occupation already suggested by the printer: that of a writer. All three occupations, sewing, sailing, writing, are linked by the one word "craft," which is also the word for the boat that the sailor sails. (*Steering the Craft* is Ursula Le Guin's happy title for a handbook on writing skills. James Merrill's tribute to Bishop is titled "Her Craft" and refers to boats.)[15] Both writer and reader may test a passage, feeling for smoothness, a term commonly used of words or of a style.[16]

"These peninsulas," says Bishop. What peninsulas? Any on that map surely, starting with Labrador, the "great Arctic Peninsula."[7] It is so huge that we seldom think of it as a peninsula, but so it is, with Hudson Bay and its straits on one side and the Atlantic with the Gulf of St. Lawrence on the other. The other side of this enormous peninsula consists of the Canadian Maritime provinces. Norway is also half of a prominent peninsula, one of more normal size. I want to make a case shortly for another peninsula as well.

The place-names reverberate yet further. They define the map as one of the North Atlantic, with two *N* words for northern territories, Newfoundland and Norway. Labrador follows immediately on Newfoundland, for they constitute one territory. (License plates on cars say "Newfoundland and Labrador.") This remains true, even though Newfoundland is an island and Labrador a sizable portion of the adjacent mainland, running north to a little over sixty degrees latitude. Virtually all critics have assumed that the map Bishop gazed at in 1934 included all of easternmost Canada — a likely assumption but not on the evidence of the place-names. The place-names of Newfoundland and Labrador have led them astray. Newfoundland and Labrador were not part of Canada when Bishop took her walking trip in Newfoundland in 1932 or when she published this poem in 1935 or when she collected it in 1946. Newfoundland and Labrador joined Canada only in 1949. When Bishop wrote this poem, Newfoundland was still a British crown colony, its constitution temporarily suspended by request in 1934, because of impending bankruptcy during the Great Depression.[18] The huge tract of adjacent mainland, annexed to Newfoundland in 1774, was disputed territory from 1902 onward. It was finally given to

Newfoundland in 1927 in "one of the most celebrated legal cases in British colonial history, the Labrador boundary dispute."[19] (Some Quebeckers do not accept it to this day.) The decision was still fresh when Bishop published her poem.

Why might this matter? A look at Norway provides a parallel. Norway's present boundaries were also established within living memory of Bishop's 1935 and 1946 readers. It separated from Sweden in 1905, a peaceful separation that is a model for conflict resolution. Bishop's two named northern territories, then, both come with a fairly recent history of boundary disputes. Even more important in the early 1930s, these were boundary disputes that were settled peacefully. The place-names of Newfoundland and Labrador, along with Norway, might remind the reader historically of Norsemen and a Norse empire. (The two areas, one on each side of the North Atlantic, are united by the prevailing spring winds, the easterlies that drove fishing ships from Norway to Greenland, and then beyond to Newfoundland and Labrador, long before Columbus came to the Americas.) The place-names might remind the reader economically of the once-huge North Atlantic fisheries, also part of the oil industry of the time. They would more likely remind the reader of recent claims to shorelines like those described with care in stanza 1. (The Labrador boundary dispute rested on questions of watersheds and shorelines.) Recent history would also remind readers of ways to decide such claims other than aggression or war.

Bishop's poems do not focus generally on war or politics or international upheavals. We do not go to them in the way we go to Yeats's or Auden's. But neither do they take place in a historical vacuum. Much more often than we think, they are rooted in their time and place. They form small worlds. So here. Sailors need to know about shorelines and boundaries, including who governs them. Citizens watch these things too.

There are also hints of another world in "The Map" beyond a public world. They come in the form of scattered affective words that could belong to a narrative. But the poem does not tell us how, nor does it even gesture toward such a reading. The affective words are unexpected but never disruptive: "unperturbed," "lovely," "excitement," "quiet," "agitation," "delicate." The tone varies. Only one remark addresses this vocabulary directly, and the tone is a little playful: "an emotion that too far exceeds its cause." The word "delicate" is puzzling as part of a puzzling last line: "More delicate than the historians' are the map-makers' colors." It surely bears on the one personal matter that the poem delicately but unmistakably intimates.[20]

The poem had its origin in an actual map, and the story is familiar. In a 1978 interview, when asked about the "extensive imagery of maps and geography" in her work, Bishop replied, "Well, my mother's family wandered a lot and loved this strange world of travel. My first poem in my first book was inspired when I was sitting on the floor, on New Year's Eve in Greenwich Village, after I graduated from college. I was staring at a map. The poem wrote itself. People will say that it corresponded to some part of me which I was unaware of at the time. This may be true."[21]

It is New Year's Eve, a time for reckoning with public and personal history. For Bishop, the year 1934 was just ending and the year 1935 about to begin. In the wide world, Hitler had begun to move aggressively toward dictatorship within Germany, and Japan's army had begun to move aggressively against its mainland neighbors. Her mother had died some seven months earlier. Bishop had not seen her for eighteen years. She died confined in an asylum, as she had lived since that scream Bishop remembered as a child. Not until 1953 could Bishop find a way to write about that scream in her story "In the Village." In 1934, on that map, she could see where her mother had died a few months earlier, across the peninsula from where she herself had lived. (I am assuming that the Canadian Maritime provinces were included, as well as the Atlantic coast further south.) She could see the Bay of Fundy as well, just as she had seen it as a child. She could see the coastlines where her great-grandfather had sailed and that a great-uncle knew too (see "Large Bad Picture"). The sight of that map helped, I think, to focus her eyes and mind as she stared at it. As David Kalstone realized, "Objects hold radiant interest for her precisely because they help her absorb numbing or threatening experiences."[22]

With the map or the writing of "The Map" came a memory of Eliot writing on excessive emotion, on Hamlet and his disgust with his mother, also called Gertrude like Bishop's own poor mother. Hamlet went mad temporarily, or was he pretending? "Rest, rest, perturbed spirit," Hamlet's blessing on his father's ghost, sounds even more appropriate as a response to Bishop's mother's ghost. Her mother had gone mad, apparently overcome by a grief that too far exceeded its cause, the early death of her husband. Bishop remembered her being fitted for a dress and the dressmaker crawling on the floor with pins in her mouth to mark the bottom hem. The dressmaker, she wrote years later, had reminded her of Nebuchadnezzar crawling on the ground and eating grass because (she did not need to write) he had gone mad. Bishop associated her mother with yard-goods. In her story, the dressmaker is moved to tears by the beauty of the fabric and of course by more. An unfinished poem is titled "A Mother Made of Dress-Goods" (EAP 156–157). In the first draft of her well-known villanelle "One Art," she wrote, "I have lost one ~~long~~ peninsula and one island" (EAP 225). Most of mainland Nova Scotia is composed of a long peninsula. "These peninsulas" together with "yard-goods" in "The Map" cannot but evoke a mother who has just died. "These peninsulas" would speak to any reader of 1935 or 1946 who knew a little about Bishop's background. Only a few close friends might perhaps think of Bishop's mother living and dying there.

The draft of "The Map" takes only two pages, and there are very few changes. In effect, as Bishop said, "the poem wrote itself." On the verso side of the second page is the earliest draft of another poem, a poem about her mother that Bishop never finished, "Swan-Boat Ride." It ends, "She raised her veil over her nose to kiss me."[23] The affective vocabulary in "The Map" can delicately evoke maternal thoughts.[24] No history of Bishop's personal life on New Year's Eve 1934 could possibly be as delicate as the intimations of this map-maker's poem.

It is more usual among critics to associate this affective vocabulary with Bishop's lesbianism, though if her memory is correct, she was not entirely aware of it at the time. "People will say that it corresponded to some part of me which I was unaware of at the time. This may be true." It is hard to see how she could have been fully aware, given the personal decisions on her mind at the time.

On that map, on New Year's Eve 1934, Bishop could see the island where she had hiked two summers before, Newfoundland. She could also see Cuttyhunk Island, off New Bedford, Massachusetts. She had spent several weeks there during July 1934, part of them on holiday with a young man who very much wanted to marry her and whom she liked.[25] Did she love him? By all evidence, the person she now loved to the point of obsession was her roommate at Vassar, Margaret Miller.[26] She was alone on New Year's Eve, having been sick with flu and asthma since Christmas Day; Miller had nursed her since then, until (Bishop said) she was exhausted; she had just left (to Frani Blough, 1 Jan. 1935, L 29). Miller had nursed her like a mother, as we say, an action likely to stir memories of an actual mother as Bishop stared at that map. "Name it 'friendship' if you want to — like names of cities printed on maps, the word is much too big, it spreads out all over the place and tells nothing of the actual *place* it means to name" — thus a journal entry written some time between 25 July 1934 and 22 August 1934 (Vassar 72A.3). If the occasion of New Year's Eve raised questions about 1934 and 1935, one of them must have been the question of marriage. And emotion that exceeds too far its cause? It is easy to speculate about all these things in hindsight and in doing so to skew the poem. The poem's affective vocabulary is a challenge for the reader. Do we read this poem as if it were a seventeenth-century poem of correspondences, the land as the beloved's body, Donne's "my America, my Newfoundland"? Bishop knew very well how seventeenth-century poetry works. If she had wanted a poem of allegorical correspondences, she would have written one.

It is possible to look back at Bishop's life in 1934, at least what we now know of it. It is possible to surmise circumstances that bear on the poem, and I have done so. But a warning about works of art is due, a warning that more than one critic has empha-sized. Works of art are not dissolvable back into the circumstances that produced them. These help to make up what Aristotle called the efficient cause of a work of art, and only that. Lyric voice in a poem is not an autobiographical voice but something other, though related.

If some personal voyage hovers in the background of "The Map," it is not the immediate business of this poem. This poem indicates a writer's voyage to be taken, a course to be followed. It intimates causes, subjects, knowledge, emotions that inform this voyage. Along the way, they may become more explicit. They are not so here. Instead, the poem tells us what an acutely observant eye can see. "Watch it closely": so Bishop ends her 1939 poem "The Monument," in which the monument is the beginning of a work of art that shelters "what is within (which after all / cannot have been intended to be seen)."

Less than two years later, Bishop wrote another poem using some of the same mapping techniques as in "The Map": "Paris, 7 A.M." That map is of a city, and it too brings with it a time, a history, an ambience, as we shall see.

Love

The third poem, "Casabianca," may show a disaster, but its art shows a young prodigy. Though it is a very different poem from "The Map," the art here is just as sure-footed.

At about the time Bishop wrote "Casabianca," she copied into her poetry notebooks a sonnet on the madness of love by the sixteenth-century Scottish poet Mark Alexander Boyd (Vassar 72.A.1, 34):

But twice unhappier is he, I lairn,
That feidis [feeds] in his hairt a mad desire,
And follows on a woman throw [through] the fire,
Led by a blind and teachit by a bairn.

The blind bairn is, of course, Cupid or Eros. In April 1936, she published "Casabianca," along with "The Colder the Air" and "The Gentleman of Shalott," in *New Democracy:* one poem of fire, one of cold air, one written against an enchantment like the Lady of Shalott's and choosing a half life instead.

"Casabianca" shows a profound intelligence about the state of first being passionately in love. All Bishop's layering works to prevent facile clichés about such a state. Why "Casabianca"? Most of all, it is the sheer chutzpah in choosing this title and this poem that strikes me. Think of it. Felicia Hemans's 1829 poem "Casabianca" is a poem of filial obedience to the death, of the highest sense of duty, of heart-wringing sentiment — supposing one can take it seriously. It became a classroom exercise, a poem for a school recital when schools still offered oral recitals. In *Tom Sawyer* (1876), the place I first learned of it, Twain's wonderful account of a school recital includes "The Boy Stood on the Burning Deck" (chapter 22). Dame Edith Sitwell (b. 1887) threw a tantrum and refused to memorize the poem, when a child.[27] And just six years before Bishop published "Casabianca," Dashiell Hammett published *The Maltese Falcon* (1930), in which Sam Spade chides his faithful, long-suffering secretary, "You're the sister of the boy who stood on the burning deck?" (chapter 14). Over forty years later, it was still well enough known for Rex Stout's Archie Goodwin to allude to it:

> "You're pretty good," she said.
> "I try hard. Whence all but me have fled."
> "What?"
> "The burning deck."
> "What burning deck?"
> "You don't read the right poems."[28]

Think of the tone of Mark Twain's school recital in *Tom Sawyer*. Think what T. S. Eliot would have made of it or, for all that, Robert Lowell.

Yet Bishop, age twenty-five, saw the possibilities of an extraordinary trope in the figure of the burning boy. Her genius was to combine the boy and Cupid. Whether the ambience of the burning boy suddenly seemed right for someone passionately in love or whether the burning boy suddenly recalled the figure of Eros we can never know.

Felicia Hemans's famous poem was based on an actual incident in the battle of the Nile, in which a son stayed on board a burning ship in order to help his father. It opens,

> The boy stood on the burning deck.

To which Bishop's poem replies, as in an antistrophe,

> Love's the boy stood on the burning deck

"Love's the boy": just for a moment, the familiar figure of the boy Eros floats before our inward eye — but no, not flying as usual but standing — and suddenly that 1829 boy is before our eye, along with the question of love. For it is love, filial love as duty, that keeps the boy there, against all sense, waiting for his father's command to leave, the father who lies dead below. Then comes Bishop's syntactic layering, corresponding to layers of feeling:

> Love's the boy stood on the burning deck
> trying to recite "The boy stood on
> the burning deck." Love's the son
>   stood stammering elocution
>   while the poor ship in flames went down.

Love as son, love as Eros, and burning, burning. How do we speak when first in love? It may sound like a recital of familiar words. It may feel like an exposure as if on a school platform. It may make us feel again like schoolboys or schoolgirls.

> . . . the swimming sailors, who
> would like a school platform, too.

Above all, there is consuming fire of love, which, unbeknownst to us, has killed the unseen parental voice that we wait for, somehow, to guide us through this. (I wonder if the poem spoke to Bishop personally long before this, as a poem about a child waiting for a parental voice, a voice that has vanished.)

The young boy suggests that this poem is about a first powerful encounter with erotic love. It is all here: the sense of desire, in the conventional phrase, "burning desire"; the sense of being inexperienced; the need to say something, hampered by self-consciousness as if one were reciting something on a stage; the consciousness that such words have been used before; a world that is overwhelmingly a world of desire. Eros is not himself a burning boy, but he is the cause of burning desire in others, thanks to his flaming arrows. "Love's the burning boy" makes perfect sense, both as classical figure and as actual human figure. The same boy makes sense for both heterosexual and homosexual desire. A burning ship is a disaster at sea: does this desire end in disaster? And in what sense?

The Elements

If "The Map" is a poem of navigating, of mapping, of sailing, what follows in Bishop's first collection? A ship close to an iceberg in the next poem, "The Imaginary Iceberg." A ship on fire in the third poem, "Casabianca." These are poems about the end of voyaging, not the beginning. The ship is not crushed by ice in "The Imaginary Iceberg," because the dangerous beautiful creature allows onlookers to come close and watch its performance. In "Casabianca," fire consumes the vessel, and it sinks. Ice and fire, Charybdis and Scylla. "Icebergs behoove the soul / . . . / to see them so . . . ," says "The Imaginary Iceberg." "Love's the boy stood on the burning deck," says "Casabianca." It is as if Petrarch's ship of love, sailing between Scylla and Charybdis, the soul and the body, were caught by the fires of courtly love conventions — those same conventions that Bishop played with in her earliest poems like "Three Valentines." (Compare Petrarch's *Canzoniere* 189.)

The first four poems of *North & South* are very early. "The Map" begins with land and water, "The Imaginary Iceberg" treats ice and water, and "Casabianca" focuses on fire. Is Bishop working with the elements? If so, the missing element is air. And what is the title of the fourth poem? "The Colder the Air" — a poem treating a "huntress of the winter air." Earth, water, fire, air. Bishop loved sixteenth- and seventeenth-century poetry, poetry from a time when the four elements were still familiar as a basic structure of physics and could also provide a pattern for poetry. Such patterns in the background here intimate that essential matters are in play, though always indirectly.

The four elements appear regularly in Bishop's work from the beginning. A recently discovered early fragment, "I am neither here nor there," reads, "Water claims me not, nor air, / Nor the light of fairy foam / On the hills."[29] The fourfold scheme of the elements also helped to shape Bishop's childhood memories.

It is the elements speaking: earth, air, fire, water.

Bishop published this line in 1953 in the *New Yorker*, as part of the ending to her great short story "In the Village."[30] In 1946, Bishop opened her first collection, *North & South*, with the elements speaking, this time in the order earth, water, fire, air. In her short story, the clang of Nate's hammer helps to ground the child. Against the reality of her mother's echoing scream, *Clang!* offers a normal reality like the touch of the earth, the sound and touch of the sea, the sound and touch of air, the look and heat of fire. Such reality has a healing quality, as other writers besides Bishop knew. It is not only objects that help Bishop to absorb numbing or threatening experiences. The elements do too, the world in its touch and taste and sight and sound and smell, its quiddity (as Gerard Manley Hopkins would say), its thereness. The elemental earth, Dame Kind, could give Bishop an anchoring place.

That is not, however, what the second, third, and fourth poems in *North & South* tell us. These poems envision the soul as ice or embody the fiery experience of first erotic love and so challenge everyday reality. Yet the reality that is *Clang!* offers another weapon to meet these challenges. James Merrill noted that the blacksmith shop showed Bishop as a child "a kind of art — the dangerous fire that . . . is in Nate's shop perilously mastered, turned into a game which still bears traces of violence ('hissing, protesting')" (*Becoming a Poet*, 164). I would add that Vulcan, the blacksmith at his forge, is the god who is the patron saint of artificers, including the poet as maker or shaper. Forms of art are mentioned or implied on all four opening poems. The first poem speaks of craft. The second two speak of artistic performance: "This is a scene where he who treads the boards / is artlessly rhetorical" and "upon a shifting stage" ("The Imaginary Iceberg"). And "stammering elocution" and "the swimming

sailors, who/would like a schoolroom platform too" ("Casabianca"). Imagining a stage performance helps an extremely shy
writer to find a voice, while the actor's discipline of "going into
character" can work for writers too. The stage-set metaphor turns
up in "The Monument" (1939), and Shakespeare's routine stage
direction for battle scenes appears in 1946 in "Little Exercise":
"Another part of the field." The fourth poem shows a performance
too, this time in a shooting gallery, with a crack shot who never
misses, an ideal for a writer. As critics have noted, Bishop makes
the same association in a 1934 essay on Gerard Manley Hopkins.

Though all four opening poems suggest art as a way of going
forward, not all four are equally successful in their execution.
"The Map" is rich and moving, once it is read with sufficient
attention. It is the kind of poem to which a reader will return.
So is "Casabianca," and it is a poem that appeals to a first-time
reader. "The Imaginary Iceberg" is attractive, though sometimes
dense, and the ending could be clearer. "The Colder the Air" is
for me simply frustrating. Some of Bishop's early crowded poems
show the influence of sixteenth- and seventeenth-century poetry,
and this is one of them. Along with a few others, it bears out
William Pritchard's judgment that some of Bishop's poems show
possible overkill in detail.[31] Bishop was a young prodigy, and
her craft is amazing: the command of diction, of form, of rhyme,
and more. But her judgment about what works for a reader is
still some distance from what it will be in her forties.

CHAPTER TWO

Elizabeth Bishop's Ordinary Diction — Yes, *But* . . .

> Writing poetry is an unnatural act. It takes great skill to make
> it seem natural.
> —Elizabeth Bishop

Time and again, Bishop's readers praise her ordinary, everyday,
down-home diction: "straightforward and almost chatty,"
"women's speech, . . . chattier syntax and diction," "diction, . . .
for the most part, simple enough for middle school students."
And there it is on the page:

> Of course, I may be remembering it all wrong
> after, after — how many years?
> ("Santarém")

> Heavens, I recognize the place. I know it!
> It's behind — I can almost remember the farmer's name.
> ("Poem")

> Oh, but it is dirty!
> — this little filling station.
> ("Filling Station")

> Miss Breen is about seventy,
> a retired police lieutenant, six feet tall,
> with beautiful bright blue eyes and a kind expression.
> ("Arrival at Santos")

So certainly, yes, ordinary, everyday, down-home diction. Or rather, yes, *but* . . . The quotations above are in reverse chronological order, starting with 1978 and ending with 1952. Bishop did not start out with this kind of ordinary diction — quite the contrary. Her earliest poems used a far different vocabulary.

When Dudley Fitts rejected a group of Bishop's poems for *Hound & Horn* in 1934, he not only called them "too mannered" and "too clever." He also said they were too much like Hopkins and Hardy. Bishop protested to her friend Frani Blough that she'd read very little Hardy, and the poems she had read were either "descriptions of funerals or the complaints of seduced milkmaids." Anyway, "why write like the usual crowd in *Hound & Horn,* with 'One sweetly solemn thought' coming to them o'er and o'er. Oh Hell—I thought I might get myself a new hat with the money at least" (2 Mar. 1934, L 17). Bishop was twenty-three years old and in her senior year at Vassar. She had already fallen in love with English sixteenth- and seventeenth-century poetry: "I was very much wrapped up in 16th & 17th century lyrics for years (still am, in a way). . . . I also wrote about a dozen strict imitations of Campion, Nashe, etc while at college" (to Anne Stevenson, 8–20 Jan. 1964, LOA 863). Anything further from the hymn "One sweetly solemn thought" is hard to find.

Bishop's head was full of hymns from her family and her school, including some very good ones: good music, good words. In October 1964, she was guest poetry editor of the monthly newsletter of the Academy of American Poets, *Poetry Pilot.* For poems, she chose seven favorite hymns: "Hierusalem, my happie home" (anon.), "The spacious Firmament on high" (Joseph Addison), "Jesus shall reign where'er the sun" (Isaac Watts), "Oh, worship the King all glorious above" (Robert Grant), "Oh, for a closer walk with God" (William Cowper), "Come, ye faithful, raise the strain of triumphant gladness" (John of Damascus, trans. John Neale), and "God moves in a mysterious way" (William Cowper). "My reasons for admiring these hymns," she wrote, "are too mixed to explain in a short space. They have almost nothing to do with theology and possibly as much to do with music as with poetry, since I can't separate the words from their familiar tunes. But that these hymns are poetry of a kind, I am fairly sure" (*Poetry Pilot*, Oct. 1964, 9).[1]

"One sweetly solemn thought" Bishop remembered for other reasons. It makes a cautionary example of ordinary language inflated into pious jargon:

> One sweetly solemn thought
> Comes to me o'er and o'er;
> Near'r to my home today am I
> Then e'er I've been before.
>
> Nearer my Father's house,
> Where many mansions be.

This is the kind of thing that gives hymns a bad name, but the lines are useful to describe a certain writing style, decidedly not Bishop's.[2] Maybe the best term for it is "the higher cliché," Bishop's wonderful phrase about a certain poet.[3] Readers and writers alike need to watch this misuse of ordinary language. When is ordinary language clear and unpretentious, faithful to a thought or feeling? When is it not?

It is one thing to absorb a rich poetic style and later begin to simplify. It is quite another never to go through this, or a similar, discipline before simplifying. Late in life, when a young poet asked Bishop for advice, she recommended a great deal of reading: "Read a lot of poetry — all the time — and *not* 20th-century poetry. Read Campion, Herbert, Pope, Tennyson, Coleridge — anything at all almost that's any good from the past" (to Miss Pearson, 28 May 1975, L 596). The object is to find out what one really likes. After that come major modern poets. And, she emphasized, don't just read in anthologies. "Read ALL of somebody" (ibid.). Then read that somebody's letters, biography, and so on. Even if a writer tries to imitate that style exactly, it will turn out differently.

Writers start where they start. Nobody tells them. But how they train themselves after that is crucial, and reading is essential. All the first-rate writers I know are prodigious readers. A writer who starts with ordinary everyday language has to work at it like any other serious writer. Bishop's early habits offer some pointers. She not only read; she also saw and heard and absorbed. Marianne Moore, recommending Bishop for the Houghton Mifflin prize in 1944, emphasized that "beneath an apparently unliterary surface was a deep grasp of the cultural past. 'In her writing, a feeling for strong personalities such as G. M. Hopkins, Franz Kafka, Dürer, Max Ernst, Eugène Atget, Purcell and other musicians is assimilated beyond detection.'"[4] To assimilate beyond detection. To absorb, to teach oneself this way, the only way.

From the first, Bishop was acutely aware of the possibilities of words as they go about their lives. She observed them with her famous scrutinizing eye as carefully as she observed objects. In "The Map," she was alert to words with a specialized meaning from a certain domain — navigation, a seafaring community — a meaning that adds to their dominant signification. She was sensitive to local usage. She was aware of the history of words. She had an almost preternatural sense of new words and fashions in words and a love of good dictionaries.

I want to look at some of Bishop's word usage in more detail, treating it as a lesson in how to write or, for all that, a lesson in how to read.

First, dictionaries. Here is Robert Lowell after reading Bishop's wonderful third collection, *Questions of Travel:* "It was fun looking up echolalia (again), chromograph, gesso, and roadstead — they all meant pretty well what I thought. Oh and taboret, an object I've known all my life, but not the name" (28 Oct. 1965, LEBRL 590). "They all meant pretty well what I thought." Quick now, how many of these words can readers define? I happen to know about "echolalia"; and I once knew about "gesso" because of T. S. Eliot ("A painter of the Umbrian school / Designed upon a gesso ground . . ."; "Mr. Eliot's Sunday Morning Service"), but I had to double-check the meaning. I assumed that I knew the meaning of "roadstead." I was wrong, and it mattered. (See the discussion of "Visits to St. Elizabeths" in Chapter 6.) Not all the words in Bishop are ordinary diction. A few require dictionaries.

For Lowell, looking up words in dictionaries was fun. It was decidedly not fun for one Harvard student who took Bishop's verse-writing course and told a friend, "Oh don't work with *her!* It's awful! She wants you to look words up in the dictionary! It isn't a bit *creative* at all!" Bishop reacted strongly: "In other words, it is better *not* to know what you're writing or reading. . . . But they mostly seem to think that poetry — to read or to write — is a snap — one just has to *feel* — and not for very long either" (to John Frederick Nims, 6 Oct. 1979, L 638–639, written and mailed on the day she died).

As for Bishop herself, dictionaries could start her writing again after a dry spell: "But I haven't really written a poem since I can't remember when. However — one always does start again, it seems. [Wallace] Stevens says in his letters (just read them all) that translating is a waste of time — but I don't agree with him completely. It gets one to going through dictionaries, and that is a helpful activity" (to May Swenson, 16 Nov. 1968, L 501). She dreamed of owning the large, multivolume *Oxford English Dictionary*, the best storyteller of them all for the life of words: "I also learned that the OED in 13 vols. — the dream of my life — costs much more in England than in Cambridge, Mass."[5]

So Bishop uses ordinary everyday diction, yes, but in poems that also accommodate slightly unusual words. The trick is to make them work together in a way that sounds natural.

Exercise: Write a short poem mostly in ordinary diction that also includes a word or two that may be hard to define precisely.

Bishop kept an eye out for words whose main meaning is clear but also have a more specialized meaning: "perturbed," "pinnacle," "duplicity." The first two are from her earliest published poems. "Perturbed" we have seen in its oceanographic context in "The Map." The word "pinnacle" in connection with an iceberg is a Newfoundland expression, so that Bishop's "glassy pinnacles" in "The Imaginary Iceberg" carry a special meaning for those who know about sea ice. The *Dictionary of Newfoundland English* defines "pinnacle ice" as "a peak of ice projecting from an iceberg or 'rafted' up in an ice-floe, . . . [also in combination] 'pinnacle ice,'" and gives an example from the *National Geographic* for 1929.[6] This usage is not listed in *Webster's* or the OED.

The word "duplicity" Bishop never used in her collected poetry, but when she was twenty-three, she made a note of it in her working journal: "The water so clear & pale that you are seeing *into* it at the same time you are looking *at* its surface. A *duplicity* — all the way through" (July 1934, Vassar 72A.3, 2; emphasis in original). The OED confirms that both meanings are in current use, though the common meaning of "double dealing" is older. One quotation speaks of duplicity in certain stars, that is, simple doubleness. Was Bishop reminding herself of something that she knew already, or was she thinking of a possible metaphor for double dealing? While the concordance to her poems shows no "duplicity," it does show one use each of "double" and "doubled": in "The Gentleman of Shalott" and much later in "The End of March." In the latter, a flame "would waver, doubled in the window" — so that the window acts as a mirror for the "lovely diaphanous blue flame" from the blazing *"grog à l'américaine"* of a dream life. There is something delicately erotic about this mirror image, a brief transitory moment. Duplicity? Not at all, except insofar as mirror images in a dream life might be unintentionally duplicitous. In "The Gentleman of Shalott," the brush strokes are broader: "He felt in modesty / his person was half looking-glass, / for why should he be doubled?" At the end, he "wishes to be quoted as saying at present / 'Half is enough.' " The assertion makes clear that the gentleman is aware of but wants no duplicity, at least for the moment.

Exercise: List a handful of words that have a common meaning and also a specialized meaning from some area of your life.

As we would expect, Bishop's own use of language is very precise. Take her word "religiousness." In a letter of June 21, 1977, to Robert Giroux, she thanked him for a review, adding, "very nice — especially as I don't think any traces of religiousness can be found in my poems."[7] Not "religion" and not "religiosity," which gets misused so often. Even as good an interviewer as Ashley Brown asked Bishop about how a poem gets started in the following terms: is it from pleasure in a stanzaic form (as in "Roosters") or does "the experience *dictate* the form?" (Schwartz and Estess 297; emphasis added). "In this case I couldn't say which came first. Sometimes the form, sometimes the subject *dominates* the mind. All other poets I've ever talked to say pretty much the same thing" (ibid.; emphasis added). How easily that silly word "dictate" slips out, as if any competent writer of integrity would allow anything to dictate what gets written. And how quietly and courteously Bishop revises it.

Exercise: Keep a file for words whose meaning you wrongly thought that you knew. This will take a bit of time, but it's salutary. And if you can't define a word exactly, check it.

Nor does ordinary diction require short, simple words all the time. Take one of the best blues singers ever, Billie Holiday. In 1944, Bishop wrote a poem with four parts called "Songs for a Colored Singer" *(North & South).* "I was hoping someone would compose the tunes for *them*," she said later. "I think I had Billie Holiday in mind. I put in a couple of big words because she sang big words well — '*conspiring* root' for instance" (Schwartz and Estess 296).

In *Questions of Travel*, Bishop combines two common words to produce an uncommon effect: "unsympathetic yellow" ("Electrical Storm"), "unwarrantable ark" ("Squatter's Children"), and notably "intangible ash" ("The Armadillo"). On *Questions of Travel*, see Chapter 6.

Bishop also kept an eye out for local idioms. Her earliest working notebooks record bits of conversation in which an unusual idiom or word appears. She picked up Newfoundland expressions from her walking trip there as an undergraduate in 1932. She took her copy of Prowse's *History of Newfoundland* to Brazil some twenty years later, presumably in part because of some poems she had in mind. Newfoundland expressions turn up in "The Imaginary Iceberg" (1935), as noted. In a 1949 poem, "Cape Breton," the mist is broken now and then "by one shag's dripping serpent-neck." I don't call them "shags." I call them "cormorants," along with other bird-watchers I know. The term was probably in local use when she visited Cape Breton, for older language was preserved there. The writer Alexander MacLeod, who lives in Cape Breton, tells me that "cormorant" is now generally used, though Acadians still say "shag." It is also used in Newfoundland (see the *Dictionary of Newfoundland English*), where it turns up in place-names like Shag Rocks or Shag Roost. Bishop heard it on the island of North Haven when she went there years later: "cormorants (called 'shags' here)" (21 Aug. 1976, LEBRL 795). I wonder if they're still called "shags" in this part of Maine. The term seems to have stuck locally along the northeastern seaboard.

So yes, use an ordinary everyday vocabulary if you wish, including other people's ordinary everyday vocabulary, especially when it is colorful or differs from your own.

Bishop's ordinary language is her own idiom. You can hear it in her poems, for example, the colloquial use of "awful" that ends "The Bight":

> Click. Click. Goes the dredge,
> and brings up a dripping jawful of marl.
> All the untidy activity continues,
> awful but cheerful.

And there is the word "awful" in her letters: "When someone says 'beautiful' about Key West, you should really take it with a grain of salt until you've seen it for yourself — in general it is really *awful* & the 'beauty' is just the light" (1 Jan. 1948, LEBRL 22). And then, dispiritedly, she writes, "I seem to remember that I once used to rhyme a mean rhyme, but it all seems awfully long ago" (to Lloyd Frankenberg and Loren MacIver, Apr.

1949, L 185). "I am awfully sorry I didn't get 'Sammy' done. Well, next time" (to Michael di Capna, 8 Jan. 1969).[8]

Ordinary language includes echoic effects, like that "Click. Click" in "The Bight." Bishop was fond of them from the start. People I know say that hens go "cluck cluck," but Bishop's option is close to the creature's actual sound. "The pet hen went chook-chook" ("Chemin de Fer"). "Roosters" plays throughout on rooster sounds: described, echoic, symbolic. In "Love Lies Sleeping," the morning begins with " 'Boom!' and a cloud of smoke. / 'Boom!' " while, less intrusive, a water wagon's spray comes "hissing." In "Over 2,000 Illustrations and a Complete Concordance" (1948), "the touching bleats of goats" are recorded, and in "Cape Breton" (1951), sheep go, "Baa, Baa." By 1971 and "Crusoe in England," goats go, *"Baa, baa, baa,"* forming a maddening antiphonal chorus with gulls that *"shriek, shriek, shriek":* *"baa . . . shriek . . . baa."* Thunder cracks in "Electrical Storm" or rather doesn't just crack: it goes,

> *Cra-ack!* — dry and light.
> The house was really struck.
> *Crack!* A tinny sound, like a dropped tumbler.

A peanut vendor's whistle goes *"peep-peep"* during the manhunt in "The Burglar of Babylon." And oilcans say softly "ESSO — so — so / to high-strung automobiles" in a wonderful metaphor at the end of "Filling Station." Feet and hooves moving through golden sand sound out *"shush, shush, shush"* ("Santarém," 1978). Bishop's echoic noises not only become more frequent and more pronounced as she matures. They also become subtler and simpler; some of the later ones are memorable.

Echoic effects give an immediacy, belonging as they do to mimesis as mimicry, not mimesis as description. "Mimesis" means representation in both senses, and Plato was the one who made the dominant meaning "description." ("Plato . . . uses the Greek word *mimeisthai* to mean 'depict,' although its ordinary meaning was 'mimic' or 'enact.'")[9] An illustration. My daughter is a natural mimic. One day when she was very young, there was a substitute teacher at school. "What was she like?" I asked. "Like this," she said, turning her small self into that teacher so that stance, gestures, words, tones all came alive before my eyes. Echoic sounds in a poem work in a similar way.

Some words are tricky, compounds, for instance. "Please be awfully careful about compounding words. Now please don't be mad — once in a while they work marvellously — when nothing else would do — but I think one should be very leery of them" (to Polly Hanson, n.d., Vassar 32.1). Bishop uses few of them, and many are color compounds that do not stand out because they are common enough, "blue-green," for example, in "Love Lies Sleeping." In *North & South*, there is also "the gun-metal blue dark" and "the gun-metal blue window" at the beginning of the militaristic section of "Roosters" (1941), a description one can almost taste. Thus also at the end of this section is the dead rooster, whose "metallic feathers oxidize." (See further on "gun-metal" later in this chapter.) Later come "blue-gray" in "The Bight" and "At the Fishhouses," several in "Brazil, January 1, 1502," and others scattered throughout, all in the ordinary range of pairings. But then there are the "rust-perforated roses" in "Faustina, or Rock Roses" (1947), as compact a description of roses starting to rot as you will find. Later there are hailstones or "dead-eye pearls" in "Song for the Rainy Season," an astonishing compound. In "The End of March," still later, "mutton-fat jade" color is wonderfully observed, another compound that is metaphorical.

Apart from color compounds, Bishop invents an "insect-gladiator" in "Sleeping on the Ceiling," which is just right. (Tough-shelled armor-encased insects come to mind, the kind that make one a bit nervous.) The word "star-splintered" does a lot of work, as does "carrier-warrior-pigeon" (see the discussion of "Paris, 7 A.M." in Chapter 3). So also with "glass-smooth dung" in "The Prodigal." Some of Bishop's compounds draw attention to themselves, like the ones in "Filling Station": "oil-soaked, oil-permeated," "oil-soaked," and then, emphasized by enjambment,

> grease-
impregnated wickerwork.

So also in the dream that makes up "Sunday, 4 A.M.": "cross- and wheel-studded / like a tick-tack-toe." So also in "The End of March" with the "proto-dream-house" that is changed to "crypto-dream-house" and caused this reader to double-check the prefixes "proto-" and "crypto-" and to think about the re-reading and correcting of dreams. At least one compound substitutes a word for something we expect to hear. Waste-disposal trucks rumble through my city regularly, but "guilt-disposal" is another matter ("Night City"). As for Bishop's compound at the end of "Poem," it is a stroke of genius: "the yet-to-be-dismantled elms, the geese."

Some awareness of the history of words is a sine qua non for writing well, an awareness that will develop along the way in reading older poets. Bishop possessed it to an acute degree: the feel of words, their origins in time and their etymological roots, their sudden new appearance. When she was twenty-three, she entered into a short, lively correspondence with Donald Stanford about her poems, and about his poems too, defending her practice and challenging some of his. "The word 'greenhouse' has a strangely Victorian feeling about it when used in such a poem — it strikes me as being out of place." (The poem centered on Hamlet.) She continued with a fierce attack on the word "charms" — "a convenient masculine label for the more exciting features of female anatomy" (15 Mar. 1934, L 19). Bishop's historical sense of words goes well beyond "greenhouse." She was aware of changes in meaning over the years. In a 1947 letter, she wrote to her friend Joseph Summers about his translations of George Herbert's Latin poems: "'Images' seems to me to be used with our modern meaning for it. I don't believe it was used that way in Herbert's time, was it? I think I'd object to the word 'knowing' for the same reason" (24 Aug. 1947, L 149).

Sometimes Bishop also implies that a reader should pay attention to word roots, for example, the "pure-colored or spotted breasts" of her birds in "Brazil, January 1, 1502" (1960). The house walls in "Song for the Rainy Season," also from 1960, are "maculate," as is the breath that has altered them. This suggestive use of "immaculate" and "maculate" goes all the way back to *North & South*, where "Seascape" (1941) includes "immaculate reflections." Of course, it helped that Eliot had emphasized the meaning of "maculate" as against the much-better-known "immaculate" in his "Sweeney among the Nightingales" (1918).

At the same time, Bishop was aware of new words. Take that fresh rewriting of metaphors about the sea as a garment in "The Map." It's not just the rewritten metaphor that is fresh. The diction itself is new. For this is apparently the first recorded use of the word "yard-goods." It predates by six years the supposed earliest illustration listed in the *Oxford English Dictionary*, "yard-goods" in *Little House on the Prairie* from 1941. "The Map" appeared in *Trial Balances* in 1935. How quiet it is, this introduction into the record by a twenty-three-year-old of an everyday working word she must have heard, perhaps in Nova Scotia. How many other poets, in the earliest poem of their first collection, first record a new word in the language?

"Love Lies Sleeping," published when Bishop was twenty-six, uses a fresh word at the time, "queer" ("queer cupids"), though it is in common use now. "The Man-Moth," published even earlier (1936), also uses the word, though the dominant meaning appears to be the common one ("the queer light on his hands"). In the 1930s, "queer" was moving into general use, so that Bishop can put both the older general meaning and the sexual meaning into play, as I think she does in "Love Lies Sleeping."¹⁰ Incidentally, *The Maltese Falcon*, published in 1930, provides earlier nonscientific use than the examples from 1931 and 1932 in the OED. Sam Spade's loyal secretary, Effie, introduces Joel Cairo in chapter 4 by saying, "This guy is queer." In chapter 7, the kicking, scratching fight with Bridget is caused by her crack about Cairo having a boy in Constantinople, while "the fairy" appears in chapter 10 and another reference to a "boyfriend" in chapter 19. None of these terms is used in the film versions, though in the classic one, Peter Lorre's dress and demeanor offer a stereotype of a gay man.

Bishop's notebook includes an entry on fashion in words "so much more subtle, even, than clothes fashions." The telling example is Auden's use of "marvellous":

> E. [Empson] tries to get the *feeling in the air* about the words (. . . the word fashion which is so much more subtle, even, than clothes fashions. Cecil Beaton's "infinitely beautiful" in 25 years will sound like "a capitol treat" of 1880.) . . . A sensitive reader, I think, familiar with the work of a poet, can *feel* what words are fashion-words, used ironically, "waked up," etc. etc.,

> *but* they tend to fall back, I believe, to the previous use — I
> mean A's [Auden's] "marvellous" will lose its slight tint of
> mystery-Oxbridge-naiveté and become anyone's "marvellous."
> (D. H. Lawrence & "manly," etc.) (EAP 267–268; ellipsis in
> original)

The adjective "gun-metal" is used twice to describe a color at
the start of "Roosters." The noun goes back to 1541, but the adjective, it turns out, is a twentieth-century adaptation, used of a
color by the fashion industry. The OED cites three well-known
British newspapers in 1905, 1923, and 1931. Where Bishop heard
or read it, I do not know, but it was fresh when she was young.
It is impossible now to recapture the "*feel*" of this word in 1941
when Bishop published the poem or of "queer" in 1938 when she
published "Love Lies Sleeping."

After Bishop's death, her editor and friend, Robert Giroux,
defended her use of the verb "slayed" in her story "A Trip to
Vigia" (1967, LOA 461–468): "it is 1920–30 slang, but she did use
it (as did Jean Stafford) to the end, and since she puts it in
quotes to indicate its quaintness, I hope you can stet it."[11] "That
slays me," meaning "that's hilarious," is an idiom that persisted
into at least the fifties and was familiar to me. Jay Macpherson
makes fine use of it as a punning riddle in "Isis": "The answer
will slay you, you'll see."[12] Bishop also enjoyed the fact that she
was the first to use the word "piss" in the *New Yorker* (to Howard
Moss, 30 Mar. and 6 Apr. 1971, LEBNY 324, 326).

Baudelaire was long a favorite poet of Bishop's, and she read
him closely enough to hear a surprising word for modern ears
and how it works: "'Les soirs illuminés par l'ardeur du charbon . . .'
where *charbon* is the telling word — surprising, accurate, *dating*
the poem, yet making it real, yet making it mysterious —"

("Writing poetry is an unnatural act . . . ," late 1950s–early 1960s, LOA 705). The line is a repeated rhyme line from Baudelaire's memorable "Le Balcon" from *Fleurs du mal.*

Exercise: Find a familiar word adopted in some new fashion, a fashion that gives it a particular tone, especially if it is a tone that has been lost. Or locate a key word used by a familiar writer in a certain individual way and define that way. And (easier) find a word in an older poem that dates it for us but is effective, and describe how.

To this exercise should be added Donald Davie's caveat about merely fashionable words and their danger. "Most poets are sufficiently sensitive to recognize the words which are fashionable. There are fashions in words for poetry, as in words for conversation." His example in 1952 for a fashionable word in poetry was "improbable." Bad poets, he wrote, adopt such words, "probably unconsciously." He added, "It is relatively easy to recognize bad poetic diction . . . [and] more difficult to recognize good diction, and to distinguish it from the bad" (*Purity of Diction,* 7).

Watching Bishop's diction turned up something unexpected. Certain words repeat from one poem to another and, even more striking, from one collection to another. Readers of Bishop might guess that "dream" is one such word, for she liked to work with dream material all her life. A few poems consist of dreams, some starting from actual dreams ("The Weed," "Sunday, 4 A.M."). In all, the concordance to her work shows thirty-eight examples of forms of the word "dream." A word not so easily guessed is "breath" in various forms, a total of twenty-two examples. But then, Bishop was asthmatic. The adjective "queer" turns up five times, though Bishop keeps the effect quiet.

Watching Bishop's diction turned up something else, her use of negatives. It is Milton who makes us most aware of the power of negative prefixes, say "un-." ("I cannot praise a fugitive and cloistered virtue, unexercised and unbreathed" [*Areopagitica*]. *Paradise Lost* is full of examples.) The concordance to Bishop shows that a high proportion of her "un-" words are unusual ones. There are few in *North & South* but several in *A Cold Spring*. She appears to have started to work with them about 1948. The ending of "Over 2,000 Illustrations and a Complete Concordance" is a case in point: "Why couldn't we have seen/this old Nativity while we were at it?/ . . . /an undisturbed, unbreathing flame." "Undisturbed" is clear, but an "unbreathing" flame? Impossible, for flames need oxygen, so that this flame is from an illustration and also supernatural as in the burning bush and also imagined, all at the same time. The effect is so quiet that we can pass it by. Not so quiet is the word "uninnocent" in "Four Songs," "I. Conversation": "Uninnocent these conversations start,/and then engage the senses." Bishop likes such compact, unobtrusive effects as variations in a prefix.

Diction is also governed by the kind of poem it is helping to build, its genre or mode. An epistolary poem will probably use informal diction, an elegy more contemplative, measured diction — thus in Bishop's "Letter to N.Y." and "North Haven." The diction is deliberately off in "Varick Street," a song after the manner of Auden. Refrain here plays against verse with a dislocating effect, as intended.

> *And I shall sell you sell you*
> *sell you of course, my dear, and you'll sell me.*

Above all, diction is governed by the tone of a poem, that most demanding and difficult of tests for any writer.

About 1965, Bishop was asked by an interviewer, "What do you like especially about [George] Herbert?" "To begin with, I like the absolute naturalness of tone. Coleridge has some good remarks on this, you remember" (Schwartz and Estess 294–295). The remarks on naturalness come in chapter 17 of Coleridge's *Biographia Literaria,* where he argues against Wordsworth, who claimed to be showing his readers "low and rustic life." Coleridge agrees that a reader does indeed find pleasure in the "naturalness, in *fact,* of the things represented." That is also true of Bishop's work and well recognized in the many remarks on her famous descriptive eye. Factual accuracy gives a lot of pleasure. But Coleridge with his superior critical mind saw that a reader's pleasure also depends on "the apparent naturalness of the *representation,* as raised and qualified by an imperceptible infusion of the author's own knowledge and talent." This last sentence deserves to be hung on a writer's wall as a rule of thumb for writing naturally.

Bishop had been intrigued by *Biographia Literaria* from an early age. In 1934, ensconced in the New York Public Library, she copied swatches of Coleridge's masterpiece, sometimes commenting on them. These include the funny catalogue of antimnemonics that she later used in "The Sea and Its Shore."

This was the type of warning that worried him: "The habit of perusing periodical works may properly be added to the catalogue of ANTI-MNEMONICS or weakeners of the memory. Also 'eating of unripe fruit; gazing on the clouds and on movable things suspended in the air (that would apply); riding among a multitude of camels; frequent laughter (no); listening to a series of jests and anecdotes; the habit of reading tombstones in churchyards, etc.'" (And these last two might.)[13]

Elsewhere Coleridge talked about ordinary language in poetry, the *lingua communis* (cf. OED, preface). This, he argues, becomes different when used in poems rather than prose. In poetry, "are those words *in those places* commonly employed in real life to express the same thought or outward thing? Are they the style used in ordinary intercourse of spoken words? No! Nor are the modes of connections: and still less the breaks and transitions" (*Biographia Literaria*, chap. 20). The order of words, the style, the connections, the breaks and transitions: all these condition choices about diction. Those choices are made "by an imperceptible infusion of the author's own knowledge and talent." Talent is given, though it needs nourishing. Knowledge may be acquired. Both Bishop and May Swenson admired Coleridge's *Biographia Literaria:* Bishop wrote to Swenson, "*Biographia Literaria* is one of the best books I know for 'ideas' — and do please send me your notes — it is filled with wonderful things — I think one of my quotations in 'The Sea & Its Shore' is from it, isn't it?"[4]

Bishop's careful tutoring of the work of a few friends who asked her for advice provides an ongoing lesson in such matters. She wrote to Ilse Barker, late in her life, "I know I am a finicky old fuddy-duddy. . . . Perhaps because of that very small school-teacher streak I am awfully aware of things like repetition, sounds, placement of adverbs, etc. etc. . . . Here & there *I think I could make it read a bit more naturally*" (24 July 1979, Barker letters; emphasis added). To take the smallest effect mentioned, how far do we think about where an adverb is placed? About word order in phrases? In "The Prodigal" from *A Cold Spring,* Bishop writes of the "brown enormous odor," whereas "enormous brown odor" would be the common order. "Enormous" in itself is unusual compared with the usual "strong," "overpowering," and the like. "Brown" is yet more unusual.

As Bishop's writing matured, she became more and more at ease incorporating ordinary and sometimes colloquial language into her poems. There is not much of it in *North & South,* it increases somewhat in *A Cold Spring,* while *Questions of Travel, Geography III,* and the late published poems use it freely — and they use it in major poems like "Santarém" and "Poem," the first two examples at the beginning of this chapter.

CHAPTER THREE

On the Move: From New York to Key West, via France

Bishop came within a hair's breadth of publishing her first collection in 1939 or 1940 when she was twenty-eight or twenty-nine. The reason she did not is simple: James Laughlin. Laughlin, an early admirer of Bishop's work, included her in his New Directions anthologies and in 1937 encouraged her to send him a book-length group of poems for publication under the New Directions imprint. Bishop replied that she did not yet have enough material. Two years later, on March 13, 1939, after checking, she sent him "the WORKS." But for some reason, Laughlin asked that she commit her next *five* books to him. To ask for the next book is standard, but five was unheard of. It was a lifetime commitment. After a struggle, Bishop suggested that her next two books could be bespoken. Laughlin was adamant. Alas, her list of "twenty-five to thirty" poems for a New Directions book is not with the company's records. It must have included some that did not pass scrutiny a little later.[1]

It's a curious thought that New Directions could have had her as their author. And it's a question how her career would look to us now if this first collection had been published. As it happened, for various reasons her first collection did not appear until 1946, when she was thirty-five. The reasons included a period of intense self-criticism and wavering about a path forward.

Bishop had more sense of a path forward in her letter of March 13, 1939, to Laughlin: "What I am working for, as you

say, is my own 'rhythm' — eventually I hope to be able to make
a whole book of poems all along the lines of 'The Weed,' 'The
Iceberg,' etc., which I feel are the most characteristic, and
best. I think my thoughts turn toward the 'allegorical' rather
than the 'conceit' — the poems are confused now, but eventually I hope to be able to put much more into them — many
more 'things,' and make them much more thorough-going"
(New Directions Publishing Corp. Records, bMS Am 2077
189). Bishop's thoughts about the conceit are likely second
thoughts about her very early poems like "Three Valentines"
and "The Reprimand." Marianne Moore chose them for publication in 1935, but they did not make it into Bishop's 1946
collection. They show a modern reworking of Renaissance
conceits:

> Love with his gilded bow and crystal arrows
> > Has slain us all,
>
> . . . .
>
> Oh sweet, sweet Love — go kick thy naughty self
> Around a cloud, or prick thy naughty self
> > Upon a gilded pin.
> ("Three Valentines," I)

> Now a conundrum Love propounds
> > My heart:
> You with himself my Love confounds
> > With perfect art,
> Until I swear I cannot tell you two apart.
> ("Three Valentines," II)

> If you taste tears too often, inquisitive tongue,
> You'll find they've something you'd not reckoned on.
> > > ("The Reprimand")

When a group of her poems was finally rejected by *Hound &
Horn* as "'too mannered,' 'too clever,'" Bishop acknowledged
that they were "not wonderful." But she did think that "to try to
develop a manner of one's own, to say the most difficult things,
and to be funny if possible . . . is more to one's credit than to go
on the way all the young *H&H* poets do" (to Frani Blough, [2
Mar. 1934], L 17). Developing a manner of one's own — we
sometimes say "a voice of one's own" — is the sine qua non for a
good writer and the hardest of challenges. Being "clever" aligns
Bishop with the moderns: Eliot, Stevens, Auden. It also helps
to account for the density of some of her early poems in *North &
South*, I think. Bishop's mapping for her poetic voyage began
originally through very different waters from her later travels,
though being funny remains throughout her writing (and is
seldom mentioned).

A few words on how Bishop shapes her first collection, a
subject about which critics say little: In August 1936, she wrote
to Marianne Moore, "I am reading Augustine's *Confessions*,
Amiel's *Journals*, and Wordsworth's *Prelude*, and this heaped-up
autobiography is having extreme results, maybe fortunate" (L 45).
The immediate results were thoughts of giving up poetry and
studying medicine or biochemistry, for she had been good at
science in college. Suddenly her accomplishment seemed like
"nothing at all" after "more than a fair trial" (ibid.). She was back
from Europe and suffering a crisis in self-confidence. Fortu-
nately it did not last, though it would recur. "The Weed" was
published in February 1937 and four more poems in July 1937.

Of those "heaped-up" autobiographies, I find Wordsworth's
Prelude the most useful when considering the shape of *North &
South*. If we think of *North & South* as a kind of prelude, we can
see that it follows Bishop's movements after her time at Vassar

much more closely than her title suggests: first of all, eight introductory poems with an emphasis on voyaging. Some of the voyaging is interior, the growth of a poet's mind. Northern settings predominate: a North Atlantic map, an iceberg, a "huntress of the winter air" ("The Colder the Air"), Wellfleet in Massachusetts, "Labrador" together with the "Strait of Belle Isle," the narrow strait between the northern tip of Newfoundland and Labrador that is a shipping channel. The last poem, "Large Bad Picture," repeats a place-name from the opening poem and rounds off the first group.

Second comes a movement "From the Country to the City," followed by three city poems, "The Man-Moth," "Love Lies Sleeping," and "A Miracle for Breakfast." They mark Bishop's move to New York after her college years, and they correspond to book 7 of *The Prelude*, "Residence in London." All three city poems suggest allegory indirectly, and Bishop then moves to three dream-like allegorical poems: "The Weed," "The Unbeliever," and "The Monument." These make up the first half of the collection, fifteen of the thirty poems. Allegorical intimations continue in the five French poems that begin with "Paris, 7 A.M." (I am including "Sleeping Standing Up" among these because it is paired with "Sleeping on the Ceiling" with its Place de la Concorde and Jardin des Plantes and because its wartime dream imagery suggests Europe in 1938, the year it was published.) They too correspond to Wordsworth's *Prelude*, this time to his sojourn in France (books 9 to 10 in the 1805 *Prelude*, books 9 to 11 in the 1850 version).

Then come the ten poems that make up the south of *North & South*, starting with "Florida," another place-name poem, and ending with "Anaphora." In the last books of Wordsworth's *Prelude*, the focus turns to his imagination and its restoration.

Bishop makes no such large claims or analysis. She published *North & South* when she was thirty-five, the same age at which Wordsworth finished the first version of *The Prelude*. (It was published in an expanded version in 1850 after his death.) Though "Imagination, How Impaired and Restored" is not Bishop's focus, the city poems and the dream-like poems each end with a sense of some restoration after impairment. As for "Anaphora," its subject is precisely restoration and impairment — daily restoration and daily impairment.

Throughout these thirty poems, sundry dream poems are interspersed, as are a few focusing on an art object. There are also some strange creatures, as if the voyage were something of an Odyssey. The order of the poems is roughly chronological, and the arrangement follows the growth of a poet through her formative adult years. It is astonishing to realize that most poems in the collection were written when Bishop was still in her twenties.[2]

Augustine's *Confessions,* Amiel's *Journals,* and Wordsworth's *Prelude:* autobiographies, yes, and with more than one thing in common. All three are writers. Amiel wrote poetry as well as his journal, and he lost both parents when young. Wordsworth was born in 1770, his mother died in 1778, and his father died in 1783. Augustine did not suffer the loss of parents, though his father hardly exists for us compared with his formidable mother. Age twenty-five, Bishop is thinking hard about how to write of her life thus far, how other writers made art out of their losses.

There is direct evidence for Bishop's sense of shaping. In a letter to her publisher about her *Complete Poems,* she is unconcerned about some rearrangement but very firm about keeping certain poems together in a group. In the *North & South* poems, for example, "The Weed," "The Unbeliever," and "The Monument" "could all change places in any way that would help the pages come out better" but should stay together as a group. In poems from *A Cold Spring*, "A Summer's Dream," "At the Fishhouses," and "Cape Breton" could also be shifted in any order but should form a group.[3]

Bishop also shaped the opening of *North & South*. In 1946, she inserted three poems near the start. The fifth poem, "Wading at Wellfleet," was retrieved from an early notebook of 1935 and so is contemporaneous with the first four poems. "Chemin de Fer" and "Large Bad Picture" were first published in 1946 just before *North & South* came out. Why these late additions just here? First, I think, because "Large Bad Picture" rounds out the opening group of eight poems before the move "From the Country to the City." Second and more important, because all three are simpler poems, much more readily taken in than the opening four. By this time, Bishop had started to work on simplifying her style.

Cityscapes and Dreamscapes

Bishop grouped her four city poems and three dream poems so that they provide two small dramas, each culminating in a Wordsworthian "spot of time." The second drama is the more powerful. "The Monument" gives a strong sense of ending to the first half of *North & South*, the northern North American half.

"From the Country to the City" offers a new note in *North & South*, with its "broad highway appearance, . . . / . . . the quick dance / Of colours, lights, and forms" (Wordsworth, *Prelude* 1805, 7.156–158). Its "tuning-fork" is struck and sends vibrations down the highway, the personified body of Bishop's long clown. For the first thirteen-line sentence, the highway is out of a Perrault fairy tale and the commedia dell'arte.

> The long, long legs,
> league-boots of land, that carry the city nowhere,
>   nowhere; the lines
> that we drive on (satin-stripes on harlequin's
>   trousers, tights);
> his tough trunk dressed in tatters, scribbled over with
>   nonsensical signs;
> his shadowy tall dunce-cap. . . .

There are the "league-boots," like Tom Thumb's seven-league boots in Perrault. There is Harlequin, the wily trickster who always gets the girl, though his traditional diamond-patterned costume has gone "nonsensical." There is the dunce cap that belongs to Pierrot, the melancholy clown in white, Harlequin's foil. This first section is wonderfully apt for rapid hypnotic travel along a highway at night. The road with its stripes goes on and on. Highway directions appear as "nonsensical signs." There are "intermeshing crowns" (intersections?) with "jeweled works" (stoplights?), "lamé with lights." But the clown becomes a "wickedest clown," a "you," and sirens appear, as if personifying the metaphor "the siren-call of the city." There is a threat of seduction, a whiff of possible disaster, a sense of overstimulus. The body begs and begs, "Subside."

The quoted phrase in line 10, "fantastic triumph," was much better known in 1937, thanks to Virginia Woolf's 1929 *A Room of One's Own*, which praises the author Aphra Behn (1640–1689), the first woman to earn her living by writing. In Bishop, it is the brain that is "throned 'in fantastic triumph.'" In Behn's "Love

Armed," it is Love. John Hayward liked Behn's poem well enough to include it in his 1955 anthology *Seventeenth Century Poetry*. The ending sounds like Pierrot reproaching Harlequin: "But my poor heart alone is harmed,/while thine the victor is, and free." Behn makes a fine figure for a young woman going to New York and hoping to earn a living by her wits, to write — and no doubt to explore love.[4]

As if in answer, "The Man-Moth" offers a second act in an ongoing drama, this time a solo act, as if one of the great mimes, wearing a white Pierrot costume with whitened face, had metamorphosed into a moth, a man-moth. A misprint gave Bishop her Kafka poem: "man-moth" for "mammoth." ("The . . . misprint seemed meant for me. An oracle spoke from the page of the *New York Times*, kindly explaining New York City to me, at least for a moment" ("On 'The Man-Moth,'" 1962, LOA 715). After a speeding car at night comes silence, whiteness, flitting in the underground, riding a subway train, or climbing out toward the unearthly light of the moon. After a "you" and "we" comes a solitary figure. In this poem, as Robert Lowell said, "you don't know what will come after any one line. It's exploring. And it's as original as Kafka. She's gotten a world, not just a way of writing."[5]

The ambience is of shrinking, fear, darkness, and a struggle toward light: "nervously," "trembles," "fearfully," "what the Man-Moth fears most he must do." The creature always sits facing backward, that is, occupying our only possible seat in the train of time, where we can't see what's coming, only what has passed. (It's a metaphor found, for example, in Walter Benjamin.) Just as subway ties recur, so also do "recurrent dreams/ . . . underlie/his rushing brain" and the compulsion to think of the deadly third rail alongside. The last stanza focuses on the Man-Moth's eye and its mysterious tear, recalling Bishop's early poems on eyes and tears.

"Love Lies Sleeping" is a dawn poem, waking to early morning light as the city starts another day. The imperative "Hang-over moons, wane, wane!" is like "Subside" at the end of "From the Country to the City." Slowly, this becomes a daylight poem, with "detail upon detail" of a city waking. Only in the last four stanzas of this fifteen-stanza poem does something very amiss happen "to one . . . whose head has fallen over the edge of his bed."

All three poems offer vignettes of New York in the thirties, three random vignettes very different in tone, perspective, and form — or on second thought, not so random. There is one unobtrusive link among all three, the brain:

>   that
> glittering arrangement of your brain consists, now,
>   of mermaid-like,
> seated, ravishing sirens. . . .
> ("From Country to City")

> Just as the ties recur beneath his train, these underlie
> his rushing brain.
> ("The Man-Moth")

> Earliest morning . . .
>
> . . . .
>
> now draw us into daylight in our beds,
> and clear away what presses on the brain.
>   ("Love Lies Sleeping")

Together the poems make a small drama with an allegory of (1) brain and body, (2) brain and — what? (3) brain and heart. It is the body that begs its brain to "Subside" in "From the Country to the City." It is the heart that is mentioned in "Love Lies Sleeping." And "The Man-Moth"? What is the part of us that mostly lives underground, timid and fearful, sometimes rising to the surface, where it aspires to reach the moon? More than aspires: is compelled, as a moth is compelled to fly toward the light and as Pierrot is drawn to the moon. The Man-Moth, much indebted to Kafka, also draws on the Pierrot figure from the commedia dell'arte, as several critics have observed. He sometimes appears as *Pierrot lunaire,* the sad moonstruck clown, and is often associated with Jules Laforgue, whom Bishop admired, though Verlaine's poem "Pierrot" with its flitting, haunting, ghostly form should not be forgotten.[6] Nor should Arnold Schönberg's 1912 dramatic song cycle *Pierrot Lunaire.* (Hopkins's "ideas about composition seem almost to forecast some of Schönberg," Bishop wrote to Marianne Moore on April 2, 1935 [L 32].) So is this poem an allegory of brain and soul? Brain and spirit? Brain and subconscious? As befits this part of our selves, Bishop keeps the creature mysterious, including his mysterious freshwater, non-human tear at the end.

"A Miracle for Breakfast" ends the first city drama, this time with an urban dawn in which a crowd of people are lined up, hoping for food. Bishop later called it "my Depression poem": "It was written shortly after the time of souplines and men selling apples, around 1936 or so. It was my 'social conscious' poem, about hunger."[7] The tone is straightforward reportage. The form is striking, a sestina, a form that lends itself to themes of repetition, like hunger and eating. Of the six repeated end words, the odd man out is "miracle," miracles being unique and rare: "coffee," "crumb," "balcony," "miracle," "sun," "river." The miracle of the loaves and fishes is most apt here, the miracle in which a few fish and loaves miraculously become thousands, enough to feed a multitude. In the first publication of the poem and nowhere else, it had an epigraph translated from Pascal's *Pensées* (part 13, section 802):

> Miracles enable us to judge of
> doctrine, and doctrine enables
> us to judge of miracles.

Naturalistic explanations of the miracle of the loaves and fishes posit a compassion that spread from Jesus to those in the crowd who had food, who were then moved to share it. If the miracle of coffee and bread appeared for a line of the hungry unemployed of the Great Depression, then, says Pascal, it would enable us to judge the doctrine of the state concerning its deprived citizens. The man who drops crumbs demonstrates his own personal doctrine about the needy.

As for Bishop's doctrine, "I can tell what I saw next: it was not a miracle." It was a "baroque white plaster balcony / added by birds," bird droppings, that is. It is a natural phenomenon and so not miraculous. But then this architecture of birds' droppings becomes the speaker's own, "made for me by a miracle, / through ages, by insects, birds, and the river / working the stone." Natural phenomena offer their own kind of miracle to an observing delighted eye, and Bishop's own doctrine readjusts itself to accommodate this kind of miracle. Like the elements, like the natural phenomena that so often steady Bishop through difficult times in her life, so with this natural miracle. The tone at the end is firm and realistic, a reclaiming of ordinary life after the hectic pace of the preceding city poems. As protest poem, however, "Miracle for Breakfast" has a mixed effect, perhaps because Bishop is trying to do too much.

The second three-act drama belongs to an interior life, and the first two poems come back to the body and the heart ("The Weed") and the body and the soul ("The Unbeliever"), while the third ("The Monument") treats an unlikely work of art rather as "A Miracle for Breakfast" treats an unlikely thing of beauty. As noted, Bishop wanted these three poems kept together.

"I dreamed that dead, and meditating,/I lay upon a grave, or bed": so begins "The Weed." The grave or bed experiences an upheaval familiar from springtime and seedbeds. Like a surreal painting in motion, a young weed starts to grow from the heart until it splits the breastbone, and two rivers begin to flow, one to each side. But then, as Bishop said, "some of Herbert's poems strike me as almost surrealistic, 'Love Unknown,' for instance," and that was the poem Bishop modeled "The Weed" on. "I was much interested in surrealism in the '30s," she added (Brown, "Interview," 294–295). The poem is also based on close observation of how a seedling grows, how it splits the seed with a head that then divides into two leaves. For this is a poem about division and about the heart, as the ending tells us: "'I grow,' it said,/'but to divide your heart again.'" As with "Love Lies Sleeping," the literal heart bears the consequences of the metaphorical heart. It gets eaten out. It gets divided by new growth.

"The Unbeliever" is not Bishop's first poem in *North & South* to treat unbelief. The end of "The Imaginary Iceberg" also does, though obliquely:

Icebergs behoove the soul
(both being self-made from elements least visible)
To see them so: fleshed, fair, erected indivisible.

The word "self-made" may do for the iceberg, but a self-made soul? This soul does not come from the hand of God. "Now shall

I make my soul," says Yeats, in a poem first published eight years earlier, "The Tower." Behind "The Imaginary Iceberg" lies many another poem in which the journey of the soul's "earth-vessel," the body, is the archetypal story of the voyage of life. Longfellow's translation of an Anglo-Saxon poem, "The Soul's Complaint against the Body," opens, "Much it behoveth / Each one of mortals / That he his soul's journey / In himself ponder." Bishop's ending is highly unorthodox, though that is not its point. She simply assumes this perspective.

And that final word, "indivisible"? Is it the soul that is indivisible? This is a traditional view. Or is it the fleshed and fair that are also indivisible, that is, the soul and body? If soul and body are one and indivisible, then a body cannot act differently from its soul. For someone struggling with the question of sexual orientation, the question matters a great deal. For someone struggling with questions of making art, it also matters a great deal in a different way. "What the artist is always looking for," Oscar Wilde wrote, "is that mode of existence in which soul and body are one and indivisible" — that is, a work of art *(De Profundis).*[8]

In "The Unbeliever," the epigraph reads, "He sleeps on the top of a mast — Bunyan," and the sentence opens the first and last stanzas. The poem begins with a fine mimesis of someone in bed suffering from a hangover, as if swaying on top of the mast.

> He sleeps on the top of a mast
> with his eyes fast closed.
> The sails fall away below him
> like the sheets of his bed,
> leaving out in the air of the night the sleeper's head.

We might call line 4 a gambit declined. Rather than punning on "sheets," Bishop turns it into explicit simile, without mentioning that a sailor's word for sails is "sheets."[9] Bunyan uses the text from Proverbs 23:34–35 twice, once in *Pilgrim's Progress* (1678) and once in *The Life and Death of Mr. Badman* (1680).[10] Proverbs links the text with drunkenness, as does *Mr. Badman*. But in the far-better-known *Pilgrim's Progress,* the text is used of three different forms of unbelief, attributed to Simple, Sloth, and Presumption. Christian warns them of their fate, but they refuse to join him on the path to salvation. Simple says, "I see no danger." Sloth says, "Yet a little more sleep." Presumption says, "Every tub must stand on its own bottom."

In Bishop, there are also three types of unbelief. The man on top of the mast is dreaming, like Christian in Bunyan's great allegory, but not dreaming of salvation. He is like Sloth. The cloud and gull who speak are both deluded that they are up-held in the air by marble. ("Marble" is a common epithet for the heavens in the seventeenth century. "Now, by yond marble heaven," says Othello [3.3.460], and Satan journeys through the "pure marble Air" [*Paradise Lost* 3.564].) "I must not fall," says the man who sleeps on the top of a mast. Like Christian warning Simple, Sloth, and Presumption, he knows that those "who sleep on the top of a mast" have "the Dead Sea under you — a gulf that hath no bottom." "I must not fall" is also a drunkard's self-admonition. Feeling as if one were floating like a cloud or flying free while actually solidly based: these are a drunkard's delusions too. The man who sleeps on the top of the mast may be dreaming, but he is a lot more realistic than gull or cloud and a lot more realistic than in Bunyan, in a nice touch of humor.

The third poem in Bishop's grouping, "The Monument," is a powerful poem with a memorable ending:

It is the beginning of a painting,
a piece of sculpture, or poem, or monument,
and all of wood. Watch it closely.

Bishop drew a rough sketch of what she had in mind for her poem, and beneath the sketch, which she introduced as "a *frottage* of this sea," she wrote the lines that are the kernel of this closing: "This is the beginning of a painting / a piece of statuary, or a poem, / or the beginning of a monument. / Suddenly it will become something. / Suddenly it will become everything."[11] The poem was "influenced, if by anything, by a set of prints I had of Max Ernst — lost long ago — called *Histoire Naturelle* (something like that) in which all the plants, etc., had been made by frottage — on wood, so the wood grain showed through" (to the Summerses, 19 Oct. 1967, L 478).

The monument sounds derelict earlier, more an end than a beginning and impossible to locate. It's "like a stage-set," objects the viewer, sky of wood, clouds full of splinters, a *frottage*. The viewer is instructed from line 1 onward: "Now can you see the monument?" So also Robert Browning opened his long poem *The Ring and the Book*, "Do you see this Ring?" and proceeded to explain just how it was made, an allegory for his own poetic method. Bishop's poem is an *ars poetica* of sorts, taking the observer firmly in hand. The unlikely construction in "The Monument" is the starting point for new growth in the hand of a maker or the eye of a beholder — thus also with any stage production. The questioner sounds like the person who wants standard mimesis. Bishop's use of allegory here works wonderfully for the mystery of a piece of art.

What makes the poem especially worth "watching" is its tone, its sense of mastery. In contrast to the many tumultuous poems between "The Map" and "The Monument," Bishop's tone has that calm authority that she possesses when she focuses on her art. Here, as David Bromwich makes clear, Bishop is at home.[12]

War

"The Map" shows us a whole world in little, much like a Vermeer painting. So does "Paris, 7 A.M.," written within two years of "The Map." The poem draws us into the midthirties at a time when doomsday in the form of a second world war "had become a commonplace," as Samuel Hynes puts it.[13] I shall not repeat the detailed reading of this poem in my 1998 *Against Coercion: Games Poets Play*.[14] But I want to emphasize again contemporary evidence from the midthirties (adding Bishop's letters to Muriel Rukyser), as well as the function of some supposedly surreal effects.

Bishop lived in Paris for three months during the winter of 1935–1936. She spent part of the summer on the Brittany coast, then moved with Louise Crane to a handsome apartment in Paris. They planned to take some courses at the Sorbonne, though they did not in the end.[15] From late March through May, they traveled to Morocco, Spain, and Mallorca before returning to New York in June. (Bishop had a small inheritance from her father, and it went a long way in the Great Depression. Louise Crane came from a wealthy and distinguished family.) Bishop traveled again in Europe from June to December 1937. She was fully aware that she was living a life of privilege. "I am sorry I am being so obstinate about 'apartments.' To me the word suggests so strongly the structure of the houses, later referred to, and suggests a 'cut-off' mode of existence so well — that I don't want to change it" (to Marianne Moore, 29 Sept. 1936, L 46). Most of us don't associate the word "apart" with "apartments," but then most of us are not poets. Bishop did and, before her, Wallace Stevens: *We are not a part of the chapel* — but apart from it. Hence, the word apartment. Hope this is clear."[16]

As with "The Map," "Paris, 7 A.M." closely observes a map — not its boundaries but its center, not land and water but a circular urban center with radiating streets and in the middle a monument. A clock face evokes the urban center, for that it is what it resembles, and the poem brilliantly superimposes the clock face on the map (and vice versa), so that the question of ticking, marching time slowly becomes acute. Place becomes place-time.

In line 5, "Time is an Etoile," and the Etoile has at its center a monument — not an isolated mysterious monument but a famous public monument, the Arc de Triomphe.[17] It is not for nothing that Bishop placed "Paris, 7 A.M." immediately after "The Monument." On a map, the Place de l'Etoile may be seen as a center for all Paris. So self-evident is this that a current children's guide to Paris offers it as a cartographic way of seeing the city. "From the Arc de Triomphe, monument to military might, one can see that Paris is bisected by a broad paved line leading straight from the Arc du Carrousel, in front of the Louvre, through the Arc de Triomphe all the way to the Grande Arche in the western suburb of La Défense, with the Champs-Elysées to the east of the arch and the avenue de la Grande Armée to the west."[18] The twelve avenues converging on the Arc de Triomphe become the hands of the clock-Etoile of Paris, measuring out the days, hour by hour and minute by minute. Eleven of the twelve avenues have military names, while the Arc de Triomphe in the heart of Paris celebrates military victories.

In the winter of 1935–1936, during Bishop's stay, economic conditions in Europe were very bad, and nationalism was burgeoning, a dangerous combination. Hitler had been in power since early 1933. In July 1935, the chancellor of Austria was murdered by Nazi agents; in October 1935, King Alexander of

Yugoslavia was assassinated in Marseilles; in March 1936, Hitler reoccupied the Rhineland. "Like so many of my contemporaries," John Lehmann wrote of 1935, "I was haunted by the feeling that time was running out for a new world war. 'How to get out of this trap?' I noted in a journal at the time. . . . How to defend oneself, to be active, not to crouch paralysed as the hawk descends?"[19]

Bishop like others was very aware of war news. On November 20, 1935, she wrote to Muriel Rukeyser, a fellow poet, college friend, and left-wing activist: "If the weak little Paris edition of the Herald Tribune can horrify us so with one column of War News I hate to think what you are in for in New York." She offered to send Rukeyser French magazines like *Commune*. "Communistic writing seems to be . . . flourishing here, led on by such exhibitionists as Gide, etc."[20] A later postcard reads, "If you stay in Stockholm long enough, I'll join you. Love, Bishop."[21]

Some of Bishop's supposedly surreal effects have nothing to do with surrealism. They are simply accurate description. To repeat: a first test for reading Bishop is always the possibility of ordinary representation — thus with the opening line and thus also with a dead "carrier-warrior-pigeon" falling from the sky.

"Paris, 7 A.M." opens with "I make a trip to each clock in the apartment" — a remark that can sound as whimsical as "Shadows, or are they shallows, at its edges." It is not. Like the shadows-shallows line, it makes perfect sense when read in context. At that time, you visited clocks daily or weekly in order to wind them up. A novel by William Maxwell set in 1918 reads, "Once a week he would wind all the clocks in the house, beginning with the grandfather's clock in the hall."[22] Robert Lowell reported in 1956 that Philip and Nathalie Rahv had "a clock that runs without winding for three years" (to Bishop, [18 June

1956], LEBRL 180). As for a "carrier-warrior-pigeon," it is a precise description, as Bishop well knew, and such birds were indeed shot down by enemy snipers.[23]

If readers are sometimes reminded of surrealism in Bishop's poem, this is because Paris in the mid-1930s *was* "surreal." "Surrealism provided a means of expressing not political ideas, but the emotions *behind* thirties politics — the fears and anxieties, the sense of unknown and terrible dangers, and of possible violence and outrage beyond the projections of reason: in short, it provided a parabolic method for the social nightmares of the time" (Hynes, *Auden Generation* 226).

When we take a step back, we note that the poem pulls quietly against its title. Why not a title like "Brazil, January 1, 1502"? "Paris, 7 A.M." suggests the lasting Paris, whose early mornings remain constant, with their promise of good coffee and fresh-baked croissants. But in 1935–1936, other things overshadow this Paris, including the question of how long it will last. Until June 1940 would be the eventual answer.

A note on the copyright page of *North & South* reads, "Most of these poems were written, or partly written, before 1942" — that is, before the United States went to war on December 7, 1941. Nonetheless the book is shot through with a sense of foreboding, both civil and personal, and there is much war imagery in the first six poems. After that, the sense of foreboding abates, only to return in force with Bishop's French poems. Her France in the thirties corresponds to Wordsworth's France just before the outbreak of the French Revolution (*The Prelude*, books 9–10, 1805; 9–11, 1850).

Another memory poem follows in the French section, personal memory this time and unspecified. "Quai d'Orléans" was

later dedicated to Margaret Miller, Bishop's dearly loved roommate in college. Rather than shake the reader with its particular
occasion, the poem that Bishop has written works for any horrifying memory that will haunt our lives. This one was a car accident in 1937 in France when Louise Crane was driving and
Bishop and Miller were passengers. Miller's right arm was se-
verely injured and had to be amputated near the elbow. She was
an aspiring painter.

> "If what we see could forget us half as easily,"
>   I want to tell you,
> "as it does itself — but for life we'll not be rid
>   of the leaves' fossils."

Three more French poems, "Sleeping on the Ceiling,"
"Sleeping Standing Up," and "Cirque d'Hiver" close this section. The first two resonate with war imagery; the second is a
Grimm fairy tale, transposed to the thirties and shot through
with frightening wartime imagery. "Cirque d'Hiver" (the Winter
Circus) is free from war imagery. (Like Marianne Moore,
Bishop was fond of circuses, and this one had just returned to
its earlier home in Paris.) The poem shows a charming mechan-
ical toy of horse and rider that perform when wound up. The
rider dressed like a ballet dancer is attached through the body
of the horse with its mane and tail "straight from Chiroco."
Bishop has returned to her allegories of body and soul: "the
little pole / that pierces both her body and her soul // and goes
through his" — not "The Imaginary Iceberg," not "The Man-
Moth," not "The Unbeliever," but a new figure. "He is the more
intelligent by far," so that perhaps we should add an allegory of
brain and body, complicating it all. Until the last line, the poem

is in third person, but then, "we stare and say, 'Well, we have come this far.'" The change of person suggests a personal journey in the first instance, while one earlier title, "History," suggests a wider journey as well.

The South

Looking back, it's hard to recognize how sharp a change Bishop's ten southern poems represent — much more than a change of place and climate. Although she told James Laughlin in March 1939 that she was turning "toward the 'allegorical,'" that did not happen. Starting in fact about 1939, she began to experiment with simplifying her work. "New styles of architecture, a change of heart," as Auden says.[24]

What were these new styles? First, as in "Florida," detailed description of a natural scene, realistically, with suggestive patterning on closer inspection. "Florida" ushers in a type of poem that Bishop will develop to perfection: "The Bight," "At the Fishhouses," "The End of March" — all coastline poems with detailed descriptions, all portrayed realistically in the first instance, all with a touch of humor: Florida's birds (see later in this chapter), the bight "awful but cheerful," a musical seal near the fishhouses, a shingled house that looks like an artichoke "but greener / (boiled with bicarbonate of soda?)" ("The End of March"). There is no realistic (or largely realistic) description of a natural landscape in the preceding twenty poems of *North & South*. There are vignettes of urban landscape, and there are bits of natural landscape in strange settings, weighted with significance. But so far Bishop's famous eye has dwelt on objects or else on scenes from fables, fantasies, allegories, dreams. Now suddenly, there is a plain poem in comparison. This is new for Bishop in *North & South,* and I think she recognized it by calling her collection what she did and dividing its two halves disproportionately.

Second, as in the next poem, "Jerónimo's House," are poems of local color. This is a genre that Bishop never quite made her own in *North & South:* local customs, local habitations, local names. "Jerónimo's House" and "Cootchie," the eighth southern poem, also published in 1941, are the two examples in *North & South.*

The third poem, "Roosters," is a war fable like "Paris, 7 A.M.," but its allegory is easily grasped, unlike the argument of "Paris, 7 A.M." More interesting as a harbinger of Bishop's later work, the poem uses juxtaposition to raise questions, juxtaposition that sets memory side by side with a current scene. She would continue to use this method, developing it in "Over 2,000 Illustrations and a Complete Concordance" and notably in "Brazil, January 1, 1502."

Fourth is an experiment in writing popular songs, as in "Songs for a Colored Singer," published in 1944 after a gap. This too demanded a discipline of simplicity. (So also Leonard Cohen moved from the world of poetry to the world of song.) She did not return to the genre in this form.

Fifth, also after a gap, is "Anaphora," the remarkable visionary closing poem, again a type of poem Bishop did not repeat — or not exactly: the late poem "Santarém" is a visionary poem layered with memory but circumscribed.

For some nine years, Bishop divided her time between New York and Key West. She and Louise Crane bought a house in Key West in 1938, though by mid-1940 they had ceased living together. By mid-1941, Bishop and Marjorie Carr Stevens had become lovers and remained so for six years, living mostly in Key West. The southern love poem "Late Air" (1938) comes from that period. It is the earliest of the southern poems (1938), followed by "Florida" (1939), then "The Fish" (1940), then four 1941 poems. From 1941 to 1944, there is a hiatus in publication. Late in 1944, Houghton Mifflin encouraged Bishop to apply for its new poetry award, having been struck by "Songs for a Colored Singer" (MacMahon 7); Marianne Moore highly recommended her, and she won over eight hundred applicants. Her first collection was finally published in 1946.

The coastline in "Florida" is seen as if by a walker, not a sailor: a place where sea creatures live and play and die and leave their skeletons. Florida is "the state that floats in brackish water," with amazing mangrove roots, whether alive or dead. On the high-tide line is a remnant, "a rag of rotted calico" from a buried Indian Princess's skirt, decorated with named shells — "Job's Tear, the Chinese Alphabet, the scarce Junonia, / parti-colored pectins and Ladies' Ears." The focus then pans outward, and the entire "monotonous, endless, sagging coast-line" becomes a memory-place. Florida is the "state full of long S-shaped birds," unidentified. They look emblematic, "S" for "South," and sure enough, looking back, we see northern birds as N's, "hanging in *n*'s on banks" — smaller birds, presumably ("Large Bad Picture"). The S-birds are in fact herons, as we know from Bishop's letters. The "unseen hysterical birds" whose rising songs or calls sound like a tantrum are also unidentified. Critics are incurious, but it's not hard to discover that they must be prairie warblers, who confusingly are not on the prairies. They are, however, "common in . . . young stands of . . . mangroves." Their song, "slow or fast, consists of buzzy notes ascending in a chromatic scale."[25] The "tanagers embarrassed by their flashiness" must be scarlet tanagers, presumably blushing at their own glorious color. Pelicans are commonly seen as clowns, and Bishop gives them ample tricks to play through their five lines and more. Among the shells, the pectenidae are scallops, and a calico scallop is parti-colored as in the "parti-colored pectin," a calico shell to match (or suggest) the "gray rag of rotted calico" of the imagined buried skirt.

The poem, whose title is a place-name, is also a poem about naming: "the prettiest name" (a touch of cuteness?), the unnamed birds, the named shells, the unnamed Indian Princess. How much does it matter that we see or hear things and have no names for them? At the very least, names help us to remember what we have seen or heard, especially when a prairie warbler is not a prairie warbler or when a calico shell precedes calico cloth, which etymologically comes from India and reminds us indirectly why the "Indian Princess" is in fact called "Indian." Bishop's method of withholding names, then providing a list of names, teases and challenges us. (Similarly with the *n*-shaped birds in "Large Bad Picture," published after "Florida": my guess is that they are murres.)

The first main verb is delayed until line 18, and the verb is "die," for an air of death permeates the poem along with the vigor of life. (The poem was published in 1939, before Eliot's 1941 "The Dry Salvages" with its portentous Massachusetts coastline and all its detritus.) Death dominates in the second half, starting with the "buzzards drifting down, down, down." The colorful noisy Florida coastline with its cycle of life and death gives way to an impoverished moonlit night scene of mosquitoes and "black specks" juxtaposed with "ugly white," "the poorest / postcard of itself." In line 41 comes a change in diction

so quiet that it can slip by: "Cold white, not bright, the moon-
light is coarse-meshed,/and the careless, corrupt state is all
black specks." "Corrupt"? But, but. "Careless" is the bridge
word: animals can also be careless, but "corrupt" is used only of
human beings, unless the old biblical meaning of "rotting" is in
play. (It's familiar from Handel's *Messiah*: "for the trumpet shall
sound, and the dead shall be raised incorruptible, and we shall
be changed. For this corruptible must put on incorruption" [1
Cor. 15:52–53].) This sense of flesh that dies and rots is present
all through "Florida," only now as corrupt. Natural description
incorporates moral judgment through an older language.

The poem ends with an alligator — not Stevens's alligator in
one of his best Florida poems, "Nomad Exquisite" (1923): "And
blessed mornings,/Meet for the eye of the young alligator." No:
an alligator that has five known calls but that in the evening
makes a different sound. That same mysterious Indian Princess
who ends the first verse paragraph is now heard resuscitated in
the sounds of its wildlife — not in one of the alligator's known
and classified sounds but through an alligator who "whimpers,
and speaks in the throat/of the Indian Princess."

"Florida" and "Seascape," the fourth poem, call out for comparison. Both have two contrasting sections. Both defer the
first main verb, in "Seascape" until line 13, when it sums up the
preceding descriptive catalogue: "this cartoon by Raphael for a
tapestry for a Pope:/it does look like heaven." Then "Seascape"
revisits the scene of "Florida," but listen to the two views of
mangrove: "when dead . . . /dotted as if bombarded, with
green hummocks/like ancient cannon-balls sprouting grass"
("Florida"); "the weightless mangrove island/with bright green
leaves . . . / . . . down to the suggestively Gothic arches of the

mangrove roots" ("Seascape"). Or listen to "skeletons" and "skel-etal": "when dead strew white swamps with skeletons" and "a skeletal lighthouse." Or listen to the adjective "white," as in "white swamps" and "white herons got up as angels." Or con-sider the adjective "black," as in "charring . . . like black velvet" and "the careless corrupt state is all black specks" ("Florida") and "a skeletal lighthouse standing there / in black and white clerical dress" ("Seascape").

The tone of "Seascape" is entirely different: relaxed, appre-ciative, and in the second part pure fun, with the clerical light-house "who lives on his nerves, thinks he knows better." Heaven is defined for him by its opposite, hell, and "when it gets dark, he will remember something / strongly worded to say on the subject." A Raphael cartoon for a tapestry versus a clerical light-house: two views of a coastline, *Paradiso* and *Inferno*, both so different from "Florida" that they seem to release Bishop's southern poems and allow them to proceed freely.[26] In the next poem, "Little Exercise," mangrove roots appear again but quite neutrally, as a place to tie a boat to.

There are, incidentally, seven famous surviving cartoons by Raphael for the ten tapestries in the Sistine Chapel. They are based on the Acts of the Apostles, and none comes close to this description. "Seascape" offers a design for an allegorical tapestry with "big symbolic birds" ("Brazil, January 1, 1502"), a tapestry of the blessed in heaven and a dark alternative represented by the lighthouse. The poem might be called an ekphrasis manqué.

"Cootchie" is also a study in black and white, unlike "Jerónimo's House," which is full of color. "Cootchie, Miss Lu-la's servant, lies in marl, / black into white she went." There is a lighthouse as well, "which will discover Cootchie's grave / and dismiss all as trivial." The sea at the end, "desperate, / will proffer wave after wave." Bishop's last line anticipates Stevie Smith's "Not waving but drowning" and at a distance recalls William Carlos Williams's poem "Yachts."

The long poem "Roosters" was published four years later than "Paris, 7 A.M." and similarly treats war, but Bishop is no longer an apprehensive bystander. She responds viscerally to the violence of war in a poem that includes corresponding violence. ("Roosters" is known as the occasion for Bishop's necessary coming-of-age break with her admired mentor, Marianne Moore, who recommended taming the poem into something much more genteel. Bishop made clear that she needed the "very important 'violence' of tone" [17 Oct. 1940, L 96–97].) It starts out as a protest against being wakened at four A.M. by roosters heralding the first light with raucous crowing:

> then one from the back fence,
> then one, with horrible insistence,
>
> . . . .
>
> grates like a wet match
> from the broccoli patch.

"Cries galore" culminate in "the uncontrolled, traditional cries" in an insistent, short-line series of triplets harassing the irritated half-awake sleeper. This is a protest poem that could stay exasperated, hyperbolic, and funny (and slight) but will now turn into a protest against much more. It's illogical to blame the rooster for its traditional cries and for being naturally "combative" (the Greeks' word for them, as Bishop points out). It's illogical to see their iridescent breast feathers as military "green-gold medals" and their noise as ordering us "how to live." It's illogical to see their "crown of red" as an "excrescence [that] makes a most virile presence" and lay on it all the burden of male aggression, including war. It's illogical in one way, yes, but all too logical in another, as Bishop ends the first section with a fight to the death between two roosters in midair. The loser "is flung / on the gray ash-heap, lies in dung." The winner presumably follows the old adage and crows from a dung heap.

By this time, the context of war is unmistakable, with the fight resembling so-called dogfights between Spitfires and Messerschmitts in the Battle of Britain, and the roosters recalling the *coq gaulois,* the French national symbol. Its fighting spirit was extolled in wartime. A World War I French recruiting poster appealing to French Canadians to help in the victory of the French cock over the Prussian eagle *(le coq gaulois sur l'aigle prussien)* shows a fierce cock clawing out feathers from the top of a larger eagle's head. Picasso's anti-Fascist cock, especially the one that appeared in *Guernica,* is well known. Bishop explicitly distinguished her roosters from his. "'Roosters' was not 'inspired,' as they say, by a Picasso rooster at all. . . . I started it and wrote all the beginning, and bits here and there, much more directly at 4 or 5 A.M. in the back yard in Key West, with the roosters carrying on just as I said" (to May Swenson, 18 Feb. 1956, L 316).

The second section abruptly changes tempo and volume — presto to adagio, forte to piano — and shows us that Bishop is perfectly aware of logic (and illogic) in symbols. She sets out the biblical scene of Peter's threefold denial of Christ in the Crucifixion narrative. "Then began he to curse and to swear, saying, I know not the man. And immediately, the cock crew. And Peter remembered the word of Jesus, which said unto him Before the cock crow, thou shalt deny me thrice. And he went

French recruiting poster for World War I, showing the French *coq gaulois* fighting *l'aigle prussien*, the German eagle (see "Roosters")

out and wept bitterly" (Matt. 26:74–75). In Bach's *St. John's Passion*, when "Petrus . . . ging hinaus und weinete bitterlich," *weinete* (wept) is a prolonged wail with chromatic effects. Shortly before publishing "Roosters," Bishop told Moore, "I wanted to keep 'to see the end' in quotes, because, although it may not be generally recognized, I have always felt that expression used of Peter in the Bible to be extremely poignant" (17 Oct. 1940, L 96–97). Peter goes in "to see the end" before his threefold denial. Peter: friend and disciple, betrayer and enemy, the bitterly repentant, the forgiven. She also put "Servants and officers" (John 18:18) in quotation marks that point up the source and invite readers to pursue it.

But betrayal and violence is long past in Bishop's second section. As against all the action in the first part, contemplation governs the second, contemplation of a work of art:

> Old holy sculpture
> could set it all together
> in one small scene, past and future.

Christ and Peter stand together with a small cock between and the inscription *gallus canit; flet Petrus* (the cock crows, Peter weeps).[27] Peter's tears are carved in the sculpture, for it depicts the moment when, "heart-sick," he "cannot guess / those cock-a-doodles yet might bless, / his dreadful rooster come to mean forgiveness." The diction pulls together "cock" and "rooster," and shifts the screams of barnyard roosters to a domesticated "cock-a-doodle-do." Bishop is describing a cock on a pillar in Vatican City, a cock that reminds everyone that roosters say more than "Deny, deny, deny."

The closing section is half again as long as the second, itself half again as long as the first. Sunshine is now "gilding the broccoli leaves" ("gilding" is repeated), swallows float above, the cocks are "almost inaudible." "How could the night have come to grief?" is an unexpected question that suggests personal as well as public conflict. The last stanza hands the reader a puzzle:

> The sun climbs in
> following "to see the end,"
> faithful as enemy, or friend.

Try omitting the last stanza and simply ending with the tranquil sunrise scene. The third part then becomes a peaceful coda after the violence and drama of the first two parts. It would distance them from our everyday experience. The last stanza prevents that. As surely as the sun rises each day, so also it sees the end. The end of what? Of the day, as its natural self. Of our lives, of necessity. As persona in this poem, it evokes the enmity and the friendship that dominate the first two sections. War and forgiveness: Bishop is setting them side by side and challenging us to think of them together.

"After such knowledge, what forgiveness?" asks Eliot in "Gerontion," a poem published some twenty years earlier, two years after World War I. In Eliot, the knowledge is historical (the recent war), physical (sexual, including history as a whore), and spiritual (an implied absence). Bishop is writing in the midst of World War II for most of the Allies ("Roosters" was published in April 1941). How do we think of violence in these circumstances? And after war is concluded, what form of forgiveness enters into a peace treaty? The question also applies to domestic conflicts.

"Roosters" (1941) is the only poem among the nine southern poems that focuses on war, yet war is hardly absent from the others. In "Florida" (1939), the mangrove roots are "dotted as if "bombarded," and their "hummocks [are]/like ancient cannon-balls." In "Little Exercise" (1946), a storm subsides "in a series/of small, badly lit battle-scenes." Someone sleeping in a rowboat is "uninjured," for the lightning has done no harm — nor has the battle, whose explosive light and thunder are from nature. The little exercise is an opusculum, a painter's term, as in Wallace Stevens's title, but it also evokes a military exercise. Part 3 of "Songs for a Colored Singer" (1944) is a wartime song in which "At sea the big ship sinks and dies,/lead in its breast." In poems published before the United States went to war in December 1941, Bishop is not simply "acutely attuned to the approach of war."[28] She is acutely attuned to the World War II already well under way for most of Europe and for the Commonwealth, in-cluding Canada. "The [war] news seems to fill me with such frantic haste," she wrote on September 1, 1940 (to Marianne Moore, L 93). France had fallen in June 1940, and the Battle of Britain had begun in July 1940.

"The Fish" sounds in one way as if it has grown out of "Florida." It is a poem of detailed description, not of a natural scene but of a natural creature. Its argument is straightforward: "I caught a tremendous fish," and then in line 110, "And I let the fish go." It is not a war poem, but it treats matters of life and death. It sounds calm and authoritative, and it is true that Bishop loved fishing. (Hemingway is said to have liked the poem.) It is not visionary, yet at the end everything is suffused with the rainbow colors of spilled oil "until everything/was rainbow, rainbow, rainbow!" This is a moment of "victory," when the rainbow overcomes and life is granted. The poem is immensely appealing and became Bishop's signature poem, to her eventual exasperation. For all too many lazy anthologists, it was as if she had never written anything more after 1940. "I seem to get requests for it every day for anthologies with titles something like *Reading as Experience,* or *Experience as Reading,* each anthologizer insisting he is doing something completely different from every other anthologizer" (to Robert Lowell, 27 Feb. 1970, L 515).

Bishop chose to end her collection with a late poem of 1945, a poem unlike any other in *North & South.* "Anaphora" takes a figure of speech, a scheme, as its title, and brilliantly extends it to the way that the entire world works. Anaphora is the repetition of a word or phrase "at the beginning of successive phrases, clauses, sentences or lines."[29] In poetry, anaphora at the beginning of the line has long been the most common form, for example, in the Hebrew poetry of the Bible. In more recent poetry, it is familiar from Whitman's catalogues. What Bishop's poem does is to convert scheme into metaphor.

In Bishop, it is as if the whole world were a poem, where each dawn is a fresh line of verse. It raises the whole matter of repetition: its different meanings and the human responses to it. It elicits other sunrise poems like Hopkins's "God's Grandeur," already quoted. Against such poetic forebears, it sets Emily Dickinson's "Guest in this stupendous place," the stupendous place that is dawn in Dickinson. It also recalls,

> The Infinite a sudden Guest
> Has been assumed to be —
> But how can that stupendous come
> Which never went away?[30]

In Bishop, that adjective "stupendous" belongs to "the beggar in the park,"

who, weary, without lamp or book,
prepares stupendous studies:
the fiery event
of every day in endless
endless assent.

The poem is a hymn of praise, praise for the "freshness deep down things," praise for a daily incarnation. As with the Christian Incarnation, this daily incarnation will fall into mortality, "victim of long intrigue." The "beggar in the park" is related to Stevens's "vagabond in metaphor" in *Notes toward a Supreme Fiction* (1942; 2.10), an unexpected human form of the ideal who appears "in the park." Visually it evokes William Blake. The form consists of two linked sonnets with much-varied line and rhyme. The turn in both parts comes after line 10, "instantly, instantly falls" after the ecstatic sunrise and "prepares stupendous studies" after the day's suffering. The word "paradise" means "park," something that Bishop would know. This fallen world is our paradise, Bishop implies — not our lost Eden as in Eliot's Adam, the "ruined millionaire" ("East Coker" IV 12). Rather, an Eden recreated fresh each morning, seemingly meant for an "ineffable creature," who duly "appears and takes his earthly nature," only to fall into our daily world. "Endless, endless" in orthodox theology belongs in the praise of the Almighty. Here, however, it belongs in the simple assent to living by all things in nature, including human beings. Against all the tensions in Bishop's book, against all the wars, against all the struggles, against all the suffering, comes this "endless / endless assent."

Bishop said that she loved George Herbert's poems, and she often kept a copy of them with her when she traveled. She especially admired his ability to write of complex matters in a simple way. I think she admired this all the more because she too wrote about complex matters, but not always simply, especially at first. She was, after all, still very young when writing her remarkable early poems. Simplifying her style while retaining richness in her poems was a challenge that took several years to meet.

CHAPTER FOUR

Diction on the Move

Concentrating too exclusively on diction can be a hazard for a writer or a reader. Listen to W. H. Auden: "None of the students seemed to be at all interested in technique. They'd talk about the *Four Quartets,* but nobody seemed at all interested in Eliot's imitation of Dante. Now that's a question you'd think a young poet would be quite concerned about. But they weren't. They mostly seemed to be imitating Hart Crane. There was some Millay, some Stevens, even some me, I'm afraid. Very bad. *They mostly imitated the diction*" (emphasis added). It was different, Auden said, with nineteenth-century poets: "particularly its minor poets, [where] I am continually struck by the contrast between the extraordinary high standard of their prosodic skill and the frequent clumsiness and inadequacy of their diction." Arthur Hugh Clough, though very inventive, could be insensitive to verbal nuances: "at one moment the diction is too flat, at another too fancy, for what he is trying to do."[1]

Yet all through the nineteenth century, "there is hardly a single poet who, in his handling of meter, cannot do exactly what he wants." The reason (Auden thought) was that most of them received a standard classical education and first wrote verses in a language very different from their own, Latin. By contrast, in his and our day, "a classical education has become a rarity, and I notice that there are a number of modern poets whom I admire greatly in many respects but whom I find prosodically inept or monotonous. I suspect that this is because prosody is not, with them, a conscious preoccupation; they try to play it by ear." In fact, Auden concluded, we have also become "so diction conscious that, if we find a modern poet's diction inadequate, we attribute this not to carelessness but to lack of talent."[2]

Excellent diction but inept or monotonous prosody? How often do poets "play it by ear" instead of preoccupying themselves with prosody? How often do we listen for the rhythm of a new poem and think about its prosody? How often do reviewers mention it, let alone online commentators? For early training, Auden recommended Walter de la Mare's fine anthology for children, *Come Hither: A Collection of Rhymes and Poems for the Young of All Ages,* which Bishop also admired. In her review, she quotes part of Auden's memorable comment: "A child brought up on such verses may break his mother's heart or die on the gallows but he will never suffer from a tin ear."[3]

Here is a remark by Elizabeth Bishop that will astonish some admirers of her ordinary language: "Writing Latin prose and verse is still probably the best possible exercise for a poet."[4] A beginning writer, especially a poet, should not miss Elise Partridge's essay on the lively teaching methods of the distinguished classicist Robert Fitzgerald, "A Dipody in a Billabong: Studying Prosody with Robert Fitzgerald."[5]

Where to start for a poet who doesn't know Latin well enough to write exercises in Latin verse, that is, nearly all? Start with older admired poets, Bishop advised, she having started with Herbert and Hopkins. For those who are prosodically challenged, like some of her students, she had two other suggestions from her own experience: hymns and nursery rhymes. In 1977, she gave a talk in a series called "Conversations," sponsored by the Academy of American Poets. The series was meant to show younger poets how well-established senior poets had absorbed their own poetic forebears and made use of them. After speaking of Herbert, Hopkins, Coleridge, Marianne Moore and others, Bishop talked about hymns and nursery rhymes as early influences. "Where I lived . . . people used to sing hymns at home in the evening. They liked to play on the piano and organ, and they'd sing and sing and sing. . . . I have friends who are Southern Methodists, who know even more hymns than I do. [When] I used to visit them, we would have a mint julep, and then we would all sing hymns."[6] Some of the hymns were ridiculous, Bishop added, and modern ones became worse and worse. But she greatly admired many earlier hymns — "superb!" It goes without saying that now, alas, this long heritage of hymns has largely faded away, though far from entirely. A beginning writer nowadays could well start with African American spirituals, then add a good hymnary with music, then find a church to hear hymns sung live or else find a CD.

As Bishop knew, "if you have these hymns in your mind, . . . you find yourself using phrases from them or even using the same meters and rhymes" ("Influences," 13). Thomas Hardy and A. E. Housman were influenced by hymns, she added, while omitting any mention of Dickinson. Among contemporary writers, Gjertrud Schnackenberg was also influenced by hymns, notably in the Lutheran tradition. "The first poems I wrote were in quatrains, which I am certain came out of those indomitable Lutheran chorales and the massive foursquare tetrameter hymns (and I believe that anyone writing poetry can learn a great deal about resolution and endings from this music — about how and where and why to end a poem)."[7] Metrically Bishop learned even more from nursery rhymes, and she notes how useful both hymns and nursery rhymes are. "I don't think you have to write in meter like the 'ti-um ti-um ti-um,' but they [some of her students]

can't do it, they can't even feel it. Yet they can feel rock and roll."
It puzzled her. "Anybody who can waltz can certainly write in
meter. . . . It's a natural thing" ("Influences," 13). As Robert
Pinsky says, prosody is "the most consciously physical mode
of language," so that poetry "is in part a bodily experience."[8]
Nursery rhymes are still widely known and provide fine ex-
amples for exercises in imitation or adaptation in poems. (See
Auden's "As I walked out one morning" or Bishop's "Visits to
St. Elizabeths.")

Bishop was stringent with her students. They needed to
practice meters and metrical exercises just as a music student
needs to practice scales and musical exercises. (Auden speaks of
de la Mare's "metrical fingering.")[9] When at the University of
Washington, she wrote, "I fought the battle of the iambic pentameter and intend to fight the 2nd battle of the iambic pentameter this quarter — no, I think I'll be even meaner and make
it heroic couplets this time" (to Jean Garrigue, 27 Mar. 1966,
NYPL: Berg). She must have made an impact, because she told
May Swenson about when she was in the hospital in Seattle,
"some students even wrote me poems in *iambic pentameter*, all
marked (about which I had been nagging incessantly)" (29 Nov.
1966, Swenson-Bishop letters). In 1974, she told her Harvard
students that her favorite line of iambic pentameter was "I hate
to see that evenin' sun go down" (quoted by Lloyd Schwartz in
his "Elizabeth Bishop, 1911–1979," Schwartz and Estess 254).

Prosody in school can sound as dull as ditchwater, but transfer
it to music and relate it to whatever music a student enjoys, and
it comes alive.[10] In fact, it can come so alive that it takes over
your head for a while. "What I don't see is how you manage to
get that effect with that metre that is so heavy the words seem
to be jostling each other's shoulders [in "Thanksgiving's Over"].

I made the mistake of reading it when I was working on a poem & it took me an hour or so to get back into my own metre" (to Robert Lowell, 18 Mar. 1948, LEBRL 30). Hearing a poem read aloud gives you the rhythm, loud or faint, regular or irregular, one beat or two beat or three or four or five beat. Accentual-syllabic poetry beats regularly in counted syllables with variations, and virtually all poetry in modern English over the centuries is accentual-syllabic. The main exceptions are the pure accentual verse found in Old English (Anglo-Saxon) poetry, a little syllabic verse like Marianne Moore's, and free verse, which became prominent in the twentieth century and dominates today.

Here is the place to observe that Bishop knew music and that some of her effects reminded Marianne Moore of "musicianly strategies." Among these "many musicianly strategies is an expert disposition of pauses."[11] Bishop "studied counterpoint and the piano for years": "I suppose I'm still 'musical.'" She said that she'd have "love[d] to be a composer!" (Brown, "Interview," 296). She owned a fine clavichord, which went to Brazil with her and then back to the United States. (Eventually she sold it to her *New Yorker* editor, Harold Ross, to his pleasure.) At one time in Brazil, she set about acquiring every Henry Purcell record she could find, because termites had eaten the labels on her old ones, leaving a sticky trail. A superb *Dido and Aeneas* with Kirsten Flagstad was a special favorite (24 Mar. 1958, Barker letters).

Some of Bishop's acoustical echoes are like musical effects. I have commented elsewhere on the near rhymes that give rise to ghost rhymes in "Wading at Wellfleet."[12] One of them links "Wading at Wellfleet" to the following poem, "Chemin de Fer."

Lying so close, they catch the sun
the spokes directed at the shin.

These are sunlit waves whose bright advance looks to Bishop like the "sharp blades" attached to the wheels of ancient Assyrian war chariots, blades that the waves at Wellfleet all too horribly resemble. One ghost rhyme of "sun"/"shin" is "shun." "Wading at Wellfleet" is a poem of terror, or so Anthony Hecht thought, following Mary McCarthy. The poem is only one reason that McCarthy, a classmate, described Bishop as a poet of terror.[13] She is a poet of fear, certainly, and of affliction, given the quoted phrase from Herbert's "Affliction." This is how the next poem, "Chemin de Fer," ends:

> "Love should be put into action!"
>   screamed the old hermit.
> Across the pond an echo
>   tried and tried to confirm it.

"Action, -shun, -shun, -shun": so the echo would go. The ghost rhyme of "shun" is subliminal, then becomes very slightly louder in this acoustical rhyme in "Chemin de Fer." It makes a subtle sound effect linking the two poems like a quiet musical motif.

Bishop keeps her skill in prosody mostly unobtrusive, a sign that she wishes her art to sound natural. Her fifteen lines of buried terza rima alternating through "From the Country to the City" have gone unobserved, as far as I know. Sometimes a reader can be well into a poem before realizing that it rhymes. Take, for example, her first poem in *North & South*, "The Map." The rhyme scheme in the two eight-line stanzas uses identical words for the *a* rhymes in the *abba* schemes. It's difficult to make this sound natural, but Bishop does it, partly by varying the grammar slightly.

I want to highlight two aspects of Bishop's mastery of rhythm in general and of prosody in particular: her early mastery of the short line and her great versatility in stanza and line, including rhyme and near rhyme.

Bishop's short lines in *North & South* are deployed in two ways: poems using a short line throughout and poems combining a short line with a longer line. Is there another major poet who makes such extensive use of the short line, that is, the two- or three-beat line, the dimeter and trimeter?

> Which eye's his eye?
> Which limb lies
> next the mirror?

Then, two poems later, comes a poem about longer lines, the highways that lead into and out of a city:

> The long, long legs,
> league-boots of land, that carry the city nowhere,
> nowhere; the lines
> that we drive on.

In "Love Lies Sleeping," the quatrains shorten their third and fourth lines, sometimes to two beats, after the two opening iambic pentameter lines. Similarly, "Quai d'Orléans" alternates one line of tetrameter and one line of dimeter:

> Each barge on the river easily tows
>   a mighty wake,
> a giant oak-leaf of gray lights
>   on duller gray.

Bishop's metaphor of an oak-leaf is wonderfully accurate (watch the wake of a boat), so that this is also a visual poem, a shape poem.

The entire poem works with the old topos of leaves, not so much Milton's leaves of Vallombrosa that descend into Shelley's revolutionary leaves blown by the wild west wind — leaves that go back to Homer's metaphor for souls of the dead. "Leaves" make such a potent figure for a poet that no competent poet will use this word and possible topos without thought. It easily widens into the leaves of a book via an English-language pun. It also widens into leave-taking via a pun — into the Sybil's mysterious leaves that must be arranged if you want an answer, as in Hopkins's "Spelt from Sybil's Leaves." Bishop evokes all three meanings but primarily makes these into the leaves of memory. That is, Bishop's work with this topos remembers the past and also looks to the future, where everything is now altered for her dearly loved friend Margaret Miller. Bishop would have known about the oaks of Dodona, which helped priestesses at the ancient oracle to prophesy, so that a fallen giant oak-leaf comes with this memory too; and the prophecy at the end follows appropriately.

Among the southern poems, "Jerónimo's House" (1941) uses a basic meter of dimeter lines. "The Fish" (1940) varies its line from a basic three-beat down to two and up to four, with a fine variation of feet also.

> I caught a tremendous fish
> and held him beside the boat
> half out of water, with my hook
> fast in a corner of his mouth.
> He didn't fight.
> He hadn't fought at all.

For part 3 of "Songs for a Colored Singer," where the lines are mostly dimeter, see below in this chapter. In part 4, the second of four lines is dimeter and the rest tetrameter.

Of poems that vary their line, the most striking is "From the Country to the City." Even the look of the poem on the page is arresting. Bishop uses a short line and a long, long line throughout, as if the lengthy lines were the turnpike itself and the short ones various crossroads. In fact, the look is something of an optical illusion, rather like nighttime effects along the highway. The long lines are not unusually long. It is the short two-stress lines that make them look so — that, combined with the descriptive force of the "long, long legs" of the highway. "From the Country to the City" draws attention to its form visually in a way that no poem thus far in *North & South* has, apart from "The Gentleman of Shalott."

"From the Country to the City" also achieves the illusion of its long-line effect because Bishop cleverly decided to open the poem with its short two-beat line. It is much more usual with a strongly varied line length to open with the longer line and have the short line follow, like a refrain or echo. Bishop also ends the poem with its short line, now lengthening it to a three-beat line and rhyming it with line 1: "The long, long legs," "'Subside,' it begs and begs." Even more remarkable: she has quietly used terza rima throughout for the short lines, opening with "legs" ("The long, long legs"), then moving to *bcb cdc ded efe fa*. The final line is "begs," the *a* rhyme, so that the scheme circles back to link with the start. The terza rima "has a powerful forward momentum" and also "a reassuring structure of continuity" — both apropos for a car trip on the turnpike. It also suggests "processes without beginning or end, a *perpetuum mobile*."[4] So does Bishop's poem. The fifteen alternate lines so rhymed resemble a terza rima sonnet (not that they read continuously as a separate poem, though they make an understandable if discontinuous poem — so do the longer lines). The effect is of a powerful interweaving warp along with the longer woof of the fabric.

A similar technique of opening with a very short line is used in the next poem, "The Man-Moth." On the page, it again produces a noticeable effect, for Bishop is using an eight-line stanza of long lines — longer than the preceding poem and slower, for there are far fewer repetitions and a sustained narrative. The short first line imitates on the page the Man-Moth's act as he climbs to try to get out of the hole at the top of wherever he is. He can't. He falls back, as if being drawn down into the density of his own stanza.

> Up the façades,
> his shadow dragging like a photographer's cloth behind him,
> he climbs fearfully . . .
>
> .   .   .   .
>
> But what the Man-Moth fears most he must do, although
> he fails, of course, and falls back scared but quite unhurt.

These poems combine a short line with a considerably longer line. "The Gentleman of Shalott," published about the same time, concludes that "Half is enough," so that the poem's two-beat line is most appropriate. It's all the more appropriate because "The Lady of Shalott" uses a four-beat line for most of its nine-line stanzas. The short line also approximates the look of the Gentleman, stretching down the page in longish verse paragraphs — half of him, that is, or the half we can see. Apparently there is another half, visible only in the mirror — or vice versa. The contrast with the rhythm of Tennyson's poem is marked, for Tennyson has written a charm poem, lulling its reader by easy-flowing verses with many repetitions. The subject itself is a charm, an enchantment, which the Lady can break only at her peril. The Gentleman seems wide awake about his difficulty. While the Lady sees actual life only as reflected in her mirror, his mirror *is* his actual life for the Gentleman, or half of it. But which half? As the poem says at the start, "Which eye's his eye?" (Or for all that, which I?) Weavers commonly used a mirror as the Lady does, but not a magic one except in romances. As for a creature who is half mirror, inverted, that sounds like a different kind of curse — or is it? It certainly offers a fine opportunity to demonstrate a gift for writing dimeter lines.

Bishop's mastery of the short line increases with the years. In *A Cold Spring*, for example, "Insomnia" uses chiefly a trimeter line, effectively varied with a tetrameter line, especially at the end, where the two last lines lengthen. The last line can even be read with five stresses:

> into that world inverted
> where left is always right,
> where the shadows are really the body,
> where we stay awake all night,
> where the heavens are shallow as the sea
> is now deep, and you love me.

The change in the rhythm of the last two lines is masterly: a sudden but smooth change to a four-beat basis. Instead of clear back-and-forth contraries in trimeters, a paradox emerges over the enjambment. The line has lengthened, and the grammar slows things down to a rocking rhythm, like the sea, while the final three words move past contraries to an imagined union.

In *Questions of Travel*, "The Riverman" uses short three-stress lines for virtually all of its 158 lines. James Merrill singled them out for praise in 1968. "I wanted to get away from pentameter, too. Do you know that wonderful poem by Elizabeth

Bishop called 'The Riverman'? . . . Wonderful pulsating lines — you hardly feel the meter at all."[5] "I'm always open to what another poet might do with *the line,* or with a stanza," he said later; "it's always very important, the phrasing of the lines." And he goes on to praise Bishop's "North Haven" for the rhythm of its lines. You felt you knew it by heart after a couple of readings. "Every line fell in the most wonderful way, which is perhaps something she learned from Herbert. You find it *there.* I think you find it very often in French poetry."[6]

"George Herbert and Thomas Hardy are the two poets I can think of who had the most varied forms of any people," Bishop said. "Hardy made up a new verse pattern for practically everything he wrote, and Herbert often did too" ("Influences," 13). Anne Ferry thought that Herbert's *The Temple* provided "a model for Bishop's experimentation" and that "the remarkable variety of metrical, linear and rhyme patterns in *North & South* may be unmatched in a single poet's collection since . . . *The Temple.*"[7] Try testing this, and the results prove astonishing. There are thirty poems in all. One of the thirty, "Songs for a Colored Singer," has four parts, each in a different form, so that the collection consists of thirty-three variously shaped poems. Of these, twenty-four have regular stanzaic forms; three of the twenty-four alternate two different stanza forms. (This two-thirds ratio of stanzaic poems remains constant through Bishop's second and third collections. Her fourth collection, *Geography III,* is too small for statistical analysis.) Other poems in *North & South* consist of those in verse paragraphs or without any break at all. All use regular meter, sometimes with much variation, especially in line length. About two-thirds of the thirty-three poems are also rhymed, though the two lists do not coincide completely. The eight-line stanzas of "Jerónimo's House" are unrhymed, while the tercets of "Little Exercise" use only a few rhymes.

The astonishing thing about the twenty-four poems in stanzas is that not one poem repeats the stanzaic structure of another. Each is unique. Each is built in a way that Bishop thought appropriate to her subject. It's amusing to observe that three poems use a three-line stanza, four use a four-line stanza, five use a five-line stanza, and three use a six-line stanza (plus the sestina, where it is required). This begins to look deliberate, like some schematic "Well-Tempered Clavier" working through different keys, though I doubt that it was. There are no poems with a seven-line stanza; four come with an eight-line, two with a nine-line, and two with an eleven-line stanza.

This kind of versatility, done so quietly, is enough to give any reader pause, once it is observed. Just as remarkable is the variation within the line. Penelope Laurans wrote well about all this in 1983, but in the thirty years since, critics have paid little attention to it — a confirmation of Auden's argument at the beginning of this chapter. Laurans rightly concludes that Bishop's expert use of technique "adds subtlety to utterance" and is "one of the less-recognized reasons that Bishop's poetry has retained its freshness and interest."[18] She uses the term "rough" for Bishop's variations in meter, though to my ear the effect is not rough unless Bishop wants it so. Rather, the meter is greatly, often subtly, varied. ("Rough" can be an unfortunate term insofar as it suggests that "smooth" is the ideal in poetry: "But most by Numbers judge a Poet's song; / And smooth or rough, with them, is right or wrong," as Pope said [*An Essay on Criticism* 2:337–338].) Coleridge notes that John Donne wrote in quite regular meter for songs and generally in irregular meter for "poems where the writer *thinks*."[19] The same is loosely true for Bishop. When, for example, she writes ballads or ballad-like poems, the beat is clear and the line smooth. "The Burglar of Babylon" is the obvious example, and other poems like "Manners" or "Chemin de Fer" bear this out. At least once, she wrote a pure accentual or strong-stress poem, in which the rhythmic base is quite different from the usual accentual-syllabic meters. The line will sound bumpy to anyone unfamiliar with this old form of writing poetry. (See Chapter 5.)

As an example of Bishop's versatility, take her three tercet poems, "Wading at Wellfleet," "Roosters," and "Little Exercise." The first was written about 1935, the second appeared in 1941, and the third appeared in 1946. In "Wading at Wellfleet," the four-beat lines are fairly regular iambic. Bishop rhymes the last lines of each pair of tercet stanzas, starting with *abc dec,* and there are other rhymes, along with some repeated end words. The effect is regular and rolling, like those Assyrian chariots and those waves that Bishop is describing. In "Little Exercise," an electrical storm summons up a dramatic scene in its seven stanzas, like a stage or movie scene, lit by flashes of lightning here and there, with growls of thunder. Many of the lines are long (about half have twelve syllables or more); many have trisyllabic feet, and the stresses are irregular, as befits a storm. The mood is imperative: "Think of the storm," and the injunction "Think" opens four of the seven stanzas. Bishop begins with a shortened third line, but by the final stanza, it is as long as the others. Only there do we find "someone sleeping in the bottom of a row-boat / tied to a mangrove root . . . / . . . barely disturbed."

"Roosters" is technically one of Bishop's most extraordinary poems: three sections totaling forty-four stanzas all rhymed *aaa.* Yet it reads easily; the rhymes are mostly unobtrusive. Bishop modulates them as if writing music and in fact said that a recording of Scarlatti got her "going again in a particular rhythm" in "Roosters" (to Anne Stephenson, 20 Mar. 1963, LOA 844). One of her technical decisions in "Roosters" has a powerful effect, and that is shortening the first line to two beats, with a few variations. The second line has three beats and the final line four beats. The stanzaic pattern is rare but not unprecedented. Bishop is following Richard Crashaw's "Wishes to his supposed mistress," a charming mid-seventeenth-century idealized love poem: three-line stanzas, rhymed *aaa,* with the first line two beat, the second three beat, the third four beat:

> Whoe'er she be
> That not impossible she
> That shall command my heart and me.

Crashaw's poem has thirty-eight stanzas, and its rhythm moves smoothly, with a pulsing effect and increasing hope. Bishop's early delight in sixteenth- and seventeenth-century poems included delight in some of Crashaw. "I've been doing quite a lot with Crashaw lately — particularly 'Music's Duel.' Do you like that? I'm translating the Parabasis of *The Birds* and the imagery and lightness of the whole thing is so like it that I am making use of it" (to Donald E. Stanford, 6 June 1934, L 24). For "Roosters," she altered the lightness of "Wishes to his supposed mistress" into the "rattletrap rhythm" of "Roosters," maintaining the metrical pattern. "Rattletrap," a defensive and slightly amused word, applies only to some sections of "Roosters."[20]

> At four o'clock
> in the gun-metal blue dark
> we hear the first crow of the first cock.

In Crashaw's poem, the meter is very regular, and virtually all the rhymes are full rhymes. Bishop's lines can vary in meter, and she demonstrates her great ability in near rhyme throughout.

Where rhymes are full, they maintain their force partly because so many of them rhyme different parts of speech: the ratio is two to one. (W. K. Wimsatt, years ago, noted that rhyme words using the same part of speech make weaker rhymes.)[21] Where the same part of speech is used, the rhyming is by no means all with nouns; it includes other parts of speech, past and present participles, for example.

For one example of what Bishop can do with these lines and stanzas, contrast two passages:

> Now in mid-air
> by twos they fight each other.
> Down comes a first flame-feather,
>
> and one is flying,
> with raging heroism defying
> even the sensation of dying.

And the opening of the second part:

> St. Peter's sin
> was worse than that of Magdalen
> whose sin was of the flesh alone;
>
> of spirit, Peter's.

The change is like a new movement in a piece of music. In the cockfight, an emphatic "Down" opens the line with a stressed syllable. Bishop then moves to present participles, with their strong effect of ongoing action. She has used the present tense all through the first part of "Roosters," from the moment that the roosters wake the speaker. Then comes the second part and the past tense: contemplation, not physical action; ethical judgment, not heroic combat. Switching tenses, Bishop said, was very like switching keys in music. Hopkins was her example, when he addressed himself saying, "Fancy, come faster." "Browning does something like this, but not so strikingly. In other words, the use of the present tense helps to convey this sense of the mind in action. . . . But switching tenses always gives effects of depth, space, foreground, background, and so on" (Brown, "Interview," 298). So it is here, in the compact and moving prelude to Bishop's second subject. "Of spirit, Peter's" is memorable.

Bishop did not return to tercets for a long time: in 1962 in "A Norther — Key West," in 1966 in "Under the Window: Ouro Prêto," and in 1979 in "Pink Dog," as well as in "One Art" (1976), which as a villanelle requires three-line stanzas. "Pink Dog" repeats the *aaa* rhyme of "Roosters," with a fine casual insouciance and a Carnival kind of rhyme:

> wear a *fantasía*.
> Tonight you simply can't afford to be a-
> n eyesore. But no one will ever see a

Her use of the quintain in *North & South* is also especially fine. "Casabianca," with layered and interwoven diction and rhymes, is a tour de force and a difficult pattern to imitate. "The Unbeliever," on the other hand, is wonderfully suggestive. Its fifth line extends far beyond the first four, so that the stanza looks and sounds like some base for that "top of a mast" — the deck, say, or more ominously, the sea. In the first stanza, lines 1 to 4 alternate three-stress and two-stress lines, while the closing line has five stresses, and then six stresses in stanzas 2 and 3. In the last stanza, a sixth line is added, also long, with a double end rhyme of "fall," then "all." The base under the mast has deepened. The rhyme resounds as if the sea were calling out, echoing with every wave, "fall," "fall."

Bishop uses a similar effect in the five-line song "Lullaby," part 3 of "Songs for a Colored Singer." Here the fourth line is lengthened, the most telling look and sound also being that of a ship:

> Lullaby.
> Adult and child
> sink to their rest.
> At sea the big ship sinks and dies,
> lead in its breast.

The other five-line stanzas are in the French poems, "Sleeping on the Ceiling" and "Cirque d'Hiver," both rhymed, the latter more tightly.

In Bishop's 1938 poem "Late Air," love contrasts itself with the easy love that some pop star of the day belts out, the "Air" of the title heard late at night. The night air brings such airs, thanks to the aerials. She follows this pun with another in the opening line:

> From a magician's midnight sleeve
>   The radio-singers

Magic, indeed, this diffusion of midnight song on the radio might well appear. But the sleeve is also the "sleeve" that is the cover for a record in days long before CDs. The DJ is a magician of sorts, offering fortune-telling about love. It falls like dew on the night lawns.

Stanza 2 shows a different kind of love, private, burning, self-enclosed. The aerials on the Navy Yard in Key West give Bishop her central trope. They are "better witnesses" to the love this stanza knows than some crooner's "love-songs." For high on them are red lights:

Five remote red lights
   keep their nest there: Phoenixes
burning quietly, where the dew cannot climb.

In stanza 1, the singers "distribute all their love-songs / over
the dew-wet lawns." Theirs is a dull sublunary love in Donne's
phrasing. It belongs to the elements of earth and water. The love
of stanza 2 belongs to the elements of air and fire. As for the
Phoenixes, a knowledgeable reader will say that only one phoenix
exists at a time. Each bird is unique; that's the point. After living
for ages, the bird self-immolates on a pyre, and from its ashes a
new bird arises. But then, again, there are Donne's lovers:

The phoenix riddle hath more wit
By us; we two being one, are it.

It is also true that lovers have the sense that they are unique. As
for love burning, "Casabianca" knows all about its obsessive de-
structive fires. This poem knows a happier flame. Why Bishop
notes the number five, I do not know. It's an auspicious number
in Pythagoras and in Plutarch at Delphi and also in Sir Thomas
Browne, whose works she bought in 1934.[22] Perhaps this crossed
her mind and pleased her. But this is not a symbolic poem.
Those phoenixes bear nothing of their long-standing symbolic
force, apart from a memory of it. They are modern, and doubtless their number is too — perhaps no more than the actual
number she saw, which was nonetheless worth making into
part of the poem. Again and again, Bishop works like this. Her
poems will include the history of their art, here the traditional
function of the phoenix and perhaps a faint memory of the uses
of the number five. The history enriches the poem with its
flavor, placing it in a much wider context. But it does not stop

the reader short. The poem remains pleasing and effective, even without this knowledge. Of course, the form helps greatly, and here the effect operates with or without historical knowledge. That's the beauty of rhyme.

Bishop's rhyme scheme is an old one, envelope rhyme, which is easy enough in a quatrain *(abba)*. This is Tennyson's stanza for *In Memoriam* (with a four-beat line). The longer the stanza, the harder the rhyme scheme. James Merrill wrote an envelope-rhyme poem of thirty-one lines, "Pearl," a tour de force. Here Bishop has expanded the stanza to six lines, using an *abccba* scheme. The scheme has been called a "nested" scheme, and I expect Bishop wanted it especially for this poem because of its sheltering nests of private love. (For a different effect in a love poem, compare Browning's six-line *abccba* stanza in "Meeting at Night.") Bishop, who can make her rhymes as loud as she wants, keeps them quiet here. She uses some near rhymes and runs on a few lines, and I suppose that is why her envelope rhyme scheme has not been observed.

I mentioned earlier that "Anaphora" converts scheme into metaphor. The word "scheme" survives today in common usage as "rhyme scheme." But the full rhetorical meaning, partly recovered now, covers all those figures of speech, those "patternings of elements of language . . . which carry no meanings per se."[23] Rhyme scheme, alliteration, assonance, chiasmus, and such do not overtly change signification. Trope, on the other hand, is a figure of speech (sometimes called a figure of thought) in which ordinary meaning is overtly changed or "turned." (The root meaning of "trope" is "turn.") Metaphor and metonymy, for example, change the ordinary meaning of words. Envelope rhyme is another example of Bishop converting scheme into trope, this time a rhyme scheme that also stands for a nest, a shelter.[24]

While no poem in *North & South* repeats a stanza form, Bishop shows her liking at the start for the favorite set form in all English poetry, the sonnet, whether the Italian (Petrarchan) sonnet or the English (Shakespearean) sonnet. Her first poem, "The Map," appears to have begun as a sonnet. In her notebook, the first version is a twelve-line poem rhymed *abba cddc effe;* the final version splits this into an eight-line opening stanza and the first half of the third stanza. Originally it needed only a two-line closing couplet to make it into a sonnet variation on both main types of sonnet. The second poem, "The Imaginary Iceberg," has an eleven-line stanza, which consists of eight lines followed by a three-line reflection that includes a final couplet. The rhyming indicates that this is again a variation on the Italian plus the English sonnet. The closing poem in *North & South,* "Anaphora," consists of two fourteen-line stanzas, a pair of linked sonnet-like poems. Bishop is well aware of the strengths of this form and exploits them throughout her writing life. Her last published poem is a virtuoso play with the form, titled simply "Sonnet."

CHAPTER FIVE

Rhythms of *A Cold Spring*

The sentence is everything — the sentence well imagined. See
the beautiful sentences in a thing like Wordsworth's To Sleep
or Herrick's To Daffodils.
—Robert Frost

Bishop published one collection for each decade of her working
life. The first was delayed until 1946. After that, the collections
followed regularly: 1955, 1965, 1976. *A Cold Spring*, her second
collection, started out as "Faustina and Other Poems," then
changed to "Concordance," and finally to *A Cold Spring*.[1] Although all its poems except the last one were published by 1952,
A Cold Spring did not appear until 1955. Its entire shape was
changed by the occasion for the final poem, "The Shampoo"
(1955), just as Bishop's entire life was changed by her stay with
Maria Carlota de Macedos Soares (Lota) in Brazil in December
1951.

A Cold Spring is shorter than *North & South*, eighteen poems
compared with thirty.[2] Most prominently, there is a change in
tone. The shadow of war that hangs over *North & South* has gone,
and so has the more general sense of menace. Bishop has moved
away from her strange fantastical creatures, her monsters: no
half-mirror man like the Gentleman of Shalott, no Kafka creation like the Man-Moth, no heart-dividing weeds. What has
increased are love poems, now larger in number and more direct in approach. It's tempting to posit that Bishop has now ac-

cepted her lesbianism and no longer feels the need of strange creatures that once embodied her own sense of strangeness about her sexuality, among other things. But then wartime images can metamorphose into strange creatures and monsters too.

There is a new focus on everyday working life, all part of the change in tone and a sense of enduring. In a classic essay on Dickens, George Orwell observes that in his novels, "anything in the nature of work takes place off stage. . . . Wonderfully as he can describe an *appearance*, Dickens does not often describe a *process*."[3] In *North & South*, Bishop's focus is on observed objects, the private life, travels, war, dreams and fantasies and visions. There is virtually no focus on a working life. All that changes in *A Cold Spring*, starting with the opening title poem, which is centered on a working farm: "a calf was born," "Four deer practised leaping over your fences," "each cow-flop," "your shadowy pastures." A dredge is shown at work in "The Bight," and "At the Fishhouses" memorably describes a working dock, where "an old man sits netting, . . . his shuttle worn and polished." In "Cape Breton," a remarkable natural landscape is inhabited by unremarkable everyday working people: bulldozer operators, bus drivers, grocery store owners, garage owners, preachers, teachers, a father with a baby. The contrast of extraordinary landscape and ordinary people is palpable. "The Prodigal" treats the work of a farm laborer in a filthy pigsty. The twelve stanzas of "Faustina, or Rock Roses" show one of the hardest jobs, caring for an old sick woman whose mental capacity is in doubt. Or is it? How far? What is happening when a visitor is not there? "Arrival at Santos" shows a working port, with a "strange and ancient" tender, "twenty-six freighters/waiting to be loaded with green coffee beans," someone clumsily handling a boat hook, and customs officials.

"Insomnia," the eighth poem, is the first without work in it and the first love poem. "Varick Street" does use the look and smells of factories, but it functions chiefly as a love poem askew. Nor is there work in "Four Poems," "Letter to N.Y.," or "Argument." In general, then, the love poems don't include work, and the rest do. "Invitation to Miss Marianne Moore" flies above all kinds of work, looking benignly down. The beautiful final poem, "The Shampoo," is the one love poem to include work, here domestic work, lovingly undertaken.

Some subjects continue. There are two travel poems, the second and the second to last, a study in contrast: "Over 2,000 Illustrations and a Complete Concordance" and "Arrival at Santos." The relation of servant and mistress continues from "Cootchie" in *North & South* through "Faustina, or Rock Roses." The city poem in *North & South* is centered on Paris; here it is on Washington, DC, in a slighter poem ("View of the Capitol from the Library of Congress"). In *Questions of Travel*, it will be Rio de Janeiro, while *Geography III* has "Night City." Bishop's strong sense of the creaturely world — fish, flesh, or fowl, as Yeats has it in "Sailing to Byzantium" — continues in *A Cold Spring*.

A Cold Spring widens the geographical sense of *North & South* by focusing on climate. The seasons are not prominent in *North & South*, not like the elements or like coastlines and harbors. They are mostly assumed. In *A Cold Spring*, seasons appear much the same way, casually. "Cape Breton," like the title poem, is set in spring, given its bawling calf and thousands of song sparrows' songs. Fireflies appear in late spring and early summer, the season of "While Someone Telephones" ("Four Songs," III). The two Brazil poems come at the end, so that the book is framed by "A Cold Spring" and "The Shampoo": cold as against the warm water of "The Shampoo"; cold as against the warm emotions of "The Shampoo"; cold with stirrings of new life outside, as against the stirrings of new life within.

The new tone of this collection is apparent with the first sign of spring in "A Cold Spring":

> Finally a grave green dust
> settled over your big and aimless hills.

The first greening of spring *does* look like a dusting of green across some fields and a few treetops. But "grave"? Is there a gravitas? Yes, with a muted echo of Whitman: grass, graves. With Whitman's example comes the ancient topos on which he was drawing, flesh as grass (going back to Isaiah) and death as a mower, all part of the cycle of life and death. The sense of a new life pervades this poem, though it is not an easy new life but one more like the difficult birth of a calf that follows. The word "aimless" quietly says no to any possible teleology that might be implied by "grave," or by Bishop's epigraph, "Nothing is so beautiful as spring," the first line of Hopkins's exquisite sonnet "Spring." Hopkins's spring is "a strain of the earth's sweet being in the beginning / In Eden garden." Bishop will have none of it. Her "big and aimless hills" also work against any echo of the biblical everlasting hills, as did Wallace Stevens's "ever-hill" in *Notes toward a Supreme Fiction* (1942, 3.4). Bishop's 1952 hills are neither for nor against an aim; they are simply without one. The next poem, "Over 2,000 Illustrations and a Complete Concordance," will come to focus on birth, an infant, and teleology par excellence.

Adjectives like "grave," "aimless," and "wretched" disappear in the rest of the poem. "Now . . . Now . . . Later" usher in the present tense and a response to the natural beauty of the scene.

Somehow the simple presence of the earth works its healing process as it did very early in Bishop's life. ("It is the elements speaking: earth, air, fire, water"; "In the Village.") At the end, there is a quiet pun in the "glowing tributes" of the fireflies, also sometimes called glowworms. "A Cold Spring" is not about an epiphany, a dramatic change. Nonetheless there is a change by the end of the poem — a tone poem with muted dissonance at the start but anticipated harmony by the end.

The book opens with a series of five longer poems and one short poem: "A Cold Spring," "Over 2,000 Illustrations and a Complete Concordance," "The Bight," "A Summer's Dream" (the short poem), "At the Fishhouses," and "Cape Breton." Except for "Over 2,000 Illustrations," they are all centered on land or water, as if once more the elements provided a sense of grounding, of sanity, even of comfort when emotions run riot. It is not that the landscapes or seascapes or coastlines are happy. It is that they are enduring. All the poems show how life goes on, even when it does not give us what we want.

> And your shadowy pastures will be able to offer
> these particular glowing tributes
> every evening now throughout the summer.
> ("A Cold Spring")

> Thus should have been our travels:
> serious, engravable.
>
> . . . .
>   Why couldn't we have seen
> this old Nativity while we were at it?
> ("Over 2,000 Illustrations and a Complete Concordance")

> All the untidy activity continues,
> awful but cheerful.
> ("The Bight")

I have seen it over and over, the same sea, the same,
slightly, indifferently swinging above the stones
("At the Fishhouses")

The birds keep on singing, a calf bawls, the bus starts.
.   .   .   .
an ancient chill is rippling the dark brooks.

("Cape Breton")

After the two opening poems, the focus is on coastline scenes,
including the dream poem.

"The Bight" is written against the American seashore poem
in which a lone figure on a seashore speaks or sings: Whitman,
Eliot, Ammons. It might be called "The Idea of Disorder at Key
West." It is also written against sea poems in which a lone figure
by the sea speaks or sings, possessed by water, sky, and air:
Byron, Baudelaire. Bishop's earlier descriptive seashore poems,
"Florida" and "Seascape," have no human inhabitants, just wild-
ness. The seashore poems in *A Cold Spring* are located in harbors with docks.

"If one were Baudelaire," says Bishop's speaker of "The Bight,
"one could probably hear it turning into marimba music." "La
musique souvent me prend comme une mer!" wrote Baudelaire
(Music often takes me like a sea [Richard Howard]). Not this
music. "The bight is littered with old correspondences." For
Baudelaire, correspondences are often sounds, scents, colors, and
in particular scents. Bishop's poem offers no scents, just sight
and lots of sound: marimba music, the dredge playing "dry perfectly off-beat claves," pelicans crashing, the dredge going
"Click. Click." "The Bight" is one of her noisiest poems.

Nova Scotia consists mostly of a peninsula and a large island
to the north that is more thinly populated, Cape Breton. A
causeway now connects it to the mainland, though not in Bishop's

day. It is famous for its scenic beauty and was once also known for its coal mines. Bishop's mother taught there briefly when young. The poem "Cape Breton" starts "Out on the high 'bird islands,' Ciboux and Hertford" where "the razorbill auks and the silly-looking puffins all stand." The two conservation islands reflect Nova Scotia's dual French-English heritage in their names and its centuries of bird habitation in the species mentioned. (And puffins can look silly with their bright broad beaks, just as pelicans can look comical to a human eye.) The poem's cinematic gaze will drop to the "silken water . . . weaving and weaving" (like shot silk, catching colors?) before looking out over valleys and gorges, then following the coastline road and eventually its small bus and passengers. The mist hangs here and there pervasively, like a character, and it ends the poem, as it "follows / the white mutations of its dream; / an ancient chill is rippling the dark brook." In "A Summer's Dream," the brook wakes the sleepers, the brook "still dreaming audibly." A brook dreams, the mist dreams.

Bishop insisted that "A Summer's Dream," "At the Fishhouses," and "Cape Breton" stay together, albeit in any order. "A Summer's Dream" gives a nighttime view of the ordinary inhabitants of Cape Breton ("two giants, an idiot, a dwarf," "a gentle storekeeper," "our kind landlady"). A "somnambulist brook / . . . / still dreaming audibly" ends the poem. As in "The Weed" and "Quai d'Orléans," the brook offers water with its own life — not its own memories but its own dreams, as it sleepwalks into the dreams of others. Two poems later, "Cape Breton" also ends with a brook, whose ancient chill recalls the ancient feel of "At the Fishhouses." The three poems provide a very full sense of place, and I expect that is why Bishop wanted them together. They end with the ordinary daylight working world; but as in other such worlds, a strange nighttime world coexists with it, and something primordial and lasting underlies it. The brook is like a character who brings "A Summer's Dream" to an end. Similarly in a later dream poem, "Sunday, 4 A.M.," "the brook feels for the stair," "the wet foot dangles." "For men may come and men may go,/But I go on forever," sang Tennyson's famous brook, against the brevity of our shorter lives ("The Brook"). Bishop quoted the lines in 1962 ("A Sentimental Tribute," LOA 708).

Sentences

When readers praise Bishop's ordinary everyday diction, they usually have in mind more than her diction. They are also praising her sentence structure, grammar and syntax both, as well as a natural speaking rhythm. But that phrase can be deceptive. James Merrill is very helpful: "Naturalness is always becoming. I'm not sure, though, that many poets know what it is. They're haunted by bugaboos like 'natural word order,' which teaches them to write 'See Jane run,' when the truly *natural* way of putting it would be something closer to 'Where on earth can that child be racing off too? Why, it's little — you know, the neighbor's brat — Jane!'"[4] In prose, too, there is an art to sounding natural. In 1979, Bishop wrote to her good friend Ilse Barker, who had sent her the manuscript of a story: "I think I could make it read a bit more naturally." It was a matter of the details "like repetition, sounds, placement of adverbs, etc." (24 July 1979, Barker letters).

I want to look briefly at the opening group of poems in *A Cold Spring*, listening for their rhythms — not only their metrical beat but also the rhythm of their sentences. How do these sentences sound so right, so natural?

> A cold spring:
> the violet was flawed on the lawn.
> For two weeks or more the trees hesitated;
> the little leaves waited,
> carefully indicating their characteristics.
> Finally a grave green dust
> settled over your big and aimless hills.

We can hear the sentence rhythms, jerky, like the start-and-stop arrival of a cold spring. First comes one sign of spring, a violet likely touched by frost, then a full stop. Then leaves are observed, waiting, also in a short line. Time seems to drag, pulled along by multisyllabic words at line's end. Lines are end-stopped until "Finally" a line flows over in enjambment, and the first permanent sign of spring appears. This is syntax heard musically, as if we heard it through a wall, sounds only and not exact words. "The best place to get the abstract sound of sense is from voices behind a door that cuts off the words."[5] It is also syntax understood objectively, as enacting a natural process through its phrasing, pauses, and stops.

Listening this way to the next poem, "Over 2,000 Illustrations and a Complete Concordance," gives us a different kind of music: an opening with slightly archaic diction and word order and a rhythm that David Bromwich hears as "broken, randomly spliced": "Thus should have been our travels:/serious, engravable" (with a submerged echo of "grave green" and anticipating a "holy grave").[6] Then come descriptions of illustrations and episodic travel accounts, a few lines apiece, in longish verse paragraphs. Finally Bishop makes a sharp change from description to conclusion. She calls attention to her sentence structure, so that grammar and syntax become an analogy for a kind of travel, a kind of life:

> Everything only connected by "and" and "and."

The sentences then change abruptly to a double imperative ("Open the book," "Open the heavy book"), followed by an intricately fashioned question and an astonishing closing line: " — and looked and looked our infant sight away."

The title clearly refers to the title page of a Bible, an English-language Bible, very likely a King James Bible, with attractions added. The word "Complete" in the title is hyperbolic and not what Bishop's family Bible (the Bulmers') said. It was sizable: "As a child, I used to look at my grandfather's Bible under a powerful reading-glass. The letters assembled beneath the lens were suddenly like a Lowell poem, as big as life and as alive, and rainbow-edged. It seemed to illuminate as it magnified; it could also be used as a burning-glass."[7] "Over 2,000 Illustrations and a Complete Concordance" is permeated by that childhood memory. Some of the illustrations are described from a child's perspective, as in the "squatting Arab, / . . . plotting . . . / against our Christian Empire."

"Everything only connected by 'and' and 'and'" suggest parataxis. It is accumulative, an aggregate, like the White Queen's sample of addition in *Alice through the Looking Glass,* to take an extreme case. It describes the disparate travel vignettes, which appear to have no center or purpose. (They are based on Bishop's own travels and connected with biblical matters only obliquely or very generally.) It may describe some sentences in the Bible, notably the genealogical lists where A begat B and B begat C. But the Christian Bible is certainly not built this way,

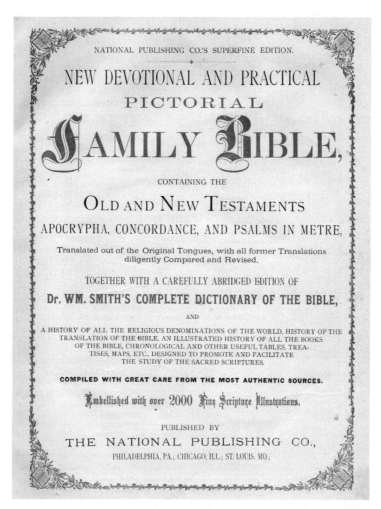

Title page of Bulmer family Bible (see "Over 2,000 Illustrations and a Complete Concordance")

not "only connected by 'and' and 'and.'" Rather its center governs all: pre-X, X, post-X, where X is the Incarnation. In typological reading, latent is followed by patent, type followed by antitype, prophecy followed by fulfillment, as in Augustine, *In Vetero Novus latet; in Novo, Vetus patet.* "Thus should have been our travels," the poem begins. They have not been.

Changing grammar tightens the poem at the end. "Open the heavy book. Why couldn't we have seen / this old Nativity . . . ?" What follows is an illustration and simultaneously an illustration-come-alive: "the dark ajar," "rocks breaking with light," "unbreathing flame," "a family with pets." (The dark ajar and rocks with light evoke the sepulcher and resurrection, appropriate as the ending to the Nativity. An unbreathing flame is at once a flame on a page of that old Bible and a miraculous flame as befits the old Nativity.) "Why couldn't we have seen / this old Nativity . . . ? / . . . / — and looked and looked our infant sight away."

The entire closing passage is extraordinary, as it incorporates a child's point of view ("a family with pets"), while also suggesting through the pun on Latin *infans* that "our infant sight" is unspeaking. Bishop knew Latin and of course had read Eliot's "The word within a word, unable to speak a word" ("Gerontion").[8] She also chose to end this poem with three "ands" — "and, lulled within," "and looked and looked our infant sight away" — so that the ten-line conclusion is framed by matters of "and," the coordinate conjunction that does so much work in English and is so easy to overlook. These coordinate conjunctions work very differently from "Everything only connected by . . ." The unexpected adverb "away" at the very end is breathtaking. A child's sight must grow up and grow away, to be sure. And looking on and on, as in "play away" to a pianist, means freedom to carry on as long as desired. John Ashbery once said, "In the almost twenty years since I first read this poem, I have been unable to exhaust the ambiguity of the last line."[9]

Writers and especially poets would do well to study Bishop's crafting of her sentences in these five longer poems. All five use a loosely similar four- or five-beat line with much variation, plus a few short two- and three-beat lines and a few long six-beat lines. Stress and partial stress are very flexible. There is a remarkable variation in feet with a high proportion of trisyllabic feet interspersed with two-syllable feet like the common iambic foot. The sentences lie so artfully over the steady but varied metrical beat that they sound entirely natural, only tightening when Bishop wants a certain tension. The endings of "Over 2,000 Illustrations and a Complete Concordance" and "At the Fishhouses" are examples. Auden speaks of "the tension between natural speech and musical demands (which should be felt in every good lyric)."[10] Frost comments that a poet "must learn to get cadences by skillfully breaking the sounds of sense with all their irregularity of accent across the regular beat of the metre" (to Bartlett, 4 July 1913, 665). All this is true, though such general principles need fine-tuning to catch something of what Bishop is developing in these poems. They show her new command of sentence structure in relation to poetic line.

How does she manage to make the sentence rhythms sound so distinct in each poem? For one thing, the grammatical mood differs in all five. In "A Cold Spring," the sentences are all indicative, and the clauses are coordinate or else simply parallel. Such grammatical construction lends itself to calm descriptive prose or poetry. It is what Josephine Miles called adjectival syntax rather than predicative or balanced. (An adjectival style uses a higher proportion of phrases and coordinate clauses, while a predicative style uses a higher proportion of adverbs and subordinate clauses.)[11] "Over 2,000 Illustrations and a Complete Concordance" calls attention to its grammar in the first line of its conclusion, "Everything only connected by 'and' and 'and,'" as noted. The sentence rhythm of "The Bight" is closer to "A Cold Spring," though there are several subordinate clauses. A number of its lines read to me like alexandrines, the six-foot line that is the standard line of French poetry. I wonder if this is a deliberate evocation of Baudelaire, who figures prominently in the poem.

"At the Fishhouses" has a strong predicative syntax with a number of subordinate clauses, starting with the opening line: "Although it is a cold evening." "Cape Breton" returns to the syntactical style of "A Cold Spring." The coordinate conjunction "and" is much used; there are hardly any subordinate clauses; some appear simply in parallel. The number of nouns and adjectives in proportion to verbs and adverbs is high. Two adjectives modifying a noun are common, and there even a few examples of three modifying adjectives. The poem uses a longer line than "A Cold Spring" and uses it much more often.

Bonnie Costello observes the art of Bishop's sentences in "Crusoe in England": "The rhythm of long sentences against short, the parentheses, dashes, ellipses, all these impersonal devices (largely ignored by critics) give a personal inflection to the speaker, create an effect of immediate voice."[12] Her parenthesis deserves attention from all writers and readers, including critics.

It's worth noting in passing how much attention Bishop paid to grammar, including often-ignored parts of speech like articles and prepositions. Look at her titles, which often use "The" or "A" but sometimes do not ("Roosters," "Sandpiper"). As for prepositions, Bishop starts off several of her own poems this way: "At low tide," "To the sagging wharf," "Out on the high 'bird islands,'" and so on. She fussed over the difference between "on" and "upon" in a letter to May Swenson: "But the stones are *in* the mouth, so wouldn't you say the mouth champs *on* them instead of *upon?*" (19 Sept. 1953, Swenson-Bishop letters). She strongly disliked the misuse of "like" for "as" or "as if," a battle now mostly lost: "please, please I wish you wouldn't use 'like' for 'as.' . . . Or were you doing it on purpose? . . . I didn't see any other evidence of deliberate low-browness" (to May Swenson, 20 May 1955, Swenson-Bishop letters). Swenson replied that the use was in fact deliberate. The skirmish recurred in 1964: "I like that poem about the plane very much — but — I hope you won't think I'm being impolite or perhaps even dumb perhaps you wanted to say that? — I can't BEAR the word 'like' used instead of 'as if.' . . . PLEASE look at Fowler, page 325 — I just hate it."[13]

Bishop's use of "shan't" in "One Art" can sound unduly fussy, because this usage has died out since Bishop was a child in school. ("Even losing you . . . / . . . I shan't have lied.") Proper grammar once taught that the first-person indicative uses "shall," while the second and third persons use "will." Where resolution or determination is meant, these verbs are reversed. Bishop is using simple indicative in "One Art," just as the speaker of "In Prison" (1938) does, repeating "should" and then "shall" several times. Third-person narrative uses "would" and "will" (*CProse* 185, 187–190). So does the speaker of "To the Botequim and Back" (1970, ibid., 73).[14]

T. S. Eliot once challenged poets, "Try to put into a sequence of simple quatrains the continuous syntactic variety of Gautier or Blake."[15] Readers can test "A Summer's Dream" and then "The Burglar of Babylon."

Love

If Bishop had published her poems in chronological order, a running narrative of love would have been evident. Except for the late poem "The Shampoo," the love poems tell a story of increasing unhappiness, especially from 1949 to 1951: "Letter to N.Y." (1940, omitted from *North & South*), "Argument" (1947), "O Breath" ("Four Poems," IV, 1949), "Conversation," "While Someone Telephones," "Rain towards Morning" ("Four Poems," I–III), and "Insomnia" (1951). Most of these poems show love that is vexed with problems, chiefly the unhappiness of a speaker whose love is not reciprocated or not reciprocated in anything like the same degree. Bishop's diction is more open about lesbian love in the 1949 poem "O Breath" and the other three poems of "Four Poems" (1951) as well as "Insomnia" (1951). The 1947 poem "Argument," placed later in the collection than the others, works for an argument between any two people who are close. The last poem in the book, "The Shampoo," is Bishop's first full-hearted love poem and a beautiful tribute to the woman with whom she would live for over fifteen years. The gap in publishing in 1950 reflects a very difficult period in Bishop's life. On the cover of her working notebook, "The Year 1950" (Vassar 77.4), she scribbled, "Just about my worst, so far —."

The love poems contrast sharply with the opening group. They are all comparatively short, especially "Four Poems." They are more compact, and some are dense. The new style and technique that started with "Florida" is wonderfully and variously advanced in the opening group. But it is a different style that Bishop is working on for the love poems: candid yet indirect, compact with implication, straightforward in some ways and veiled in others. The sentences are generally shorter, as are the lines, and the rhythms more abrupt.

Bishop at first thought she could not publish the poems that finally appeared as "Four Poems," earlier called "Love Poems."[16] They must have seemed too intimate, too personal. They were written when she was struggling with depression, a recurring drinking problem, and above all, fear of losing her gift for writing. There are several long, desperate letters to an old friend in July 1949, concluding, "Well, I suppose nobody's heart is really good for much until it has been smashed to little bits" (to Loren MacIver, 19 July 1949, L 191). Some lines follow for "the third of this unfortunate sequence — or is it too clumsy?"

> *Your eyes two darkened theatres*
> *in which I thought I saw you — saw you!*
> *but only played most miserably my doubled self.*

In the end, Bishop rejected these lines, and the third part became "While Someone Telephones" (L 189). All in all, Bishop wrote to May Swenson later, "the *Four Poems* are pretty mysterious, I'm afraid. I hoped they'd have enough emotional value in themselves so that I wouldn't have to be more specific. . . . Any meanings you want to attach are all right, I'm sure — the wilder the better. It should be a sketch for an acute, neurotic, 'modern' drama — or 'affair,' that's all" (6 Sept. 1955, LOA 805–806). That's all, indeed.

The last in the series, "O Breath," appeared first, in 1949, the other three in January 1951: I, "Conversation"; II, "Rain towards Morning"; III, "While Someone Telephones." All are short, intense poems, possessed by strong and different emotions. Much is clear, but much is implied or hardly even implied but delicately intimated and left for the reader to puzzle out. Bishop thought of them as four lyrics belonging to a sequence. To more than one friend, including Swenson, she wrote that they were meant to resemble the lyric intervals in Tennyson's *Maud,* and the comparison is telling. Some ten years earlier, Bishop filled three pages of her notebook with quotations from *Maud,* whose speaker is afflicted by the curse of hereditary madness, though how far, he does not know. Nor is the reader altogether sure. It goes without saying that such a poem would speak to Bishop, as it did to Tennyson, who also came from a family afflicted with madness. *Maud* is a narrative love poem, marked in the end by violence and failure, then a final turn toward public life. Some of Tennyson's most exquisite lyrics are here, and Bishop copied some in her notebook, including "Oh let the solid ground / Not fail beneath my feet" (part 2, XI) and "She is coming, my own, my sweet" (part 2, XXII). At the end of three pages, she wrote, "Mad-house scenes in general —" and "What *we*'d do if *we* were mad —" (Vassar 72.A.2).

The poems that make up "Four Poems" are written from the viewpoint of a single lover. (*Maud* is subtitled *A Monodrama,* i.e., a drama spoken by one person.) All are short (12, 9, 14, and 15 lines, respectively), each takes a different form, and each has some diction that quietly stops us short. By such diction, Bishop blocks any plot that relies on stereotypes. By such quietness, she indicates that she is not interested in shock tactics. Like the woman in "Rain towards Morning," we are also set a "puzzle" in the implied narrative. "Conversation" is highly condensed. What is "the same tone of voice"? Tentative hope? Surprise? Suppressed anxiety? Bishop throws us back on our own experience, actual or imagined. What does the final couplet imply: "until a name / and all its connotation are the same"? *All* its connotation? And what name? "Love"? "Passion"? A proper name? In any case, the full-ness, the essence, the quiddity, of a name; the place at which name and thing come together, fully realized, or seem to; the place in which we find ourselves in love. And what is an "uninnocent" conversation? Experienced conversation? Guilty? Some mixture of the two? Or? The adjective asks for a little thought about the complexities of lesbian love at this time.

Bishop overestimated, I think, the extent to which readers would be interested in connecting the poems. "Four Poems" lives chiefly as separate love poems. The love poem that attains simplicity shows Bishop's remarkable art at its best: "The Shampoo."

Bishop placed a 1947 poem after "Four Poems" and "Letter to N.Y." (1940). "Argument" is also a love poem, not as forceful as those discussed already but with memorable phrasing. It is more sanguine, determined to conquer whatever it is that has divided two lovers. "Days" and "distances," time and space, have intervened between them, and Bishop goes on to create something close to two characters, "distance" and "days." Her "hideous calendar" is memorably stamped "Compliments of Never & Forever, Inc." The ending is peaceful, with days and distance "gone / both for good and from the gentle battleground." "*Argument* is just the old complaint of separation — with a slightly optimistic ending," Bishop wrote to May Swenson (6 Sept. 1955, LOA 806). By 1949 and "Four Poems," the battleground is far from gentle.

In December 1951, Bishop decided to stay in Brazil with Lota. She published "Arrival at Santos" in 1952, and the first edition of *A Cold Spring* included it; Bishop later reprinted it as the first poem of *Questions of Travel* (1965). She published no poetry in 1953 or 1954, when her writing energy was taken up by two short stories, including the masterpiece "In the Village." In 1955 came the first poems published in three years, "The Shampoo," "Manners," and "Filling Station." Like her 1953 stories, the latter two poems are built on her Nova Scotia childhood. But she marked her new life by ending *A Cold Spring* with "The Shampoo." *Poems:*

North & South — *A Cold Spring* was published in July 1955 and won the Pulitzer Prize.

As love poem, the tone of "The Shampoo" could hardly be more different from the tone of all her published love poems to date. It centers on a small everyday domestic task, washing someone's hair. And yet this is also an expression of love, a poem of "O Hair" that does not need that form of address. (It began as "Gray Hair.") Bishop's characteristic focus is on a little everyday domestic task that slowly and quietly and calmly intimates an entire world. Similarly, the work of the "women feeling for the smoothness of yard-goods" in "The Map" intimates an entire world.

The poem has three six-line stanzas with three rhymes per stanza and a variable line length. In *A Cold Spring,* only one other poem uses a six-line stanza, also with three rhymes per stanza, also three stanzas in all. It is "Insomnia," an unhappy love poem. The one metrical difference is that "The Shampoo" has a much less regular line length. "Insomnia," with its mirror and moon world, its "world inverted," is a lesbian love poem.

> By the Universe deserted,
> *she*'d tell it to go to hell,
> and she'd find a body of water,
> or a mirror, on which to dwell.

The moon in "The Shampoo" is embodied in a simile:

> —Come, let me wash it in this big tin basin,
> battered and shiny like the moon.

Here the speaker has captured the moon in a tangible object, shiny, yes, but also battered, as if to acknowledge personal and public difficulties in lesbian love along with the gleam of love itself. The washing of hair hints — no more — that this might resemble a ritual, a symbolic act.

Wyrd

I want now to look at "O Breath," a poem that hopes for some way to live with a beloved who seems unknowable. Even when asleep, and so apparently vulnerable and open — even then, the heart is hidden:

> I cannot fathom   even a ripple.

The poem opens on a preposition of place and comes back to it at the end:

> Beneath that loved   and celebrated breast
> . . . .
> something that maybe I could bargain with
> and make a separate peace   beneath
> within   if never with.

The mystery of this lover's heart remains closed. The fifteen-line poem breaks into three sentences: an indicative sentence setting out the problem; an imperative sentence in a parenthesis, showing desire "almost intolerably" and referring to a "you"; thoughts of negotiation for some kind of livable arrangement, peace of sorts.

Bishop laid out "O Breath" so that each line has a space in the middle, and the space runs irregularly down the length of the poem. Why this form? In 1949, while at Yaddo, she was working on a poem about breath, to follow David Wagoner:

> She asked what punctuation might be strongest
> For catching her breath, for breath catching.

Wagoner's "Poem about Breath" goes on to say that Bishop rejected ellipses or blank spaces but thought about a double colon or dashes like Dickinson's.[17] He himself continues thinking about asthma, breathing, and poetic rhythms. Critics have routinely followed Wagoner's lead and taken the spacing in "O Breath" as Bishop's own invention, a picture on the page of what it feels like to be an asthmatic and how to read the poem aloud.

And yet, and yet: the full answer is much more interesting. The first time that I saw this poem, I thought, Ah, Old English (Anglo-Saxon) poetry, because that is exactly how it is laid out on the page. Glance at a page of *Beowulf,* and there is the same spacing running down the entire page. A number of poets have adapted this oldest of English-language poetry, often for subjects related to the themes of Old English poetry. Auden has a masterly one, "Doom is dark and deeper than any sea-dingle." Bishop used it for a modern theme.

The spacing was there from the beginning, when "O Breath" first appeared in the *Partisan Review* in 1949 (16: 894). What could be more appropriate? Old English poetry depends on breath even more than most other poetry. For one thing, it was largely an oral poetry. For another, it uses strong-stress (or pure accentual) meter, that is, meter with a set number of stresses and an irregular number of unstressed syllables. It is unlike most later metrical poetry (accentual-syllabic), because only the stressed syllables are counted. Imagine a small harp thrumming a regular beat, four beats or stresses to the line, like a jazz accompaniment. The poet recites the lines in time to the beat and then fits in a variable number of unstressed syllables. The number may change but must fit into a single breath, which is taken at a break.

The style of Old English poetry is the alliterative style, in which the line is bound together with one or often two sounds, commonly at the beginning of words. The lines are not rhymed, though occasionally end rhyme or midline rhyme is used, as are assonance and consonance. In Bishop's poem, the use of the Anglo-Saxon verse line is more regular at the start:

Beneath that loved and celebrated breast,
silent, bored really   blindly veined

In line 1, the dominant alliteration is on the *b* that starts things in the title, "O Breath" (be-, bra-, bre-), and it continues in line 2 (bo-, bli-), with the last *b* picking up the secondary alliteration on *l*. The line lengths shrink from ten to eight to six to four syllables, but in strong-stress or pure accentual verse, this does not matter. The four beats continue, with fewer and fewer intervening syllables, so that the first four lines sound as if they are gradually running down. In music, the pauses would become longer and longer.

The grammar requires attention. Word order is reversed, so that a series of verbs comes first: "grieves maybe, lives and lets / live, passes bets." And what grieves, bets, and so on? Bishop does not offer a conjunction, so we cannot even say "grieves or bets." The poem builds on apposition, units of grammar lying side by side like these lovers. Apposition invites us to think a bit about the relation of the appositive words or phrases or clauses. Mostly we assume a simple parallel (as we might of lovers), but apposition can shift a parallel in greater or lesser degree. The subject of the verbs here is apparently "something moving," so that something moving "grieves, maybe," or in contrast "lives and lets / live." Or something moving "passes," as say an expression might pass over a face. Or something moving "bets" on — what? A new lover? The present lover doing what? But something moving moves "invisibly" and without noise:

and with what clamor   why restrained
I cannot fathom   even a ripple.

Old English poetry uses rhyme sparingly, but Bishop has used an intricate scheme of end and internal rhyme in this fifteen-line poem.

When I first saw the poem and recognized its pattern, I also smiled because Bishop is addressing a "loved and celebrated breast." Here is a visual rather than an oral patterning, with the space down the middle representing the valley between the two breasts. As it happens, the word "breast" (Old English *breost*) in its general sense is fairly common in Old English poetry, both in a battlefield context where the breast may be full of valor or may be wounded, say, and in a context of love, both erotic and other. As with breath, so also with breast. The diction is just right.

The word "breath" appears only once in "O Breath":

(See the thin flying   of nine black hairs
four around one five the other nipple,
flying almost intolerably on your own breath.)

Breath means life, of course. In its Latinate etymology rather than its Old English root, it branches out into inspiration. "Breathe on me, breath of God," says the old hymn, recalling Genesis and the Hebrew word for "breath" in the creation story. Bishop's poem concentrates on the physical signs of breathing, but what lives beneath the observable effects of breathing, the speaker cannot tell. The title sounds like an Old English riddle poem, the type in which the answer is given in the title and the poem expounds the object's characteristics. As for the mysterious adjective "celebrated," it comes from a different world, a Latinate world, not an Old English world.

In the end, Bishop plays "equivocal" against "equivalents" (and her verse form depends on equivalents) and leaves us with a riddle. The gap in the verse line is a metaphor for the division between these two lovers. Although "what we have in common's bound to be there," the two lovers cannot be open with each other or mend their differences openly. Bishop's speaker can "maybe" strike some kind of bargain for continuing this affair. But peace between the lovers is another matter:

> and make a separate peace   beneath
> within   if never with.

This lover must make peace within herself, beneath the surface, keeping in mind "what we have in common." And the word "celebrated" remains uncomfortably bedded in line 1. The breasts themselves remain blind.

Does it seem improbable that Bishop would call on this old form, Old English poetry? That she knew it hardly needs proving. Bishop's knowledge of things poetic was formidable, as is the range of her known reading. Then, too, Bishop published "O Breath" in 1949. In 1947, she published another poem in which the echoes of Old English poetry are unmistakable to my ear. Here is the sea in "At the Fishhouses":

> element bearable to no mortal,
> to fish and to seals . . .

"At the Fishhouses" does not begin this way. It begins as a Wordsworthian poem. The forty-line opening verse paragraph describes a wharf and its fishhouses at dusk, the details lovingly observed with a Wordsworth's or a Darwin's eye. The scene is not a conventional thing of beauty, but Bishop's eye sees the working tools and the iridescent patterns of countless fish scales as if in a painting. The verse paragraph ends by focusing on a single lone figure, an old man, a fish scaler, somewhat resembling the title character in Wordsworth's poem *Michael*. He accepts a cigarette, he knew the speaker's grandfather, they discuss fish populations. This first section ends by focusing on his scaling knife, a knife as used and worn as Crusoe's in the later "Crusoe in England." Then comes a transitional six-line paragraph leading the eye down the ramp to the sea.

The long final verse paragraph (thirty-seven lines) opens with a move away from any Wordsworthian tradition:

> Cold dark deep and absolutely clear,
> element bearable to no mortal,
> to fish and to seals . . .

Wordsworth is a poet of land and inland waters, not of the sea. Suddenly this poem's conversational tone has been interrupted with reverse word order, the use of the word "mortal," the sea as "element," and creatures of the sea that evoke Old English kennings or standard epithets. The sea can be called not the "sea" but "a whale-road" or "a home for fishes." Seamus Heaney, in several fine pages on "At the Fishhouses," observes how just here "a rhythmic heave . . . suggests that something other is about to happen." Then Bishop reverts to a conversational tone. She will repeat the line that precedes these two lines, "Cold dark deep and absolutely clear" later in the poem, a refrain followed this time by "the clear gray icy water" and similarly by an ellipsis that marks a break in thought. The sea is almost a character in itself in Old English poetry, bountiful in providing food but dangerous and unpredictable. Bishop's brief evocation of the oldest English-language poetry also evokes the ageless sea (as it might appear) and what it has meant to humankind.

As Heaney says, "it is a different, estranging and fearful element which ultimately fascinates her, . . . this poet enduring the cold sea-light of her own *wyrd* and her own mortality."[18] *Wyrd* means "fate," and Heaney has chosen it (I think) because this translator of *Beowulf* recognizes the Old English sense of the sea at work here.

Bishop also explicitly reminds the reader of the elements in "At the Fishhouses," the four elements that steady her as a child in her story about Great Village, the four elements that started her poems in *North & South*. All four are present in this poem. Air and earth open the poem, but water, Bishop's own element, comes to dominate. Fire is suggested by the cigarette, a Lucky Strike, then explicitly toward the end. If you dip your hand in the sea,

> your hand would burn
> as if the water were a transmutation of fire
> that feeds on stones and burns with a dark gray flame.

For all that, the poem evokes all five senses as well. Sight and sound are obvious, a strong smell of cod appears in line 7, and at the end come touch and then taste, again like burning:

> If you tasted it, it would first taste bitter,
> then briny, then surely burn your tongue.

Tone, rhythm, syntax, and diction all change in the opening lines:

> Cold dark deep and absolutely clear,
> element bearable to no mortal,
> to fish and seals . . . One seal particularly
> I have seen here evening after evening.

Bishop inserts no commas between her adjectives, as the lines follow fish and seals into an ellipsis, with the sentence incomplete as if the poem had slipped down into the deeper sea. Then comes another change of tone, with another kind of conversation, this time with the curious seal, funny and engaging. "Clear dark deep and absolutely clear" is repeated, followed by "the clear gray icy water . . ." and again that ellipsis.

Another change of focus follows, and then Bishop's slow development of the end of this third movement. The poem is like a piece of music. Two conditional sentences lead to the astonishingly rich ending ("If you should dip your hand in," "If you tasted it"):

> It is like what we imagine knowledge to be:
> dark, salt, clear, moving, utterly free,
> drawn from the cold hard mouth
> of the world, derived from the rocky breasts
> forever, flowing and drawn, and since
> our knowledge is historical, flowing and flown.

To draw, drawn; to know, known; to flow, flowed. But wait. There appears to be no past participle for "to flow" like the past participles "drawn" and "known." "Flown" nowadays is the past participle of "to fly," not "to flow." There is a historical reason for this. All four verbs are Old English in origin, and the difference in the past participles depends on whether a given Old English verb is strong or weak. You don't have to know this to write poetry, though the *Oxford English Dictionary* will tell you. But you do have to know something about word roots, and Bishop knew a lot, as we have seen. She is playing with the difference, evoking the verb "to fly." She is also continuing to draw on one of two major streams that flow together to make the English language: the Germanic stream, Old English. That too gives knowledge; on that too we draw perforce every time we speak; that too flows; that too has flown in some ways. "Since knowledge is historical," yes, including knowledge of the language, and not just knowledge of the old words — the first forms of "the sea," "to know," "dark," "free," "hard," "mouth," "world," "breast," "forever," "to draw," "to flow," "to fly" — but wide and deep knowledge, including the "fearful and estranging" knowledge of our own *wyrd* and mortality, knowledge as felt in the bones and in the mouth, the way Seamus Heaney felt it.

CHAPTER SIX

Kinds of Travel, Kinds of Home, Kinds of Poem: *Questions of Travel*

From the start, *Questions of Travel* has yet a different tone from Bishop's two earlier collections. It is the collection of Bishop's forties, not of her tumultuous twenties or anxious thirties. It is dedicated to Lota, and it shows a Bishop who has now fully realized her poetic powers. The first poem, "Arrival at Santos," was published in June 1952 shortly after Bishop's arrival in Brazil. (Santos is the port of São Paulo, where Bishop first landed after her seventeen-day voyage [to Alfred Kazin, Dec. 1951, L 226].) She included it at the end of *A Cold Spring*, then used it again to open *Questions of Travel*. She is playful throughout the poem, and that includes the playfulness of her technical bravado. This is a map of sorts ("Here is a coast; here is a harbor") but not the reflective map that locates her life as a twenty-three-year-old starting out in "The Map." Nor is it a gravely meditative local mapping, anchoring itself in a farm and the steadiness of everyday work as in "A Cold Spring." No, Bishop is ebullient. She is happy. It ends, "We leave Santos at once;/we are driving to the interior." That sense of a tourist approaching from the outside in so many different ways is part of the poem. So too is the sense that what follows will move into the interior of a new country, a new people, a new life.

Something is freed in Bishop in this third collection. In *A Cold Spring*, some poems appear burdened or else stripped of certain feelings. Here the poems show a fuller response than ever from her senses, feelings, thinking. There is also a fuller literary response than ever, so that Robert Lowell marveled at how she changes styles, unlike other writers who can command only one style. "I think you never do a poem without your own intuition. You are about the only poet now who calls her own tune — rather different from Pound or Miss Moore, who built original styles then continue them — but yours, especially the last dozen or so, are all unpredictably different" (12 July 1960, LEBRL 331). Bishop demurred that this sounded "too much like facility" (27 [?] July 1960, LEBRL 333), and when Lowell wrote the jacket blurb for *Questions of Travel*, he made his point clearer: "What cuts so deep is that each poem is inspired by her own tone." Her voice remains uniquely her own, while she returns to the same or similar subjects: ekphrasis in a map or tapestry, dreams, love poems, war, the creaturely world. She extends her command of diction and line, even amusing herself with the run-over line in the opening poem. What is most remarkable in her style in this collection is, I think, her expanded repertoire of genres.

Bishop divided *Questions of Travel* into two sections, "Brazil" and "Elsewhere," with her short story "In the Village" placed between. What if anything unites these two sections? A number of things. The animal kingdom, for one, which appears throughout, as if to say that all geography includes creatures. Species differ, of course, but the creatures themselves catch Bishop's eye, as the creaturely world always has. Every poem in this collection except for the first and last refers to the world of creatures, though one ("Sestina") does so only through metaphor. Both halves include a poem focusing on one kind of creature, "The Armadillo" and "Sandpiper." Both halves include domestic animals. Both halves include birds, some free, some captive. The cattle in Anthony Trollope's account are poor, sick animals, raised for slaughter, their plight being emblematic of the times; they are the last creatures to appear in the book. The house of Bedlam in the last poem, "Visits to St. Elizabeths," admits no animals or birds or insects. The story "In the Village" shows an observant child watching a handsome horse being shod, meeting two dogs (one deaf and indulged), herding Nelly the cow, avoiding the sounds of a pig being slaughtered, and watching trout in a stream. "Sunday, 4 A.M." is a dream poem with a dream horse that needs shoeing, like the actual horse being shod in "In the Village."

Overview: Brazil

The "Brazil" section consists of eleven poems and is centered on two intimate household poems, "Electrical Storm" and "Song for the Rainy Season." These are poems of being at home, outwardly and inwardly, and the second is an exquisite love-song-cum-country-house poem. After "Arrival at Santos" and "we are driving to the interior," the rest of the section moves into that interior.

"Arrival at Santos" is a prologue of sorts. "Of sorts" because a prologue poem usually opens a continuous work, not a collection. Yet this poem brings the reader to Brazil and starts off a trio of introductory poems. It is a slighter poem than the two that follow, "Brazil, January 1, 1502" and "Questions of Travel," but it provides an attractive, funny scene of embarkation, drawing us into this new world. "Here is a coast; here is a harbor," it begins, sounding a little like Dickens's Wemmick ("Here is a church"; *Great Expectations,* chapter 55) or like someone pointing a finger at a map. But no, this is from the deck of a ship: "here, after a meager diet

of horizon, is some scenery" — a disappointing scene for those
hoping for the sublime or at least the picturesque. The poem has
at least two voices, an outward tourist's voice and an inner voice
of conscience, a public and a private persona. The second voice
suddenly interrupts the description to ask,

>   Oh, tourist,
> is this how this country is going to answer you
>
> and your immodest demands for a different world,
> and a better life, and complete comprehension
> of both at last, and immediately . . . ?

Then the tourist's conversational voice takes over, as passengers
prepare to embark.

Bishop is sure enough by now of her technique that she allows herself a little fun in enjambment, twice over, in the process of embarkation. Enjambment here is not on the usual scale
of walking around the curve at the right-hand side of the line, a
scale that runs from a gentle curve to a sharp hairpin curve. No,
this walk takes a step across from a ship's ladder to a tender,
guided by seamen. One is a boy with a boat hook.

> Please, boy, do be more careful with that boat hook!
> Watch out! Oh! It has caught Miss Breen's
>
> skirt! There! Miss Breen is about seventy,
> a retired police lieutenant, six feet tall,
> with beautiful bright blue eyes and a kind expression.
> Her home, when she is at home, is in Glens Fall
>
> s, New York. There. We are settled.

Now that *is* mischievous. William Pritchard says he once heard
James Merrill read this poem. "His wonderfully nuanced voice

did an especially fine job with 'Watch out! Oh! It has caught Miss Breen's // skirt!'" — exclamations he delivered in a mock-horrified, somewhat campy mode that Bishop herself would surely have loved."[1] John Hollander calls this effect of enjambment "almost at the edge of whimsy" and the break across "Glens Fall // s" an "e. e. cummings sort of fracture," because it is "modulated by rhyme, tone, subject and narrative. . . . It is no cheap effect."[2] "I marvel how you do so much so simply," Katherine White wrote to Bishop, accepting the poem for the *New Yorker* (31 Mar. 1952, LEBNY 79).

Bishop added the date to the end of "Arrival at Santos": "January, 1952." The second poem is titled "Brazil, January 1, 1502." Two Brazil poems, dated 450 years apart. And how does "Brazil, January 1, 1502" begin? "Januaries, Nature greets our eyes / exactly as she must have greeted theirs." How much work those deceptively simple twelve opening words are doing. It only becomes apparent when we pause over them and enter into the entire world that Bishop patiently, slowly creates. "Brazil, January 1, 1502" is a magnificent ekphrastic poem, Bishop's most accomplished to date. It continues her work on "The Map," "Large Bad Picture," and the like, and prepares the way for her late "Poem." It also metamorphoses into a war poem, with links to "Paris, 7 A.M." and "Roosters." Of course, ekphrasis began in Western writing with a work of art inextricably connected with war: the shield of Achilles, forged by the master craftsman the god Hephaestus, or Vulcan. Bishop's poem does not offer the terrible postwar vision of Auden's 1952 "The Shield of Achilles," but nor does it avert its eyes from the cost of empire, especially for the defeated.

By the end, the travelers are also implicated in the Portuguese conquest (but just how, and how far?). This sense of history is sandwiched between the immediate arrival by boat and the start of driving to the interior. For a tourist, it might occupy a brief moment's thought, but not to a traveler, especially one who will reflect on questions of travel and of home. Those early explorers traveled certainly, and they came to other people's homes. "Brazil, January 1, 1502" also ends with "driving to the interior" in a quite different sense, a military sense. I want to look at the poem in more detail at the end of this chapter.

The third poem, "Questions of Travel," returns to the present, beginning almost querulously with complaints about the landscape, as if the fussy tourist in "Arrival at Santos" had reappeared.

> There are too many waterfalls here; the crowded streams
> hurry too rapidly down to the sea.
>
> .   .   .   .
>
> But if the streams and clouds keep travelling, travelling,
> the mountains look like the hulls of capsized ships,
> slime-hung and barnacled.

The poem moves from the echoing Brazilian rain forest to the question of why people bother to travel at all. The question is then sidestepped with the observation that "surely it would have been a pity" not to have experienced some things on this trip: pink trees like a pantomime along the road, then the filling station on which the poem pauses to focus. The attendant's wooden clogs make a tune of sorts, while a bird sings from within an intricately fashioned bamboo birdcage. Why do the "crudest wooden footwear" exist alongside the "careful and finicky/ . . . whittled fantasies of wooden cages"? You could study history through this question, the traveler reflects — an unusual traveler.

For as with "Arrival at Santos," a second voice also speaks, a close observer and a questioner. The traveler sees some of the results of the Portuguese invasion as described in "Brazil, January 1, 1502," the birdhouse, for example, that is "a bamboo church of Jesuit baroque." The prevailing voice, the questioner about travel, ends the poem by writing in a notebook, layering "Questions of Travel" in a way reminiscent of Wallace Stevens.

> *"Is it lack of imagination that makes us come*
> *to imagined places, not just stay at home?*
> *Or could Pascal have been not entirely right*
> *about just sitting quietly in one's room?*
>
> *Continent, city, country, society:*
> *the choice is never wide and never free.*
> *And here, or there . . . No. Should we have stayed at home,*
> *wherever that may be?"*[3]

The effect here is not, as in "Arrival at Santos," of an inner bemused, ironic voice, perhaps of the same chatty practical tourist who narrates most of the poem. Here the effect is of a dialogue between the tourist who is becoming a traveler and a thinker reflecting on the whole matter of travel.

Once we introduce the term "dialogue" in relation to genre, the poem lights up, all the more when we remember yet again how much Bishop loved, and steeped herself in, Renaissance writing. For here is another probable combining of genres, travel poem and dialogue poem, the latter a genre widely practiced in the Renaissance and often associated with educational poetry.[4]

The last lines (*"home, / wherever that may be?"*) hover over the rest of the Brazil section, beginning with the two poems that follow these three introductory ones, "Squatter's Children" and "Manuelzinho."

In what sense are the squatter's children at home, as they play with their dog on the distant hills above? By definition, they are there on sufferance, a precarious existence. "Squatter's Children" is fashioned in expertly rhymed eight-line stanzas, and it asserts the children's rights at the end through a biblical echo. "Children,"

> you stand among
> the mansions you may choose
> out of a bigger house than yours,
> whose lawfulness endures.

The only way this makes sense is as an echo of the biblical text, "In my Father's house are many mansions" (John 14:2). A hymn that Bishop once cited paraphrases the text: "Nearer my Father's house, / Where many mansions be" ("One sweetly solemn thought," see Chapter 2). The text reads ironically against the plight of these children and resonates as a reminder to those who observe them at a comfortable distance — if they care to pay attention, that is.

As for home, *wherever that may be,* the answer is clear for Manuelzinho and his employer in the fifth poem. "Manuelzinho" is a long dramatic monologue in Lota's voice addressing her impossible, necessary gardener and again showing Bishop's facility with a short three-beat line. Manuelzinho is also a squatter, or rather "Half squatter, half tenant (no rent)" (l. 1). The poem is Bishop's first dramatic monologue. She had previously published songs with dramatic voices and one soliloquy, "Jerónimo's House." A dramatic monologue differs from a soliloquy in having an auditor who conditions what is said. In classic form, the speaker of a dramatic monologue also unwittingly discloses something about himself or herself, though the speaker in "Manuelzinho" seems fully self-aware. The poem provides the speaker's dramatized voice and character as the exasperated, funny, finally responsible landowner, and it sketches her gardener of sorts, impossible yet also impossible to abandon. Readers who find it condescending or worse need to answer the question, What would you do? How would you behave in a society where servants are needed and count on being employed? How would you behave in a diplomatic or military posting with a long-established servant like Manuelzinho?

The first group of Brazil poems is centered on outsiders: tourists, explorers, travelers. The second group is centered on occupants who are at home only on sufferance: squatters and a "half-squatter" gardener of sorts. With the third group, we come to true poems of home, first the dawn poem "Electrical Storm" and then the most thoroughly "at home" poem, "Song for the Rainy Season." It is as if Bishop herself in the persona of a traveler felt tentative at first in this book, even something of a squatter. But by now, this is where home is. "Electrical Storm," a slighter poem, is a scene of domestic intimacy and tranquility, despite the lightning strike on the house. Dawn, a couple in bed: is this a variation on an aubade? Are lovers threatened with parting at dawn? Quite the contrary. Rather than moving outward, the action moves inward toward the bed, which becomes a secure center in the fierce electrical storm. The poem opens, "Dawn an unsympathetic yellow." A regular aubade would develop the unsympathetic color into a sign of unsympathetic forces parting lovers. But no, it comes as a sign of an imminent storm. There is no threat of parting, no urgent call to stay just a little longer. What threat there is comes from the elements. "*Cra-aack!* — dry and light. / The house was really struck."

A lightning strike is an alarming experience, shared by the cat who is seen by lightning heading for the bed, "silent, his eyes bleached white, his fur on end." That's familiar to families with pets. (I remember a fierce lightning storm in a cottage in the woods, when our bed also contained two children, a shivering dog, and an irritated cat.) The couple wait out the storm, then rise "to find the wiring fused, / no lights, a smell of saltpetre, / and the telephone dead." Bishop adds a line break, then the conclusion, in which the cat stays "in the warm sheets" and the Lent trees have shed their petals "among the dead-eye pearls," the hail. As with Dead-Eye Dick in *H.M.S. Pinafore,* these are eyes no longer lustrous, as we say of both eyes and good pearls. It's a little spooky to think of pearls as eyes ("Those are pearls that were his eyes"), to say nothing of hailstones. Earlier the largest hailstones are the size of "artificial pearls, / Dead-white, wax-white, cold," and then, "diplomats' wives' favors / from an old moon party." A social world far removed from this scene of intimacy and a dead-white, not a shiny, moon inform this variation on an aubade. The sense of privacy leads into the next poem.

"Song for the Rainy Season" is one of Bishop's most beautiful poems and is in general underappreciated. It is a pastoral love song and a country-house poem all in one, written in ten-line stanzas like "First Death in Nova Scotia," with short lines and also rhymed, though more regularly. The effect is different, for this poem flows with ongoing life. Bishop's earlier love poem "Late Air" celebrated the privacy of lovers, enveloped in a nest. "Hidden, oh hidden" is equally a celebration of a special place for lovers and the retirement attendant on a country house, hidden from the turmoil of city life. Bishop's element is par excellence the element of water, and it was part of her new love for Lota in "The Shampoo." Now water has taken over in this land where there are not four seasons but two, the dry and the rainy seasons.

> Hidden, oh hidden
> in the high fog
> the house we live in,
> beneath the magnetic rock,
> rain-, rainbow-ridden,
> where blood-black
> bromelias, lichens,
> owls, and the lint
> of the waterfalls cling,
> familiar, unbidden.

There is no main verb, so that this is an exclamatory sentence, albeit a quiet one — a hidden one, so to speak. The properties here — magnetic rock, rain and rainbow, owls, waterfall — will recur in the last stanza, where the sun and heat will have destroyed this idyllic place, this *locus amoenus*. Traditionally, the *locus amoenus* belongs to a temperate climate and comes with streams, flowery meadows, trees, perhaps singing birds. Bishop's ideal place is in a subtropical climate in the rainy season. There is no problem with water, then, or with flowers, but where are the trees and singing birds? The equivalent of a tree is the "giant fern," the samambaia, literally "tree fern," which gave its name to the house and appears routinely as an address in Bishop's letters. The birds find their equivalent in "the ordinary brown/owl," which stamps five times before flying off in search of nearby frogs. Privacy or shelter is also intrinsic to the *locus amoenus.* It differs from a country-house locale in that it gives pleasure and is "not cultivated for useful purposes."[5] The country house's bountiful harvests are a sine qua non, but Bishop finds a way of including both kinds of attribute.

The metamorphosis from rain to rainbow hardly needs comment, a rainbow commonly being a sign of fortune and sometimes as for Noah a sign of covenant. A rainbow is crucial at the end of "The Fish," and Bishop's "rainbow-bird" is free, gay, happy in her last published poem, "Sonnet." The figure of a waterfall seeming to deposit lint, like fabric being laundered, evokes "one more folded sunset, still quite warm" from "Questions of Travel," though that is sun-dried laundry and this is damp. It may also evoke Tennyson's waterfalls in "The Lotos-Eaters" (ll. 10–11), also fabric:

> A land of streams! some, like a downward smoke,
> Slow-dropping veils of thinnest lawn, did go.

The clinging lichen recalls Bishop's memorable opening trope in "The Shampoo" for the love between her and Lota: "The still explosions on the rocks, / the lichens, grow."

The brook "sings loud / from a rib cage / of giant fern," the tree fern. A rib cage makes a fine metaphor for both fern and brook, and it does something more. It takes us back to Bishop's 1937 dream poem "The Weed," in which a weed sprouts and grows, then two rivers gush up ("the ribs made of them two cascades"). Why? The weed has sprouted "but to divide your heart again." Now the stream from a rib cage sings, as if with human voice and with one voice, undivided. The climbing vapor ends by enclosing "house and rock, / in a private cloud." (In myth, enclosing things in a private cloud is a prerogative of the gods, as in the battles of the *Iliad* or as with Zeus and Io.) Hidden, private, and further, a house built on a rock — "house built on a sure foundation," as in the African American spiritual based on the gospel parable about a house built on sand and a house built on rock.

The third stanza listens closely to night sounds from an owl and fat frogs, courting. With the fourth stanza comes a dawn address to the house itself, opening with a line echoing line 1: "House, open house." The phrase might be taken from any country-house poem, where it is mandatory that the house be generous and open to tenants and guests. So is this one, except that the tenants and guests are not human but animal and vegetable: "membership / of silver fish, mouse, / bookworms, / big moths." In the poem's first appearance in the *New Yorker*, Bishop wrote, "too indulgent, perhaps," to these creatures, then changed it to "kind to the eyes, / to membership." Membership? Well, members of a household, even if not the house's owners or (come to think of it) tenants or invited guests or even squatters. It almost sounds like a census. There is even a site for "the mildew's / ignorant map," a wall. Houses in hot, wet climates are prone to mildew, all the more if human breath contributes to it. Bishop's key word "breath" governs the last clause of this sentence, breath that comes with a warm touch, as it will if close enough, breath that is "cherished," a lover's breath; but before the adjective "cherished," breath is said to be "maculate," an odd-sounding choice of words. To be sure, the Latinate meaning of "maculate" is spotted, and there is that mildew map to demonstrate how breath can spot. Yet this hardly seems sufficient for so unusual a modifier for breath. Did Bishop want to emphasize that this is mortal and not eternal love? That she wants to make no hyperbolic claims, even if this is a place like Eden? This sentence stretches over fifteen lines, into the fifth stanza, where the address to the house proves to be an apostrophe, ending as it does in midline with an exclamatory "rejoice!"

What follows is an apprehension of "a later / era" quite different from the "dim age / of water." Another exclamatory sentence addresses the "difference that kills, / or intimidates" and then envisions the site without water: the rock bare and dry, water and rainbows and waterfalls gone, as they "shrivel / in the steady sun" that ends the poem. The rock "will stare / unmagnetized," and in fact magnetic rock can lose its magnetic charge over long periods of time. Bishop has used magnetism and the magnetic pole as symbols of lesbian attraction. The Man-Moth in his first stanza "makes an inverted pin, the point magnetized to the moon," the moon with her "queer light." In a draft of "Sonnet," the magnetic or "false north" influences the compass. The country-house poem has metamorphosed into a poem like Oliver Goldsmith's "The Deserted Village," a poem wondering about the future fate of the house and much more of the site.

The poem is a song for the rainy season in two senses of the preposition "for." The dominant sense is the usual one, but this is also a song for, or on behalf of, the rainy season, as if the season had a voice of its own and were singing. In the last stanza, the season sings apprehensively of the future, when these householders have long gone. Who will succeed them, and will they or can they nourish and cherish this special site, this present *locus amoenus?*

The house in the Brazil section is an extended house. The squatter's children have already been spotted from it, the gardener Manuelzinho already pictured, and "The Armadillo," which follows "Song for the Rainy Season," will focus on a creature existing with others on the hillside behind the house.

"The Armadillo" recounts what can be seen from Bishop and Lota's home, a first-person narrative describing a festival celebration — describing it so matter-of-factly that it takes a moment to recognize the complete change in tone of the final italicized stanza. For the animals are at home too, thus the sense of violation when we recognize what is happening on the ground. The disaster foreseen at the end of "Song for the Rainy Season" has come in the form of fire for some of the creatures in the hillside behind the ideal house. For the first half of this ten-stanza poem, all is festive. The quatrains, mostly rhymed *abcb* and mostly in trimester and tetrameter lines like an adapted ballad form, read easily. The poem sounds a little like a travel poem. (The fire balloons rise "toward a saint / still honored in these parts.") The paper balloons, filled with fire, produce a "light / that comes and goes, like hearts." Dedicated to St. John, they might be another of the sacred heart depictions in Roman Catholicism (or, Bishop suggests, sotto voce, secular hearts that also come and go, hearts dedicated to Eros). As they rise against the sky, they give the illusion of taking their places among the planets and stars in an appropriately heavenly existence. They are in fact illegal, and the poem will now show why. If the air is still, they rise, receding "or, in the downdraft from a peak, suddenly turning dangerous."

> Last night another big one fell.
> It splattered like an egg of fire
> against the cliff behind the house.
> The flame ran down. We saw the pair
>
> of owls who nest there. . . .

Bishop holds back from any affective diction here and will do so until the final stanza. But the ghost rhymes in this stanza tell us something. The near rhyme of "fire/pair" gives us ghost rhymes of "fair" and "pyre." The scene looks fair enough, pretty enough, from a distance, but it is in fact a pyre.[6]

These creatures are part of the extended household, part of the estate, so to speak, of this country-house poem. But they have their own homes too, in Bishop's extended exploration of *"home,/wherever that may be."* And these homes have now been invaded, as the original Portuguese invade Brazil six poems earlier in "Brazil, January 1, 1502." (The Christians' armor from the earlier poem echoes in "The Armadillo," the armed creature, to very different effect.) Are the owls that happily surround the house in "Song" the same ones that nest in the hill behind, where an "ancient owls' nest must have burned"? In the sun-parched vision at the end of "Song," "the owls will move on," but in "The Armadillo," human carelessness causes a pair of nesting owls to fly up "until/they shrieked up out of sight." Their eggs or chicks have been burned alive. The distant fire underneath them makes them look "stained bright pink underneath." Bishop holds back from empathy here, so that the pink stain, the shrieking, the ancient burned nest can register as pure description. It is as if she were testing the reader a little, wondering at what point a reader would say, Yes, but . . .

Bishop's metaphor of "intangible ash" toward the end of the poem has a powerful effect:

> and then a baby rabbit jumped out,
> *short*-eared to our surprise.
> So soft! — a handful of intangible ash
> With fixed ignited eyes.

How dispassionate that adjective "short-eared" sounds: the observation of a naturalist seeing an unexpected species. The adjective "intangible" is not unusual in itself, but in combination it would be an oxymoron if the scene were not far away from actual touch. (Even the softest wood ash is still slightly tangible in the hand. Bishop's phrase makes us think about "ashes . . . soft to the touch," as her 1937 story "The Sea and Its Shore" has it [LOA 581].) The ash is intangible here because it is far removed. Then we realize that this is the point of the poem: that suffering is a spectacle when it is far enough away. We have to remind ourselves of what it would be like if we were close to it, let alone part of it. William Pritchard also notes quite rightly that the last stanza is in some ways commenting on the stanzas preceding it ("Bishop's Time," 328–329).

> *Too pretty, dreamlike mimicry!*
> *O falling fire and piercing cry*
> *and panic, and a weak mailed fist*
> *clenched ignorant against the sky!*

The change of tone at the end makes "The Armadillo" into a poem about homes destroyed and at a distance a war poem — not a historical poem, like "Brazil, January 1, 1502," but a comment on current war. The echo of Arnold's well-known closing line to "Dover Beach" supports this: "where ignorant armies clash by night." Robert Lowell called it "one of your absolutely top poems, your greatest quatrain poem, I mean it has a wonderful formal-informal grandeur — I see the bomb in it in a delicate way" (28 Oct. 1965, LEBRL 591). Bishop replied, "I love your expression, 'the bomb in it in a delicate way!' That was my idea exactly, I suppose" (18 Nov. 1965, LEBRL 594).[7] It is generically a protest poem, of far greater subtlety and force than most.

With "The Riverman," the dominant element moves back from fire to water. It also moves to an uncanny way of being at home, through the embodied spirit of a place, here a river. Robert Lowell called it a "fairy story in verse" (28 Apr. 1960, LEBRL 321) and later an initiation poem, parallel to "Arrival at Santos" (28 Oct. 1965, LEBRL 591). The short, flowing, river-like lines of this long poem are a tour de force. "I wanted to get away from pentameter, too," James Merrill once said, adding, "Do you know that wonderful poem by Elizabeth Bishop called 'The Riverman?' . . . Wonderful, fluid, pulsing lines — you hardly feel the meter at all."[8] Northrop Frye in his fine essay "Charms and Riddles" describes the rhetoric of charm poetry as "incantatory," "repetitive," "hypnotic," and the words exactly suit "The Riverman."[9] As noted in Chapter 7, charm is present in this poem as a mode.

The Riverman recounts in his soliloquy how he is drawn by the Dolphin to follow him and finally to meet the bewitching spirit of the river: "yes, Luandinha, none other." As the opening note tells us, the story was based on Charles Wagley's *Amazon Town: A Study of Man in the Tropics* (1953). River legends like this seem universal. The Scots name for such a spirit is a water-kelpie, as in Robert Burns's "Address to the Deil." The OED has an entire category given over to them ("water," Compounds, C1.q). With flowing, riverine lines, long, sinuous sentences, and repetitions, "The Riverman" is a charm poem par excellence, all the more because the subject itself is charm or enchantment. All the signs are there: moonlit night, magic mirror, compulsion, bodily change, tokens: "I don't eat fish any more," "I look yellow, my wife says," "Every moonlit night/I'm to go back again."

I need a virgin mirror
no one's ever looked at,
that's never looked back at anyone

.   .   .   .

but each time I picked one up
a neighbor looked over my shoulder
and then that one was spoiled —

When finally the Riverman attains the rank of "a serious *sacaca*"
like others he knows, with a "magic cloak of fish," he says,

then I will go to work
to get you health and money.
The Dolphin singled me out;
Luandinha seconded it.

Chinua Achebe recorded an African legend: "The other thing
legend said about [Dr.] Stuart Young was that he had been be-
friended by the mermaid of the River Niger, with whom he
made a pact to remain single in return for great riches."[10] The
best poems in a charm mode, like Tennyson's "Lotos-Eaters" or
"The Lady of Shalott," take charm or enchantment as their subject. So here.

Another festival, another child, another song, another allusion: "Twelfth Morning; or What You Will." "We are staying
up [in Samambaia] until the 6th — maybe even the 7th — it depends how much of a holiday the 'Day of Kings' — the 6th, our
12th Night — is — You'd think they'd *know* by now, after several
hundred years of celebrating it and thousands of little boys
named Balthazzar, Melchior, etc. — but as Lota said, without a
trace of humor — 'no one ever knows.' This country can still

surprise me" (to May Swenson, 3 Jan. 1964, Swenson-Bishop letters). (Twelfth Night is the end of the twelve days of Christmas, mostly known now from the old carol; the days end on January 6 with the Feast of the Epiphany, the Feast of Kings.) The holiday is celebrated less now than in Shakespeare's day or in the late nineteenth century, when French children anticipated the Feast of Kings with great excitement, to follow Frédéric Mistral's *Memoirs* (chap. 3, "The Magi"). At the end of the poem, its place is given: Cabo Frio, Brazil's famous seashore, Cold Cape — "the purest, whitest, most unviolated dunes ever seen, miles of them — with streaky purple-and-green and bluing-water sea all along them" (15 Dec. 1958, Barker letters). Bishop's setting is, however, seen with a traveler's and not a tourist's eye:

> Like a first coat of whitewash when it's wet,
> the thin gray mist lets everything show through:
> the black boy Balthazár, a fence, a horse,
>   a foundered house,
>
> — cement and rafters sticking from a dune.

Against a dispiriting landscape seen with a whimsical eye, there arrives a modern epiphany: a flashing four-gallon can on the head of Balthazár, announcing "that the world's a pearl, *and I, / I am // its highlight!*" — not just an oyster: this world's a pearl. Balthazár's own song can be heard as he approaches: "'Today's my Anniversary,' he sings, / 'the Day of Kings.'" Like the squatter's children, Balthazár is at home in his world and for today both king and cherished child. (There are long-standing traditions of portraying one of the Magi as black or as native.)[11] Bishop has written the poem in quatrains with the last line resembling the last line of a Sapphic stanza (a dactyl followed by a trochee, as in "*this* is a *house*wreck"). The last line, "*I am*" must slow way down to keep the beat, and the highlight stays with the boy. In the end, it is a joyous poem.

"Twelfth Morning; or What You Will" has a summing-up quality before Bishop's closing Brazil poem, a ballad, "The Burglar of Babylon." One of Bishop's grandmothers used to read old ballads to her when she was young, and she absorbed them easily.[12] She was fascinated by local Brazilian ballads.[13] The style of her poem, she commented to her *New Yorker* editor, is, "of course, repetitious & a bit clumsy on purpose" (to Howard Moss, 20 May 1964, LEBNY 264). (She varies the common form by using three stresses in all four lines.)

"The Burglar of Babylon" is a poem of someone very much at home in some ways and not at all in others. As with "The Armadillo," viewers from the safety of home can watch the drama unfolding on the hillside, this time a manhunt for the burglar in one of the favelas around Rio de Janeiro. To May Swenson, she wrote that the story was "all quite true — I watched it. . . . Well — the names of the slums are beautiful and fearful — it was just a matter of choosing" (10–11 Dec. 1964, Swenson-Bishop letters). She begins with them.

> On the fair green hills of Rio
>   There grows a fearful stain.
>
> . . . .
>
> There's one hill called the Chicken,
>   And one called Catacomb;
>
> There's the hill of Kerosene,
>   And the hill of the Skeleton,
> The hill of Astonishment,
>   And the hill of Babylon.

Unlike most of her poems, this one came very quickly after Bishop saw the manhunt.

The poem appropriately includes a buzzard, as well as goats far away, but the telling creatures are the ones in an opening simile about the Rio favelas:

> On the hills a million people,
>> A million sparrows nest,
> Like a confused migration
>> That's had to light and rest.

"Are not five sparrows sold for two farthings, and not one of them is forgotten before God?" (Luke 12:6). As in "Squatter's Children," the echo of a biblical text, though faint, is telling. The example in both Matthew and Luke illustrates a warning not to fear those that kill the body but those that kill the soul. And this is a poem about a killing, two in fact. One victim dies committing his soul to God and "in hope of Heaven," while the other curses the sun in the morning. Do the two deaths divide into the contrast in the biblical text? The start and finish of the poem work to prevent any such neat division while implicitly raising a question of the souls and bodies of those in Rio watching the hillside securely.

Overview: Elsewhere

Questions of Travel is a diptych, a double-sided book, with a hinge in the form of Bishop's masterly short story "In the Village," connecting "Brazil" and "Elsewhere." Robert Giroux, Bishop's editor at Farrar, Straus and Giroux, discussed the order of the material with her. (He had persuaded her to move to his firm for this third collection, and it proved a good match.) On March 22, 1965, he wrote that he found the new order of contents much better. "In the old version, starting off with 'Filling Station' seemed definitely wrong (it seemed at first to be the filling station in the Brazil section!) and I was going to suggest that 'Manners' lead off, as it now does."[4] With "In the Village," the question of travel becomes the question of time-travel back in memory and especially the question of home. The first three poems of the "Elsewhere" section continue the historical period of the short story, as Bishop returns to her Nova Scotia roots. The perspective in the three poems is also a child's. "I am a little embarrassed about having to go to Brazil to experience total recall about Nova Scotia; geography must be more mysterious than we think" (to Katharine White, 10 Oct. 1952, LEBNY 85). "Elsewhere" offers travel to a different interior.

The first poem, "Manners," is "for a child of 1918," as its epigraph says, a child who would be seven years old if born in 1911 like Bishop. I am bemused by discussions of this poem as an overbearing grandfather's snobbish social rules, for they seem a serious misreading. The poem's simplicity has misled readers, perhaps even the word "manners."

In "Manners," the child and her grandfather are strongly part of a community, traveling in horse-and-buggy and greeting everyone on the road. It is a child's verse, ballad-like, with its four-line *abcb* stanza and typical slight awkwardness now and again. (See the rhythm of lines 3–4: "Be sure to remember to always/speak to everyone you meet.") It is also didactic like some children's verses and some ballads. Bishop was drawn to writing children's literature and even thought of making a collection. A memo of 1961 in the Robert Giroux Papers mentions several projects, including "The Big Pink River," the working title of a children's book started some years before, based on a trip up the Amazon. In 1962, she noted how Aesop's fables, from the sixth century B.C., come down in a "small, pure, literary stream or rivulet" to children's literature today and how she finds this "both touching and miraculous" ("A Sentimental Tribute," LOA 708).

As for criticism of the poem that takes umbrage at the lesson in manners, see Bishop's long letter of January 8, 1964, to Anne Stevenson (LOA 864). After remarks on Kafka, Buster Keaton, and Hopkins, Bishop sums up the tone of a good artist: "It may amount to a kind of 'good manners,' I'm not sure. The good artist assumes a certain amount of sensitivity in his audience and doesn't attempt to flay himself in order to get sympathy or understanding." In an early letter, she noted, "The Negroes [in Key West] have such soft voices and such beautifully tactful manners — I suppose it is farfetched, but their attitude keeps reminding me of the *tone* of George Herbert: 'Take the gentle path,' etc." (to Marianne Moore, 31 Jan. 1938, L 68). In 1963, she commented on the manners of John Dewey: "Another friend who influenced me — *not* with his books but with his character — was John Dewey, whom I knew well and was very fond of. He and Marianne are the most truly 'democratic' people I've known, I think. — He had almost the best manners I have ever encountered, always had *time,* took an interest in everything, — no detail, no word or stone or cat or old woman was unimportant to him" (to Anne Stevenson, 20 Mar. 1963, LOA 846). That is her definition of good manners. As for the grandfather's lessons in manners for "a child of 1918," this was in Nova Scotia. In 1908, in another Maritime province, exactly the same social convention was expected as a courtesy: "In Prince Edward Island you are supposed to nod to all and sundry you meet [while driving a buggy] on the road whether you know them or not" (Lucy Maud Montgomery, *Anne of Green Gables,* chap. 2).

Bishop's small masterpiece "Sestina" follows, also with a small child and this time a grandmother. It apparently began as "Early Sorrow" (May Swenson, 28 Oct. 1955, Swenson-Bishop letters), but Bishop rejected the "hammy title" (4 Nov. 1955, Swenson-Bishop letters). Some readers have found "Sestina" mysterious, but it was not in *Questions of Travel,* because it was preceded by "In the Village," including this episode: "My grandmother is sitting in the kitchen stirring potato mash for tomorrow's bread and crying into it. She gives me a spoonful and it tastes wonderful but wrong. In it I think I taste my grandmother's tears; then I kiss her and taste them on her cheek" (*CProse* 259). She is crying because her daughter, Bishop's mother, has had to go back to the mental hospital. The poem brings alive a kitchen scene within the house with grandmother, child, stove, almanac, and tears. (The last six nouns are the six rotating end words, as required by the sestina.) "Tears" is the anomalous and defining word, tears like the equinoctial rain (the adjective is very much an almanac word), tears dancing on the hot iron stove (drops of water, really) so that a cup of tea becomes "hot brown tears." So do the buttons on a man drawn by the child in front of a house, and the moons in the almanac. *"Time to plant tears,* says the almanac" in the envoy, which ends with the child drawing another "inscrutable house." The kitchen world seems to speak: the almanac, the "Little Marvel Stove."

Just as the child expresses her sorrow through drawing — what we would now call art therapy — so Bishop constructs a sestina, a six-part house, so to speak. The unusual conventions of the form help to order a difficult memory, the memory of an aching absence in the kitchen, the drawing, the memory.

There follows yet another small masterpiece, "First Death in Nova Scotia," again from a child's perspective. The poem begins with a nursery-rhyme rhythm after its allusive title that suggests antielegy. This first encounter with death comes at so young an age that the child does not really take it in. It can only be understood — partly understood — in the language of other worlds that she knows through pictures and anthems and hymns: a world of royalty, a biblical world. I want to return later to this poem that is a little world.

"Filling Station," the fourth poem, shifts perspective and tone. What can Bishop make of this way station, so common a sight yet so generally ignored? A good deal, never condescending when condescension would be so easy, just describing and reflecting on this necessary adjunct to the automobile.

"Filling Station" moves to an adult persona and to descriptive detail. The subject is unpromising, yet Bishop sees it without condescension, down to the embroidered and crocheted doilies. It is a descriptive poem, yes, but I think Bishop may be writing an ekphrasis of sorts, an ekphrasis of a painting that should exist, a shadow painting. Look at Edwin Hopper's painting *Gas* (1940), a painting acquired by the Museum of Modern Art in 1943. Point for point, "Filling Station" is the opposite. Hopper's is meticulously clean, as against "Oh, but it is dirty!" The owner shutting it down in the evening is dressed in a white shirt and tie, as against Father dressed in an ill-fitting "dirty, / oil-soaked monkey suit." There is no outer porch with "grease- / impregnated wickerwork," dog, comic books, taboret with a doily and "a big hirsute begonia" (a fine touch). Bishop's poem depicts a filling station that is more challenging as subject than Hopper's

Edward Hopper, *Gas*, in black-and-white (see "Filling Station")

painting. Hopper depicts pride in ordinary work done meticulously, a gas station seen as aesthetic object and an ordinary
highway seen as a worthy setting. Bishop's poem depicts casual,
even careless work ("Be careful with that match!"), adding a
woman's touch, a touch that has long since given up fighting the
all-pervasive oil of the place. (The domestic embroidery briefly
links the poem with "Brazil, January 1, 1502" — an object that
reflects its ambience, this time oil and not rainforest. The doily,
embroidered with daisies and presumably with a wide crocheted
border, has come from indoors.) May Swenson greatly admired
"how the poem is funny and serious both, how it points up the
foolishness and squalor-trying-to-be-homey features of the people
living there, and at the same time is so indulgent of them" (9 Dec.
1955, Swenson-Bishop letters).

Nonetheless the station does calm the nervous horses of a car's horsepower, so that it runs smoothly and quietly. You don't have to get out and walk when your horse is tired, as in "Manners." "Somebody embroidered the doily./Somebody waters the plant/ . . . Somebody arranges the rows of cans/so that they say/ESSO — so — so — so/to highstrung automobiles./Somebody loves us all." Bishop thought the "ESSO — so — so — so" might well need a footnote in an anthology: most students "might well not know that so-so-so was — perhaps still is in some places — the phrase people use to calm and soothe horses" (to John Frederick Nims, 6 Oct. 1979, L 638). As for the closing line, "Somebody loves us all," Swenson and her partner, Blackie, discussed it:

> B. . . . thinks the line means the people believe in god just like they believe in doilies, hairy begonias, etc., and I said, no, it means just as the person who waters the plant, etc., loves it, *somebody* loves these people (the poet, as an instance) and, by extension, somebody loves the poet. . . . Which meaning, straight or satirical, shall we take? and the answer, of course, is *both*. I'll bet James never write a sentence as chinese-boxy as that. (9 Dec. 1955, Swenson-Bishop letters)

Bishop replied, "I'd say you & Blackie are both right — maybe you're a little righter, if anything" (27 Jan. 1956, Swenson-Bishop letters).

A dream poem, "Sunday 4 A.M.," ends this first sequence, a dream poem also with ordinary working tools but a strange, even sinister air — "really about Breughel, more or less," as Bishop said (23 Oct. 1958, Barker letters). To Randall Jarrell, she simply wrote, "I hope you like the Flemish — painting — influence in my dreams!"[15] The poem retrospectively casts a dreamlike haze over "Filling Station." It follows the stanzaic pattern of "Manners," but its rhythm is very different. "Manners" follows the calm rhythm of the mare drawing the wagon. "Sunday, 4 A.M." has the jerky rhythm of a restless sleeper dreaming a strange bad dream and finally wakened by a cat. Dream poem it is, and also a fragmented ekphrasis of a painting, as we know from the reference to the donor. Donors sometimes appeared as minor figures in a painting, but this one (or is it Mary?) has wandered outside the frame. *"If you're the donor, / you might do that much!"* — a dream sentence in which "that" is unclear. Bishop has in mind one or more Breughel paintings, with Mary in traditional blue as ancillary figure:

> An endless and flooded
> dreamland, lying low,
> cross- and wheel-studded
> like a tick-tack-toe.
>
> At the right, ancillary,
> "Mary" 's close and blue.

The dream threatens to turn into a crucifixion scene before relief arrives in the form of a cat who interrupts sleep. It is a cousin of the cat in "Electrical Storm," and it carries a bit of the dream painting in its mouth: "black-and-gold gesso," a moth. The awakening to dawn birdsong is exquisite:

> The world seldom changes,
> but the wet foot dangles
> until a bird arranges
> two notes at right angles.

Instead of a scary brook that "feels for the stair" with its right angles, the "right angles" here are made by two song notes, either dropping or rising sharply, so that in musical notation they would form a right angle — and make things right too, as waking can after a sinister dream.

The sixth poem, "Sandpiper," returns to Bishop's favorite creatures, birds, almost as if brought there by the bird that ends her dream poem. "Sandpiper" belongs fully to a waking world, a world infused with the supra-wakefulness of William Blake — or, say, his kind of dream, a visionary dream that can see the world in a grain of sand. The sandpiper has turned up before in this collection:

> The sea's off somewhere, doing nothing. Listen.
> An expelled breath. And faint, faint, faint
> (or are you hearing things) the sandpipers'
> heart-broken cries.
> ("Twelfth Morning; or What You Will")

The sandpiper from "Elsewhere" is not uttering cries but hunting for food, obsessively it appears to a human eye. It is a seashore sandpiper with dark feet, doubtless a sanderling, recognizable by its "obsessive wave-chasing habits," as well as its black legs and feet. A sanderling is also a bird with enormous range, breeding only on the High Arctic tundra, but wintering "on most of the sandy beaches of the world." The map of their range shows them along North and South American coastlines, including the Brazil coastline where Bishop lived and the New England and Florida coastlines where she had lived earlier; they migrate through the Maritimes. This bird is a traveler par excellence, a bird that Bishop could have seen in both Brazil and elsewhere.[16] The bird's obsessive habits may well make it an apt figure for Bishop, the poet obsessed with getting it right. I think the sanderling also makes a most appropriate figure for Bishop the traveler.

Finally there are two Washington poems, very different from each other and from what has come before, "From Trollope's Journal" and "Visits to St. Elizabeths." Bishop had already published a 1951 poem based on her Washington sojourn, and collected in *A Cold Spring*, "View of the Capitol from the Library of Congress." These two later Washington poems are a good deal more powerful. "From Trollope's Journal" adopts Trollope's voice in a soliloquy, drawn from Trollope's writing. "Visits to St. Elizabeths" is in the third person, using the nursery rhyme "The House That Jack Built" as its formal and generic base.

I cannot be the only reader who has felt for some time that the two final poems seem a little disconnected from what has just preceded them in "Elsewhere" and even that they do not quite measure up to the book thus far. I have changed my mind about this, realizing that both poems require some reflection to see how they enhance questions of travel and questions of home. Anthony Trollope was of course a traveler in Washington, DC, a British traveler, on Post Office business in the Caribbean before he decided to tour the United States in the fraught days of the Civil War.[17] He offers an outsider's viewpoint. Bishop found the atmosphere that he described in Washington similar to what she had experienced during a different war-like period in 1949–1950. The poem is thereby linked with other poems in the collection that reflect on war: "Brazil, January 1, 1502" and "The Armadillo."

Found Poetry, Found Worlds: Washington, 1861–1862 and 1949–1950

I have not heard Bishop's poem "From Trollope's Journal" called a found poem, but that is what it is. And as elsewhere, Bishop has reconfigured the type of poem. In 1960, she sent the draft to

Robert Lowell, who suggested that the two halves, both sonnets, be run together. He also said in passing, "I mightn't have known this was yours" (12 July 1960, LEBRL 331). Bishop followed his advice about rearranging, then added, "The whole thing should really be in quotation marks, I suppose; the reason it doesn't sound like me is because it sounds like Trollope. . . . Have you ever read his *North America?* I just copied out some of the Washington chapter" (27 [?] July 1960, LEBRL 333). Later she acknowledged, "[It] was actually an anti-Eisenhower poem, I think — although it's really almost all Trollope — phrase after phrase" (18 Nov. 1965, LEBRL 594).

Ezra Pound is regularly cited as a modern example of someone who incorporated "found poems" into his work, as for example papal or government documents in his *Cantos.* William Carlos Williams later followed his practice in *Paterson,* as did others in long poems. Or an entire poem could consist of a "found poem." Bishop follows neither strategy. She has absorbed Trollope's language and his viewpoint, and they become seamlessly part of her poem's fabric. Only two phrases are incorporated without change into the poem, though three more appear minus Trollope's bland adjectives. Other single words are used, and a powerful, slightly reworded quotation sums up the poem. It occurs when a doctor is lancing some "anthrax" (we would say "a boil") on Trollope's face, an example from Trollope's letters rather than the Washington chapter. Bishop's invention of a fictitious journal for her title, "From Trollope's Journal," gives her this latitude.

Lowell remarked to Bishop, "your rhythm and riming are extraordinary, and of course unobtrusive" (28 Oct. 1965, LEBRL 591), and so they are. The rhythm imitates something close to conversational speech, which is Trollope's style too. But Bishop has pared and disciplined Trollope's writing, occasionally inserting a wonderfully apt word like "hoof-pocked" to describe cattle prints in the mud in a Washington beset by sickness. The run-on lines mask her rhyme in this double sonnet. The end rhyme is simple and mostly of monosyllables (twenty-one of twenty-eight rhyme words). Sometimes the rhyme has the effect of enacting the argument. In the opening lines, for example, "Washingtons" and "foster sons" may rhyme, but the historical relation is hardly one of concord. Bishop has rewritten Trollope and yet has absorbed his point of view so thoroughly that what we are reading is in effect a better Trollope or rather a poetic Trollope.

Bishop spent a year in Washington in 1949–1950 as Consultant in Poetry to the Library of Congress, a position that later evolved into Poet Laureate. Anthony Trollope's account must have seemed prescient. He was touring North America, and he was in Washington during the Civil War in the winter of 1861–1862; his *North America* was first published in 1862. In a sense, "From Trollope's Journal" is yet another map poem, with a map of Trollope's 1861–1862 Washington superimposed on a map of 1949–1950 Washington. The difference that some ninety years' growth has made is less striking than the similarities in public mood during wartime, for the United States was at war with Korea beginning in June 1950. By the time the poem was published in book form in November 1965, Vietnam War protests were widespread. In June 1965, Lowell publicly refused Lyndon Johnson's invitation to the White House Festival of the Arts as an act of protest.

Trollope had a decidedly mixed view of Washington as a capital city. He admired some of the architecture but found the edges of the small city still rural and messy and the site badly chosen. Washington is built on swampy ground, hardly a healthy terrain in the nineteenth century and earlier, before it was drained. From Trollope's chapter, Bishop chose to begin with statues: "Statuary at Washington runs too much on two subjects," George Washington and the "red Indian," Trollope wrote. Washington, "stiff, steady-looking, healthy but ugly, . . . appears to be thoroughly ill-natured." The typical Indian, on the other hand, appears "a melancholy, weak figure." He "is generally supposed to be receiving comfort; but it is manifest that he never enjoys the comfort ministered to him."[18]

> As far as statues go, so far there's not
> much choice: they're either Washingtons
> or Indians, a whitewashed, stubby lot,
> His country's Father or His foster sons.

Why start with this? It links the poem, as Margaret Dickie noted, with Bishop's other poems on public monuments.[19] It encapsulates history, the reason that the city is called Washington at all. It also draws attention not only to the indigenous inhabitants but also to minorities. In 1949–1950 and even more in 1960, when Bishop completed the poem, the minority increasingly in the public eye was the African American minority. This is just before the civil rights movement began to gain force. Reread Trollope and substitute "African American" for "Indian," and see the effect. And in either case, note the resonance of Bishop's "whitewashed."

As for Massachusetts Avenue, Trollope wrote that it ran the whole length of the city and ended "out of town, away among the fields . . . in an uncultivated, undrained wilderness. Tucking your trowsers up to your knees you will wade through the bogs, you will lose yourself among rude hillocks, you will be out of the reach of humanity" (6). The President's house was "nice to look at," he judged, "but it is built on marshy ground, not much above the level of the Potomac, and is very unhealthy. I was told that all who live there become subject to fever and ague, and that few who now live there have escaped it altogether" (18). Here Bishop stays close to her source:

> The White House in a sad, unhealthy spot
> just higher than Potomac's swampy brim,
> —they say the present President has got
> ague or fever in each backwoods limb.

That word "backwoods" is a persuasive Trollope touch, and so is the subdued pun on "limb"; "White House" echoes "white-washed" two lines earlier.

Trollope's observation of the wretched cattle herded for slaughter was bound to speak to Bishop the animal lover: "Around me on all sides were cattle in great numbers, — steers and bog oxen, — lowing in their hunger for a meal. They were beef for the army, and never again I suppose would it be allowed them to fill their big maws and chew the patient cud" (20). Here is Bishop's adaptation into poetry:

> There all around me in the ugly mud
> — hoof-pocked, uncultivated — herds of cattle,
> numberless, wond'ring steers and oxen, stood:
> beef for the Army, after the next battle.
> . . . .
> Poor, starving, dumb
> or lowing creatures, never to chew the cud
> or fill their maws again! . . .

The creatures take up nearly eight lines of the twenty-eight-line poem.

Trollope himself found the air bracing (he called it "exhilarating"), but, he wrote, "I was hardly out of the doctor's hands while I was there, and he did not support my theory as to the goodness of the air. 'It is poisoned by the soldiers,' he said, 'and everybody is ill'" (21) — or, in Bishop's memorable rhyme and rhythm, "he croaked out, 'Sir, I do declare / everyone's sick! The soldiers poison the air.'"

What Bishop chose to ignore in Trollope's Washington chapter is just as interesting. It says a lot about her preferred method of indirection that she does not make use of Trollope's repeated assessment of the mood in Washington: "Washington was at that time, — the Christmas of 1861–62, — a melancholy place. This was partly owing to the despondent tone in which so many Americans then spoke of their affairs" (27). "They were mainly indifferent, but with that sort of indifference which arises from a break down of faith in anything" (28). His chapter ends with a discussion of the war: "All this made the place somewhat melancholy" (30).

Robert Lowell made a passing remark to Bishop about "Visits to St. Elizabeths" that lit up the poem in a new way for me. He called it "marvelous," adding, "you get bits of your old monument in it, nicely" (28 Oct. 1965, LEBRL 591). This puzzled me until I went back to the boards that are repeated several times with variations in the nursery-rhyme format of "Visits." I also checked "roadstead" and discovered with chagrin that I had assumed a quite wrong meaning, on the analogy of "homestead" — all the more chagrin because that was one word whose meaning Lowell himself double-checked, though as it turned out, he knew the meaning, being a sailor. "It was fun looking up echolalia (again), chromograph, gesso, and roadstead — they all meant pretty well what I thought" (ibid., 590). "Roadstead" is a nautical term, meaning a sheltered place near the shore, though not a harbor, where ships may ride safely at anchor. "Here is a coast; here is a harbor" starts off *Questions of Travel,* and here at the end is a roadstead.

In "Visits to St. Elizabeths," the board is the sea, the sea that looks just like wood in "The Monument." The sky and clouds also look like wood in "The Monument." In "Visits to St. Elizabeths," the sailor is the second character after Ezra Pound to appear on the ward, and he eventually sails on the sea of board. Then a Jew, weeping, dances over the creaking sea of board. The board lines continue: "a weaving board," "the parting seas of board," and finally "walking the plank of a coffin board" — the Jew, that is, with the sailor. The entire metaphor captures wonderfully the sense of instability in the ward, interweaving it with terrible memories. The boards are seas, yes, but unsteady like ships at sea, as the sailor knows well. The ward itself resembles a ship where any patient may find himself walking the plank, the plank of a coffin board. The Jew is walking or dancing his way to death in memory or imagination, again and again. A roadstead is a shelter, but this roadstead offers no shelter from mental torment for some.

The poem parallels the final poem of "Brazil," "The Burglar of Babylon." Both center on a criminal, though the treason charges against Pound were stayed because he was judged not sane enough to stand trial and was committed to St. Elizabeths hospital.[20] Much more, it rounds out the collection by its links with the opening poem, "Arrival at Santos." In *Questions of Travel,* Bishop inserted "1950" under the title "Visits to St. Elizabeths," while the end of the poem is dated "November, 1951."

(She retained only the title date in her 1969 *Complete Poems*.) "Arrival at Santos" is dated at the end "January 1952," so that the collection is framed by the dates of Bishop's own voyage and commitment. The word "roadstead" establishes the final poem as a sailing poem metaphorically, a poem of a sad arrival and the end of travel, a poem of being returned home after betraying that home and being confined — this of a man who wrote so persuasively about voyaging by sea: "And then went down to the ship . . ." (*Canto* 1:10).

"Brazil, January 1, 1502"

I want to end by looking in detail at two poems that present whole worlds in little, one from each section: "Brazil, January 1, 1502" and "First Death in Nova Scotia." Both help us read Bishop, the first visually and the second aurally.

"We are driving into the interior": so ends the first poem, "Arrival at Santos." We can almost hear the tour guide explaining that Rio de Janeiro means "River of January" because the Portuguese explorers who reached Rio's wonderful harbor on January 1, 1502, assumed that it must be the mouth of a river. Bishop was in Rio or in the hills nearby in January 1952. She had just decided to live there with Lota de Macedo Soares, and the 450th-anniversary date must have struck her. The poem was published by design in the January 1960 *New Yorker*, the "New Year's poem," Bishop called it (to Robert Lowell, 15 Feb. 1960, LEBRL 310).

The epigraph from Kenneth Clark's *Landscape into Art* reads, "embroidered nature . . . tapestried landscape." An embroidery or tapestry may convert "landscape into art," but then a landscape itself may look as if it were a piece of embroidery or

tapestry. "I finally had to do something with the cliché about the landscape looking like a tapestry, I suppose," Bishop wrote (15 Feb. 1960, LEBRL 310). Earlier she told another friend that after a storm, the "Quaresma" trees "were shedding their purple petals — the trees now look *exactly* like some old bits of embroidery with the brown stitching showing and a few purple sequins left hanging" (to Polly Hanson, 8 Apr. 1954, Vassar 32.2). Her epigraph tells us that the act of looking is not simple. So does E. H. Gombrich in his *Art and Illusion,* the book that Bishop read shortly after writing this poem. (See the Introduction.)

Looking at something with a painter's or a scientist's eye is also a way of remembering it. For Darwin, "Delight . . . is a weak term to express the feelings of a naturalist who, for the first time, has been wandering by himself in a Brazilian forest. . . . Such a day as this brings with it a deeper pleasure than he ever can hope to experience again." Over four years later, in 1836, he stood looking and looking for the last time at this forest in order to commit it to memory:

> To paint the effect is a hopeless endeavour. Who from seeing choice plants in a hothouse can magnify some into the dimensions of forest trees, and crowd others into an entangled jungle? . . . The dense splendid foliage of the mango . . . with its darkest shade, . . . the upper branches . . . of the most brilliant green. . . . In my last walk, I stopped again and again to gaze on these beauties, and endeavoured to fix for ever in my mind an impression, which at the time I knew, sooner or later, must fail. The form of the orange-tree, . . . the banana, will remain clear and separate; but the thousand beauties which unite these into one perfect scene must fade away; yet they will leave, like a tale heard in childhood, a picture full of indistinct, but most beautiful figures.[21]

In Bishop's first section, we are in such a world.

"Januaries, Nature greets our eyes / exactly as it must have greeted theirs." We sometimes casually read this as if it said, "We are seeing this rain forest just as the early explorers saw it." We aren't of course, and that is why Bishop says that *Nature* greets our eyes as it did theirs. Nature, the world before us, the evidence we see — as, say, Darwin saw the Brazilian forest — that remains constant. Its phenomena may change, but that outside world persists.

In the first of three sections, the focus is on the tapestried landscape, described as both tapestry and landscape at the same time. We might be looking at either. We might be seeing the colors as if we were weavers, choosing exactly what skein we want; the "satin underleaf" suggests satin stitch for embroiderers. If embroidery or weaving sounds like a private hobby, we need to recall great older tapestries. The *Circa 1492* exhibition in the National Gallery of Art in Washington, DC, in 1992 included several large, impressive Portuguese tapestries, some celebrating military victories.

> every square inch filling in with foliage —
> big leaves, little leaves, and giant leaves,
> blue, blue-green, and olive.

This can sound finicky unless we visualize it, moving at a slow pace, the pace of someone looking closely at an actual scene or a painting — or a tapestry or embroidery — moving as Fairfield Porter suggests we move (see Chapter 1) and as Darwin's description moves. It is a short lesson in looking at a work of art or a landscape. Bishop looks, then modifies her looking. Later there will be "monster ferns" and "giant water lilies." One monster fern in Brazil is the samambaia, which gave its name to the house in

Petropolis as it grew nearby. "Blue" modifies to shades of blue and then to olive, as will colors of flowers later. This is a world that looks newly created, as the strange New World could to the European explorers, as our world does in the spring, "solid but airy; fresh as if just finished/and taken off the frame." In the spring after the poem was published, Bishop took her first trip up the Amazon into a landscape that looked "like the very beginning of the world."[22] "It is the fifth day of creation, as some Brazilian poet said," she wrote to May Swenson (5 Mar. 1960, EAP 324). So far in Bishop's poem, it is only a vegetable world. If this is biblical creation, it has come as far as the fourth day of creation.

That word "frame" is informed by Bishop's knowledge of words. It signifies an embroidery frame, a tapestry frame, yes, but it can also "be applied to the heaven, earth, etc., regarded as a structure" (OED, s.v. "frame," 8). Shakespeare, Milton, and Wordsworth all use it this way. "This goodly frame, the Earth," says Hamlet (*Hamlet* 2.2.268). For all that, God the Creator was conceived "now as weaver, now as needleworker, now as potter, now as smith," and the metaphors go back a long way.[23]

Bishop's second act introduces creatures, the fifth day of creation, and a lot more besides. It introduces history, as if the vegetable world in itself were innocent. A sense of history, though still without humans, starts with the birds in line 5:

> and perching there in profile, beaks agape,
> the big symbolic birds keep quiet,
> each showing only half his puffed and padded,
> pure-colored or spotted breast.
> Still in the foreground there is Sin.

Birds that are symbolic? Are we seeing a landscape and recalling symbolism, or are we seeing a tapestry iconographically?

Either way, the birds' breasts mutely tell us what is at stake. They are immaculate or maculate — or would be if Bishop used the Latinate terms meaning "pure" and "spotted."[24] Tapestry, weaving, texture, text: the relation of weaving and the actual represented world also has an extended history. It was a subject that had long attracted Bishop, who was widely interested in the *techne,* the craft, of any art. There is a link from "The Gentleman of Shalott" through "Seascape" to "Brazil, January 1, 1502," and it is the art of weaving.

As for Sin, it is embodied in "five sooty dragons near some massy rocks." They turn out to be lizards, and lizards plus birds make clear that we are now in a fallen world. Even the vegetation has turned symbolic:

The rocks are worked with lichens, gray moonbursts
splattered and overlapping,
threatened from underneath by moss
in lovely hell-green flames,
attacked above
by scaling-ladder vines, oblique and neat,
"one leaf yes and one leaf no" (in Portuguese).

Those gray moonbursts in "The Shampoo," "still explosions on the rocks, / the lichens," are a figure for the love between Bishop and Lota and their long-term commitment. Why are they under attack here? Or is this a reminder of how they would be attacked in a world divided between hell and heaven? The tone is playful in any case, as it is with the lizards that conclude, though the play is a little different:

The lizards scarcely breathe: all eyes
are on the smaller, female one, back-to,

her wicked tail straight up and over,
red as a red-hot wire.

The shift from "Sin" to this "wicked" is a lovely exercise in the
control of tone. How do we read "wicked"? Along with "red-hot"
and the female lizard's sexual posture, "wicked" comes with a
sense of danger more than sin. Is this female related to Eliot's
"Madame Sosostris, famous clairvoyante," "With a wicked pack
of cards" (*The Waste Land*, ll. 43, 46)? Not quite, but the challenge
of reading the tone of "wicked" is similar.

Bishop does not tell us overtly that her gaze is moving
through historical perspectives. Her language tells us. Stevens
in 1942 had done much the same thing in his falling angel canto
from *Notes toward a Supreme Fiction* (part 3, canto 8), starting
with the Miltonic phrase "gaze serene," through "spredden wing,"
and so on. Bishop simply moves from innocent, newly created
nature to fallen nature ("spotted"), then to later natural science,
where sex, not sin, provides the explanation of things. "Wicked"
is not wicked in a biblical sense. The whole context has changed.

And then the third section, and with it the high point of creation on the sixth day, humankind: "Just so, the Christians . . .
/ . . . came and found it all." "How I envy the historical stretch
at the end, so beautifully coming out of the vegetation," Lowell
wrote (28 Oct. 1965, LEBRL 591). For the tapestry now comes
alive beyond animal activity. Now sound begins: creaking armor,
a tune humming, and finally the voices of the women — or are
they birds? — with which the poem ends. The tune is "L'Homme
armé" (The Armed Man), a popular tune that formed the basis
for about thirty Masses from the fourteenth to the sixteenth
centuries. As for the heaven and hell, immaculate and maculate, all that is left behind in the Mass. An old dream takes

over: "wealth and luxury." Plus "a brand-new pleasure," catching native women:

> Directly after Mass, humming perhaps
> *L'Homme armé* or some such tune,
> they ripped away into the hanging fabric,
> each out to catch an Indian for himself —
> those maddening little women who kept calling,
> calling to each other (or had the birds waked up?)
> and retreating, always retreating, behind it.

There were debates in the Roman Catholic Church about whether native people were human or not. In 1537, Pope Paul III decreed that they were, but in 1502, the question was still open. If these "maddening little women" are animal creatures, then sin doesn't enter into it. "Maddening little women": the phrase invites the reader to work out its tone too, especially when they "kept calling." Who uses such a phrase, and what follows from it?

Bishop's poem ends with "behind it," behind "the hanging fabric," the tapestry that starts the poem. There is a famous classical tapestry that spoke with a silent voice, "the voice of the shuttle" in Sophocles's words.[25] There too is a rape, a rape woven into the fabric so that a woman can see how her husband raped her sister, then cut out her tongue to silence her. Similarly the native women here are voiceless, except as birds. In the classical tale, the two women and the rapist husband, Tereus the King, are all transformed into birds, just as he draws his sword to kill them both. The sisters, Philomel and Procne, are changed into a nightingale and a swallow, and the king into a hoopoe. The nightingale's exquisite song is the victim's, while the hoopoe's crest corresponds to the king's armor. Ovid makes the metamorphosis happen over the line break, with a wonderful explosion of sound:

> . . . pennis pendere putares:
> pendebant pennis.

(. . . you would think that the bodies of the two Athenians were poised on wings; they *were* poised on wings) (*Metamorphoses* 6.667–668, Loeb ed.; emphasis added)

As for Tereus, he

> Became a Bird upon whose top a tuft of feathers light
> In likeness of a Helmets crest doth trimly stand upright.
> In stead of his long sword, his bill shootes out a passing space:
> A Lapwing named is this bird, all armed seems his face.

This is Arthur Golding's fine translation of Ovid, in which the phallic implications of the sword crest (Ovid's *vertice crista* or "crest . . . upright" in Golding's version) are clear.[26] The lapwing is simply Golding's nearest approximation to the hoopoe, a bird that does not inhabit England. The word "Christ" means "the anointed one" and comes from Greek, not Latin, *crista* or crest, but these "Christians" are armored soldiers acting like a Tereus.

It was some time after I committed this view to print that I read Bishop's 1955 letter to Lowell: "I remember reading Golding by the hour, when I was at college" (21 May 1955, LEBRL 162).

"Januaries, Nature greets our eyes," "each out to catch an Indian for himself." Bishop leaves to us the judgment of where we stand in relation to this tapestry of history. She herself had read Darwin's diary on the slaughter of the Indians in Brazil: "Who would believe in this age in a Christian civilized country that such atrocities were committed?"[27] "The march of empire, colonization, and obliteration has made the raped and dispossessed people simultaneously haunting and unattainable, a violent emblem of the past as unrecoverable yet operative, and vaguely shaming" — thus Robert Pinsky on Philip Freneau's "The Indian Burying Ground."[28] It makes a just response to Bishop's poem as well.

"First Death in Nova Scotia"

From the start, "First Death in Nova Scotia" (1962) is presented as a world in little, a child's world, based on Bishop's memories like the story "In the Village" and the poems "Manners" and "Sestina" that just precede it. Its geographical place is given, and so is its place in a child's inner life. Dylan Thomas is surely right in the closing line of "A Refusal to Mourn the Death, by Fire, of a Child in London": "After the first death, there is no other." Bishop quoted his opening lines in her "Writing poetry is an unnatural act . . ." (late 1950s–early 1960s, LOA 705), but the simple last line is the one that sticks in the memory. It used to be more familiar. Our first encounter with death, usually when young, is memorable, and other deaths are not quite as death-like, though they may be far more affecting. The subject of Bishop's poem is her first cousin Frank Elwood Bulmer, who died in 1915 at the age of two months. Bishop was four years old.

   The poem is one of those in which, as James Merrill said of "North Haven," the lines fall so perfectly into place that it memorizes itself, so to speak, in our heads ("An Interview with J. D. McClatchy," *Recitative* 79). Its short lines come with a strong trimeter rhythm and varying feet, with a high proportion of feminine endings at the start. (The loon stanza comes with firm masculine end words, as does little Arthur, while the chromographs and other forms of consolation waver a little with their feminine end words. The two effects merge at the end.) I hear "First Death in Nova Scotia" as a strong-stress poem, rather than accentual-syllabic, and it sounds to my ear like a nursery rhyme.

> In the cold, cold parlor
> my mother laid out Arthur
> beneath the chromographs:
> Edward, Prince of Wales,
> with Princess Alexandra,
> and King George with Queen Mary.

The voice that opens the poem is an older voice, remembering and translating experience as if reliving the hard earlier time. At the end, as if by hypnosis, the child's voice has taken over. Yet the child's voice is partly there at the start, in the repetitions and nursery-rhyme rhythms.

Royalty dates the poem and establishes the traditional tone of the household. King George ascended the throne in May 1910. His father, Edward VII, was Prince of Wales until January 1901 following the death of his mother, Queen Victoria. Nonetheless, years later, Edward's pre-1901 photograph and Princess Alexandra's — chromograph, rather — still hangs on the wall. That word for a hand-tinted photo also dates the event. A chromograph is a nineteenth-century invention, superseded by more advanced methods of color photography. Bishop uses it in 1932 in her diary of a walking trip in Newfoundland, referring to "the usual chromos of the sinking of the Lusitania" (Vassar

77.1, TS, 6). The "cold, cold parlor" establishes the kind of household: not a grand house, where the parlor would be kept warm constantly, but a modest house, where the parlor was reserved for more formal occasions and heated then. ("In the winter afternoons, a fire was made in the grate because my Grandmother, from three o'clock till tea-time everyday had 'callers' on her mind.")[29] A cold parlor is, needless to say, a good place to keep a body as well as a good place for a visitation before the funeral. Some southern Ontario rural households still had "cold funeral-smelling front rooms" much later.[30]

In fact, though Bishop recalled this scene vividly, she misremembered it as happening in the dead of winter. Her baby cousin's gravestone lists his death date as June 1915. Another baby, his older sister, died in January 1909. Both had small heart-shaped gravestones that Bishop would have seen, and possibly she mixed up the dates.[31] The cogent reason is surely the cold in the room and, above all, the cold little baby. I don't know if children are still introduced to death by touching the dead body of someone they have known. I was, and still remember the physical sensation of cold inert solidity. On December 24, 1878, the Reverend Francis Kilvert recorded visiting a family whose child had died and kissing him on the forehead. "It was as cold and hard as marble. This is always a fresh surprise. I had not touched death for more than 30 years, and it brought back the sudden shock that I felt when as a child I was taken into a room at Hardenhuish Rectory where our little sister lay dead and was told to touch her hand."[32] Bishop read *Kilvert's Diary* in 1950, and this remark would have spoken to her own vivid memory of her dead cousin. The correct death date incidentally accounts for the lily of the valley in the poem.[33]

"My mother laid out Arthur." Most of us know little about this, for the task is now routinely done by trained undertakers. That did not happen in small-town Nova Scotia in the early twentieth century. The room, the chromographs, the table with the stuffed loon: the poem's eye lights on these first before it comes to the coffin, as if the child were taking in the familiar parts of the room before allowing her eye to rest on the coffin. It is like a camera filming a scene and coming only at the end to the dead child.

The last four lines of the first stanza and all of the second stanza in this five-stanza poem are given over to the stuffed loon on the table under the chromographs. It entrances the child, the "I" of the poem whose perspective is wonderfully realized by Bishop. It entrances us too, as if it were another character in the room: the mother, the child, the small dead cousin, plus the dead loon looking very much alive, all presided over by benevolent royalty. The house is her cousin's house and not her own, so that the loon is familiar but not an everyday sight. A chance to pat its breast, "deep and white,/cold and caressable," did not come every day. And its "red glass" eyes were "much to be desired," in the faintly biblical phrasing that ends the second stanza. The second stanza also introduces the poem's color palette, which is red and white and is developed in the last two stanzas: two flesh colors, two symbolic colors (for St. George, and so for England with its patron saint and its St. George's Cross as part of the Union Jack, and so for the royal dress in the chromographs with the red of the trains and the white ermine trim). In the second stanza, the loon with its red eye, looking as if alive but frozen, is somehow of the same order of reality as the royal couples above it. Its breast is caressable but cold, like the parlor — and like cousin Arthur, though the child does not record this.

As in a child's nursery rhyme, there is repetition throughout the poem, starting with the first line. Most of all, the name "Arthur" is repeated:

> "Come," said my mother,
> "Come and say good-bye
> to your little cousin Arthur."
> I was lifted up and given
> one lily of the valley
> to put in Arthur's hand.
> Arthur's coffin was
> a little frosted cake,
> and the red-eyed loon eyed it
> from his white, frozen lake.

The coffin, seen from above, proves to be a child's white coffin, with a pleated or frilled interior to hold the small body. The child's visual association sees the swirls of a frosted icing on a cake, while her aural association hears "frosted" and then "frozen" and shortly afterward "Jack Frost":

> Arthur was very small.
> He was all white, like a doll,
> that hadn't been painted yet.
> Jack Frost had started to paint him
> the way he always painted
> the Maple Leaf (Forever).

"In the Primer Class there [Nova Scotia] we use to have to sing 'O Maple Leaf, Our Emblem Dear' [*The* Maple Leaf?] every morning, as well as 'Rule Britannia'" (to Marianne Moore, 28

Sept. 1942, L III). It was of course wartime. In 1961, Bishop wrote to Lowell, "As you may not know, "The Maple Leaf Forever" is the un-official Canadian anthem — sung in school constantly" (25 Sept. 1961, LEBRL 379). Bishop means in English-speaking Canada. It could hardly be the official national anthem, as some critics suppose. It opens,

> In days of yore from Britain's shore,
> Wolfe the dauntless hero came
> And planted firm Britannia's flag
> On Canada's fair domain.

That would be on the Plains of Abraham near Quebec City on September 13, 1759, when Wolfe conquered Montcalm and the British took the French colony. The event is still commemorated by the motto of Quebec license plates, "Je me souviens" (I remember). Canada does include French Canadians, both in Quebec and elsewhere.[34]

In the closing question, the child is puzzled but assumes some kind of future life for Arthur, perhaps a page at court. Where does such a notion come from? From the chromographs of royalty, "gracious" royalty. ("At my left sat a beautiful boy named Royal Something. His name made him doubly attractive to me, stuffed as I was with the English royal family, although I realized he wasn't really royal.")[35] "Gracious" is not part of a small child's vocabulary, or so a reader will naturally think. But this is a child who has been regularly singing the national anthem, "God Save the King," as Bishop's story "The Country Mouse" tells us. ("In my Canadian schooling, . . . we had started every day with 'God Save the King' and 'The Maple Leaf Forever'" [*CProse* 26].) And how does that national anthem open? "God save our gracious king." The word is one of those that dates a poem at the same time that it reminds us of how children absorb language.

And where has the idea of royalty governing a future life come from? Surely from the hymns that run through the child's head, just as the patriotic song "The Maple Leaf Forever" runs through her head. How many hymns use the phrasing "King of Heaven"? "Praise, my soul, the King of Heaven" is just one. Or "King"? "O worship the King, / All glorious above" is one that Bishop certainly knew. ("I think I have one nice title, for a change: 'It Streams from the Hills.' (In case you don't know — it's from a good old protestant hymn.)" [26 Jan. 1957, Barker letters). And it is in oratorios, including the best-known Christian one, Handel's *Messiah,* with its memorable Hallelujah chorus that repeats "King of Kings." There is also a well-known hymn that opens "Pleasant are Thy courts above" and used to give rise to various tennis-court jokes. Corresponding texts from the King James Bible ("enter into His gates with thanksgiving / And into His courts with praise" [Ps. 100:4]) were commonly read in services that a child would attend from an early age.

Then there is the loon, looking so alive, even if "Since Uncle Arthur fired / a bullet into him, / he hadn't said a word" — not "it" but "he" and "him" and "his." That soft, white feathered breast: how can it not be alive in some strange way?

What about the closing question itself?

> But how could Arthur go,
> clutching his tiny lily,
> with his eyes shut up so tight
> and the roads deep in snow?

It's a child's thought, to be sure, but the last line reflects the adults' concern for a funeral in midwinter. When the ground was frozen hard, caskets with bodies sometimes had to wait until a thaw. They were stored outside in freezing-cold temperatures, and the burial and committal service took place later. Floating about the child are bits of adult life and conversation, beyond her mother's reported words, suspending her in a world both real and imagined. It is impossible for her to tell what is real and what imagined and how they are related. Meanwhile, the solid, unmoving, caressable stuffed loon remains a tangible object of delight and desire.

CHAPTER SEVEN

Brief Interlude on Genre

Writers have to know about genres, though readers don't pay much attention to them unless writers like Margaret Atwood or Anne Carson (to mention Canadian writers) compel them to do so. This is true in spades for poets. We casually call short poems "lyrics," and that is an end of the matter, unless a word like "ballad" or "elegy" appears in the title. Elizabeth Bishop gave a working title to a poem in progress for her deceased lover, Lota: "Aubade and Elegy" — a lovers' dawn poem and a farewell poem, all in one. When Bishop died suddenly, age sixty-eight, she left this poem in manuscript fragments, a poem that would likely have been among the great elegies in English poetry.

Of course Bishop knew about genres. She had been practicing different kinds of poems all her life, starting in her teens. Certain kinds came with the territory when she imitated some sixteenth- and seventeenth-century poetic styles. Take a look at her earliest work in "Uncollected Poems," plus the earlier poems of "Unpublished Poems and Drafts" (LOA 203–213) and sections 1 and 2 in *Edgar Allan Poe & the Jukebox*. (The selections of unpublished material overlap but not completely.) Though many poems are exercises in imitation, they are also more than exercises. Wittily self-aware, they provided practice in genres: ballad, invocation, charm poetry, riddle, parody. Bishop has an affinity for comic verse. "The Ballad of the Subway Train" (LOA 183–184), by a fifteen- or sixteen-year-old, works in a regular ballad form (*abcb* rhyme and alternating four- and three-beat iambic lines). The fall of celestial dragons into subway trains, by divine fiat, comes from someone who knows her Milton, while the "Ten thousand thousand years they lived" plays with the biblical-Miltonic formula of "ten thousand," a formula also adopted by the ballad. (The old folk ballad "Fare Thee Well" has "ten thousand miles," as does Burns's "My love is like a red, red rose.") As for subway trains as dragons, readers regularly recall "The Man-Moth," written some ten years later. "I introduce Penelope Gwyn," written about the same time, is a comic manifesto against interfering aunts and in favor of the beau monde.[1] The imitation of Hopkins, "Hymn to the Virgin," is a wicked parody, though Hopkins would become one of Bishop's favorite poets. Among the most interesting poems generically is the late 1920s poem "Once on a hill I met a man." It is a species of charm poem, a mode that Bishop developed to perfection in "The Riverman."

Bishop also wrote or translated dramatic poetry. As an undergraduate, she translated a chorus from Aristophanes's comedy *The Birds* (LOA 267), condensing the Greek. She experimented when young with writing a masque, combining words and music. "Lord, I'd like to attempt that kind of thing [a masque-like entertainment]. Now I remember that Eliot has just written a masque, too — a liturgical thing for one of his churches [*The Rock*, 1934]" (to Frani Blough, 1 Apr. 1934, L 22). "I came away [to Paris] with a large pad of paper, and Ben Jonson's *Masques* to study, with the express purpose of writing something like that" (to Frani Blough, 20 Oct. 1935, L 36). She also spoke of writing prose poems, though she did not publish one until her fourth collection, *Geography III*. A later ambition was to write pantoums.[2]

Recent discussions of genre, including genre theory, all too often begin with an attack on genre as pigeonhole, on trying to fit works into categories. Surely by now any well-informed reader has come past that. A pigeonhole is simply a misleading metaphor and pretty stale too. Taxonomies are always interpretive. They vary one from another, and they change over time. "The taxonomic order is a record of history," as Stephen Jay Gould once said.[3] Genres and their taxonomies help us to read. Children distinguish genres along with conventions of storytelling at a very young age. I have yet to meet a child who takes *Alice in Wonderland* literally.

One useful basic distinction is between genre and mode, as defined in Alastair Fowler's indispensable *Kinds of Literature*.[4] John Frow in his *Genre*, the most helpful recent guide, maintains the distinction.[5] Modes are commonly defined by adjective, and they turn up in different genres; pastoral is an obvious example. "Charm" like "riddle" can be a genre or a mode.[6] A riddle poem resembles the Old English riddles, asking "Who am I?" or presenting the answer in the title and piling up characteristics in many metaphors. A charm can be an entire poem seeking to cast a spell like the love spell in the second *Idyl* of Theocritus. Or it can be a mode in which charm effects are prominent, as in "The Lady of Shalott" or Bishop's "The Riverman."

Frow has elsewhere challenged modern genre theory, stretching its boundaries and offering a series of guidelines and hypotheses.[7] Some are wide, demonstrating how genres work as part of verbal knowledge in general. Among the more specific suggestions, I find two very useful for any given writer. First, Frow says, "All texts are informed by generic frameworks; any text may be read through more than one generic frame; many texts participate in multiple genres" ("Reproducibles," 1633). One example is *Robinson Crusoe*, which may be read as an adventure story or a salvation narrative. Bishop's work in genre suggests something beyond this guideline, something I'll return to after offering the evidence.

Second, Frow also posits that "genres are differentially weighted constellations of thematic, formal, and rhetorical dimensions" ("Reproducibles," 1633). The statement is especially interesting because the usual tension in genre is between theme and form. A field theory of genre, that is, a theory in which substance and form have a constant if varying relation, has appeared difficult if not impossible. A sestina, for example, is called a "form" by David Caplan, and that is what I would call it too. But it merits a chapter in *A Companion to Poetic Genre*, as do the villanelle, the sonnet, and more. Genres of course change historically, so that elegy in classical writing is defined by form but now primarily by theme. It is Frow's third term whose prominence is new.[8] Some genres, Frow observed, come with specific rhetoric, the riddle and curse, for example ("Reproducibles," 1631).

The sestina makes an interesting case in the question of form and genre. By definition, it is a form: "six stanzas of six lines, and a three-line envoy (or 'send-off')," with the terminal words of the lines in the first stanza repeated in different order.[9] Anthony Hecht persuasively suggests one way in which the sestina might function as genre: "I was thinking of how various sestinas I knew operated. And it occurred to me that because of the persistent reiteration of those terminal words, over and over in stanza after stanza, the sestina seemed to lend itself especially well to a topic felt obsessively, unremittently."[10] For him, in "The Book of Yolek," these were grim wartime memories. For Eliot, in the sestina portion of "The Dry Salvages" (part 2, "Where is there an end of it . . . ?"), it is the anguish of everyday time repeating meaninglessly with only a faint possibility of Christian hope. Bishop's earlier sestina "Miracle for Breakfast" shows that the sestina can be used for simple repetition like a daily routine but is not especially apt. "Sestina" is different. The repeated end words — "house," "grandmother," "child," "stove," "almanac," "tears" — are rung as by an expert bell ringer, notably the word "tears."[11]

Theory follows evidence, and Bishop's remarkable work suggests further questions and suggestions for modern genre theory.

Questions of Travel contains an unusually varied number of genres: a prologue of sorts, an ekphrasis, a dramatic monologue, a love song, a soliloquy, a ballad, a children's verse, a dream poem, a found poem, a nursery rhyme. At least ten of the nineteen poems in *Questions of Travel* are in different genres, probably even more. "Questions of Travel" might well be called a dialogue poem, while "Electrical Storm" looks like an unusual aubade and "First Death in Nova Scotia" opens with rhythms and repetitions like a nursery rhyme's. The book also includes a sestina. It's as if the multitudinous variety of Brazil and of earlier memories called for a variety of genres, notably the variety of voices that these different kinds of writing elicit. In *North & South*, Bishop displays her virtuosity with forms by shaping every poem differently. In *Questions of Travel*, it is her mastery of kinds or genres that comes to the fore.

What is most striking is not simply the wide variety of genres. It is Bishop's great originality in combining genres or else genre and mode. Look again at the poems mentioned. The ekphrastic poem "Brazil, January 1, 1502" develops into a war poem in the last section. I have thought for some time that the love song "Song for the Rainy Season" is also a country-house poem, and now Stephen Burt has independently suggested this.[12] The soliloquy "The Riverman" is a charm poem modally. The children's verse "Manners" is also a didactic poem. The dream poem "Sunday, 4 A.M." is also an ekphrastic poem, though it takes unusual observation (or Bishop's letters) to realize this. The soliloquy "From Trollope's Journal" is also a found poem, perhaps predominantly a found poem. And while the allusive title of "First Death in Nova Scotia" suggests an antielegy, the poem gives the effect of sidestepping or burying elegy altogether. It is, then, Bishop's remarkable blending of genres in different degrees and kinds that makes a reader sit up. It also suggests a path for later poets.

The result is a sense of fullness, of being rounded, so that the Brazil portion seems to offer a society in little, seen from certain perspectives, well identified. The world in "Elsewhere" works in a similar way. The different genres create a whole that is larger than its parts. Some genres are (or were) associated with certain strata of society. There is little sense of this in modern poetry, though Bishop is perfectly aware that the ballad, for example, was a popular form that could be used for low-life adventures, misfortunes, and so on — thus in "The Burglar of Babylon." "Manners" is a didactic poem that itself reinforces social convention.

Dramatic voices emerge here, for virtually the first time. Bishop earlier wrote "Songs for a Colored Singer" and "Varick Street," but they are not dramatic monologues, spoken by an individual. Nor are they soliloquies. "Jerónimo's House" is the only early example. Now in *Questions of Travel*, we have the very different dramatic voices of "Manuelzinho" and "The Riverman," the child's voice throughout "Manners" and taking over "First Death in Nova Scotia," Trollope's voice in "From Trollope's Journal." I doubt that Bishop could have written her powerful later soliloquy "Crusoe in England" without this previous work. We also have the "campy," fussy tourist voice in "Arrival at Santos," which reads like a self-consciously dramatized part of Bishop's own persona that her better self keeps an eye on.

One reason that critics pay little attention to Bishop's highly original work with genre is that her work sounds so natural, so unforced, and all the more so as the work matures. In 1963, May Swenson commented on the art behind this effect: "I would like to find the casual and absolutely natural tone that you have in your poems — they are never over-colored or forced the least little bit — they are very honest, and never call attention to their effects. Their brilliance is inside, and not on the surface. And they are subtle, not obvious" (12 July 1963, Swenson-Bishop letters).

Frow's observation that some genres come with a specific rhetoric has as example the riddle or the curse. Northrop Frye's essay "Charms and Riddles" shows that poetry using a charm mode also comes with a specific rhetoric. He notes that a modern poet "interested in charm techniques is likely to be interested in riddle techniques also, if only because both present technical problems."[13] Bishop's "The Riverman" is her charm poem. Her riddle poem she wrote early, and it is an accomplished one: "The Gentleman of Shalott." Both poems make use of mirrors. The spell on the Lady of Shalott in Tennyson's poem forbids her to look outside at the actual world of men and women moving downstream to Camelot. Instead she sees it all reflected in a mirror. The Gentleman of Shalott does not hold a mirror up to nature. He *is* half mirror: that is his nature. The Lady can turn away from her mirror, look out at actuality, see Sir Lancelot, and fulfilling her doom, die slowly as she floats singing down to Camelot. The Gentleman cannot escape his mirror or else doesn't want to.

Is Bishop further implying that it is never that easy to hold a mirror up to nature? That the mirror is always partly of our own making, from our own nature? All the more if that nature is gay or lesbian. Here the nature of a mirror itself comes into play, for a mirror always shows an inverted image in which left shows as right and so on. A mirror is "that world inverted/where left is always right" ("Insomnia"). The mirror makes a natural trope for gay and lesbian matters. The Gentleman cannot step out of his nature into a heterosexual world, like the Lady. He does reflect on it, though. "Which eye's his eye?" He's unusual in being a riddle to himself rather than a riddle challenging the outsider. In either case, this is a riddle of identity, one of those "Who am I?" riddles.

As for the closing poem of *Questions of Travel*, "Visits to St. Elizabeths," the genre is very clear: nursery rhyme. Frow neatly characterizes it: "The genre of the nursery rhyme is defined above all by its situation of address: it is characteristically spoken or sung, to or by a child, and is usually short, strongly rhythmical, and may involve a play with nonsense words; it may accompany such activities as skipping, clapping or counting, or being sung to sleep. In a sense it is a conglomerate genre. . . . Because it often proceeds by word association or by a play on sound, its logic is often close to that of dreams" (*Genre*, 110). Bishop, recalling influences on her work, spoke in 1977 of one of her grandmothers: "[She] was great at reading old English ballads, nursery rhymes, riddles and so on, and I think I took to it in that way very easily, without thinking much about it. I still think nursery rhymes are one of the greatest things to get started with. If you want to write poems, and can't, just read a few of the good old nursery rhymes."[4] Her charming occasional poem for the Barkers' small son ("To T. C. B.," 1964–1965, EAP 139) is modeled on the nursery rhyme "The king was in his counting-house." Here the model is "The house that Jack built," in which repetition upon repetition build the poem. Repetitions embody the compulsive repetitive actions of some patients, while the variations in the adjective for Pound catch Bishop's very mixed emotions about the finally "wretched" man, "wretched" both subjectively (with whatever sympathy one can muster for a talent so degraded) and objectively (for his wartime actions).

I spoke of "combining" genres, choosing a neutral word to cover all occasions and saying little about how this works. Frow simply states that "texts may be read through more than one generic frame." But the effect of some of Bishop's combinations is not either-or. It is both-and. "Song for the Rainy Season" is not a love song *or* a country-house poem. It is both in one. It raises further questions about the genre of love songs: what house shelters the lover(s)? If none, does this matter? If the house is grand or simple, does this matter? If many love songs appear to have no setting at all, does this tell us anything about the genre? As for the genre of country-house poems, it implies another type of love, communal and charitable. A love that is erotic in one aspect and communal and charitable in another is rich indeed.

The dialogue poem in the Renaissance was "determined by the form — the play of ideas, the abstraction, the dominant voice carrying the burden of instruction, and so forth" (Fowler, *Kinds of Literature*, 112). The travel poem is dominated by its subject. The title "Questions of Travel" combines dialogue in the form of questions and travel, or does it divide them? Is this a combining of the two genres, travel poem and dialogue poem? Or does dialogue dominate, as it does at the end? If the latter, Fowler's useful category of subgenre is suggestive: this would be a dialogue poem combined with a subgenre of travel poem. Yet the answer refuses to come neatly clear, as if all travel entailed questions (and all questions entailed travel, at least mental travel). These generic matters come to hover over the entire collection *Questions of Travel.*

Bishop's later work will also demonstrate mastery of genre and a variety of genres, including new ones for her and new combinations.

CHAPTER EIGHT

Geography III

Geography III, Bishop's fourth collection, was published in 1976, eleven years after *Questions of Travel* and nine years after Lota's death from an overdose in September 1967 in New York. In retrospect, the serious rift between the two women that culminated in Lota's death can be seen growing slowly, as in a Greek tragedy.

What began happily in 1961 with an invitation to Lota to design a large-scale waterfront park on Rio's Flamingo Beach deteriorated over the years. It was an ideal assignment for Lota, given her talent in architectural design, and the commitment was for only two years. Bishop rejoiced on her behalf, and the two women moved to Lota's large waterfront apartment in Rio. But Lota was perforce occupied day and night, and Bishop found herself in charge of a very busy household when in residence, in addition to her literary activities. She now had limited time and no private place to write. Tackling her problem at the beginning might have averted the eventual crisis — or not.

Meanwhile, Lota was enjoying widespread popularity, especially after her children's playground was completed.[1] Dealing with Brazilian bureaucracy was another matter and slowly sapped her energy. Then in 1964, a military coup struck. Lota supported it; Bishop followed her lead. Brazilian currency plunged, not for the first time. Late in 1965, the year when *Questions of Travel* was published, Lota was invited to take on another project. Meanwhile Bishop was invited to teach for a term at the Uni-

versity of Washington — a chance to earn U.S. dollars and to
escape the pressures now weighing on her. She urged Lota to
take a holiday with her and delayed her own decision unconscio-
nably into December. But Lota said yes to the new assignment,
and the next day Bishop said yes to the University of Washington.
From then on, the break was predictable.

In the United States, Bishop, isolated and lonely, fell back
on the support alcohol provided. A needy older student provided another kind of support, and Bishop began an affair with
her. Meanwhile she sent money to Lota for a travel fund, and
Lota, impulsive as ever, spent it on a new sports car. On Bishop's return, Lota learned of the affair at about the same time as
serious problems developed over her public project. Professional
jealousy appeared to account for some of it, just at the time when
personal jealousy was racking her. They tried a trip to England;
but Lota's health gave way, and she suffered a nervous break-
down, as did Bishop. Both women were hospitalized, Bishop
only briefly, while Lota received insulin shock treatments over
several months. Bishop, forbidden to see her, finally flew to New
York in 1967 for a stay. Lota was to join her in December. But
on September 19, 1967, Lota talked her doctor into allowing her
to fly and took the long flight north. The day after arriving, she
took an overdose of Valium, spent a week in a coma, and then died.
Bishop, overcome with guilt, was advised by her doctor not to
accompany Lota's body home. Many of Bishop's Brazilian friends
blamed her for Lota's death, while Bishop blamed Brazil in
large part because of its destruction of Lota's career. Her private
guilt she kept mostly to herself.

In 1965, Bishop had bought an old house in Ouro Preto,
hoping to interest Lota in restoring it. She kept it for several
years but finally sold it. She also realized some money from

property left her in Lota's will. She tried living on the West Coast of the United States with her new partner; but these years were very difficult, and the new alliance did not last. Eventually she settled in Boston, teaching part-time at Harvard, starting with the fall term of 1970. She traveled a good deal, as always, and began to spend summers on the Maine island North Haven, which she loved. She and Alice Methfessel, who was working at Harvard when Bishop began to teach there, became partners, and her life gradually steadied after so much turbulence.

For well over two years after Lota's death, Bishop could not write to any effect. But in June 1970, she told her doctor and friend Anny Baumann, "I've . . . just sold the *New Yorker* the first poem I have been able to finish in over three years ["In the Waiting Room"] and really can't believe this. I have finished two more old ones and am well along with a brand-new one" (17 June 1970, L 528).[2] *Geography III* is largely the work of Bishop's early sixties. It is her shortest collection, at only ten poems, one of them a translation. Yet the book has the heft of a much longer work, so rich is the poetry. For all the vicissitudes Bishop endured in her personal life, mastery of her art remained.

The title and dust jacket link this last collection to the titles and dust jackets of *North & South* with its compass rose and *Questions of Travel* with its sixteenth-century map. *A Cold Spring* seems to be omitted; yet its geography belongs with that of *North & South*, and it was published along with the earlier collection. Bishop is connecting all her work and inviting the reader to look at earlier poems behind the poems of *Geography III*. Her dust jackets tell us much indirectly. The dust jacket of *North & South* shows a streaked background of greenish gray with "*North &*" in deep red and "*South*" in white. The dust jacket

Geography III / Elizabeth Bishop

FARRAR, STRAUS AND GIROUX / NEW YORK

Title page of *Geography III*

of *Poems: North & South — A Cold Spring* is divided vertically by white and blue with a bright yellow-green leaf holding the titles. The dust jacket of *Questions of Travel* rejoices in rich tropical colors, deep purple and greenish blue. *Geography III* looks subdued in comparison: a tan background with an ink sketch identical to the sketch on the title page. It shows a geographer's working instruments: a globe, a mounted theodolite, sundry books, a pen and inkwell, paper knives, maps. The color palette is somber compared with earlier backgrounds, but more than ever, attention is directed to the art and craft of making poems.

"Yesterday I actually got out my watercolors and designed my own book jacket for . . . *Geography III*. . . . [It] looks like an old-fashioned school-book, I hope" (to Anny Baumann, 24 Dec. 1975, L 602).

That art is evident in the arrangement of the ten poems. They appear in roughly chronological order, but only roughly, so that, for example, the latest poem, "One Art" (1976), is placed seventh. There are five long, substantial narrative poems, "In the Waiting-Room," "Crusoe in England," "The Moose," "Poem," and "The End of March." So powerful are these poems, as well as the other five, "Night City," "12 O'Clock News," "One Art," "Objects & Apparitions," and "Five Flights Up," that each builds a world of its own. Critics have duly given them much attention, though less to "Objects & Apparitions," an homage to Joseph Cornell by Octavio Paz, translated by Bishop in consultation with Paz. The poems are commonly read separately, but I want to argue that *Geography III*, like Bishop's other collections, has a shape that matters. The poems speak to each other in ways that light up all of them.

Starting Again

I think that it is no accident that "In the Waiting Room" and "Crusoe in England" open this fourth collection and no accident that they are adjacent. Bishop's June 1970 letter quoted earlier suggests that "In the Waiting Room" released the poetic energy to begin writing again. For in one way, she was starting again at age fifty-nine. "In the Waiting Room" is set in the same place she had unhappily restarted her childhood, age six: in Worcester in the Boston area. In Brazil, the mystery of geography had evoked her Nova Scotia childhood. Here geography is working differently. Here she feels even more like Crusoe than when she started that poem in 1964 under the title "Crusoe at Home" (LOA 913). Daniel Defoe's Robinson Crusoe was marooned for years, possibly somewhere off the coast of Brazil. Bishop too was back after many years in Brazil; "Crusoe in England" might be subtitled "Bishop in Boston."

These two poems are the only long poems that Bishop places together. From now on, she alternates the longer narrative poems with shorter poems that belong to a different life. I think she meant these opening poems to be read together. For one thing, both are soliloquies and both use first-person singular. Both have as narrator someone who is or was solitary, though the sense of being solitary is very different: two solitaries amid society, two souls who feel isolated and alien, though by rights they should feel at home. In this sequel to Defoe's *Robinson Crusoe*, Crusoe has returned home after many years of being marooned but finds that home is no longer home. The little girl is with family, an aunt, but she is far from feeling at home. Even her opening line hints at this: "In Worcester, Massachusetts." Surely a child would simply say "In Worcester" ("I live in Worcester" or "I'm visiting Worcester"). "Worcester, Massachusetts" sounds like a postal address or like something said by a child trying to accustom herself to a new and strange place.[3]

Even before the first poem, Bishop indicates that she is starting again. The epigraph includes the place where she began her writing, a map. The source is listed at the top of the page, not in the usual place at the end, with the result that the epigraph resembles the poems proper. It might well be called a found poem generically as well as an epigraph, another example of

Bishop's fertile mixing of genres. It is taken from an 1884 edition of James Monteith's schoolbook *First Lessons in Geography* (1856) and fills an entire page, starting with Lesson VI:

LESSON VI
What is Geography?
A description of the Earth's surface.

Lesson X follows, and the series of questions begins to sound odd, starting with "*In what direction from the center of the picture is the Island? North,*" then "*In what direction is the Volcano?*" and a paragraph of queries. In the original textbook, the questions all make sense, for there is a simple map invented to teach directions, with Island, Volcano, and the like marked on it. (Monteith's book is subtitled *On the Plan of Object Teaching*, and here is an object designed to teach.) What likely caught Bishop's eye was this teaching map. For it appears to be modeled on the isthmus of Panama with adjacent parts of North and South America. The volcano is even handily off the coast of South America, like Crusoe's possible island. The map and questions seem particularly suited to her at this time, given her return to North America bearing all her Brazilian memories, given, too, her moving about in different directions for several years before settling in Boston, given, too, her need to think about directions in her life and work after her very difficult first years following Lota's death. In the original, some questions at the end of the epigraph are on separate lines. Bunching them into a paragraph gives a tone of urgency, nerves, near panic.

The use of the preposition "in" is very striking, not only in the epigraph but also in the first two poems, "In the Waiting Room" and "Crusoe in England." The epigraph's final paragraph reads thus:

NATIONAL GEOGRAPHICAL SERIES.

FIRST LESSONS

IN

GEOGRAPHY:

ON THE

PLAN OF OBJECT TEACHING.

DESIGNED FOR BEGINNERS.

BY JAMES MONTEITH,

AUTHOR OF A SERIES OF GEOGRAPHIES, MAPS, ATLASES, AND A POPULAR SCIENCE READER.

A. S. BARNES & COMPANY,

NEW YORK, AND CHICAGO.

Cover of James Monteith, *First Lessons in Geography* (see epigraph of *Geography III*)

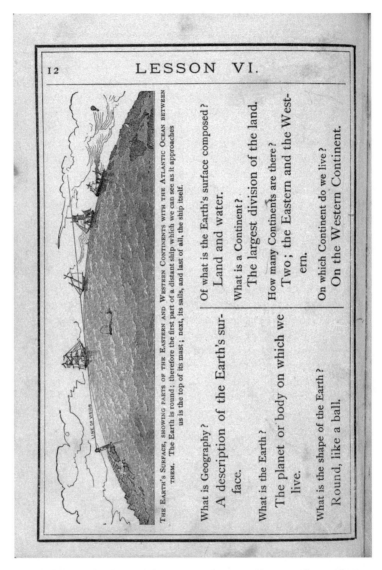

Lesson VI, James Monteith, *First Lessons in Geography* (see epigraph of *Geography III*)

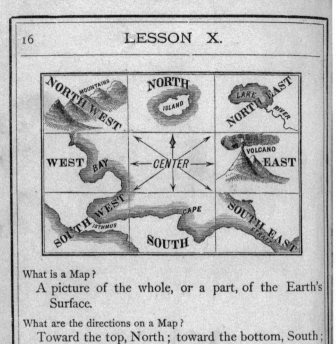

16   LESSON X.

What is a Map?
   A picture of the whole, or a part, of the Earth's Surface.

What are the directions on a Map?
   Toward the top, North; toward the bottom, South; to the right, East; to the left, West.

In what direction from the center of the picture is the Island?
   North.

In what direction is the volcano? The Cape?

The Bay? The Lake? The Strait? The Mountains?

The Isthmus?

What is in the East? In the West? In the South? In the North? In the Northwest? In the Southeast? In the Northeast? In the Southwest?

Lesson X and map, James Monteith, *First Lessons in Geography* (see epigraph of *Geography III*)

What is in the East? In the West? In the South? In the North?
In the Northwest? In the Southeast? In the Northeast? In the
Southwest?

This paragraph takes us right back to the compass rose in its simplest form. Bishop instructs our eye to follow the epigraph's *"directions on a Map"* and look left, then right, along a horizontal line, as in our conventional orientation. After that, we follow a vertical line, from bottom to top, then two crosswise lines dividing the compass rose into forty-five-degree angles. Bishop had an acute need to orient herself, to steady herself again on this earth, coming back to North America and then to Boston. Both "In the Waiting Room" and "Crusoe in England" show people trying to orient themselves in strange conditions.

The last paragraph does something more. It leads directly into the first title, *"What is in the East?"* then to *"In . . . ?"* seven more times, then to "In the Waiting Room." *What* is in the waiting room? The first line speaks to geography with yet another "in": "In Worcester, Massachusetts." Forms of "in" gather emphasis throughout: "My aunt was inside," "the inside of a volcano," "in rivulets of fire," "it was *me:*/ my voice, in my mouth," "into cold, blue-black space," "the family voice/I felt in my throat," "Then I was back in it./The War was on. Outside,/in Worcester, Massachusetts." A number of critics have commented on the use of inside and outside here, sometimes making it a black-white distinction.[4] I find the varieties of "in" suggestive and shall return to them.

The poem begins with place and ends with place and time: "In Worcester, Massachusetts," "it was still the fifth/of February, 1918." Ending with the precise date reminds us again that place is always seen historically, that geography is never divorced from history. The date of 1918 reaches back to another geography and a poem written "for a child of 1918," "Manners." Nothing in that poem or the two other childhood poems and the story in *Questions of Travel* is as confining, stifling, alienating for the child as this dentist's waiting room. In the earlier writing, Bishop's persona is at home in Nova Scotia, supported by family and her small community, for all her sad situation. In Worcester, she is in foreign territory, and she is alone.

The poem is written in three-beat lines with much-varied feet, resembling a strong-stress poem. It is divided into four long verse paragraphs, then two final stanzas of four and six lines. The opening sets the scene in the dentist's waiting room in Worcester, Massachusetts, full of grown-up people and their winter gear. The child of six, nearly seven, waiting for her aunt inside, reads the *National Geographic* ("I could read"). She sees an inert and then an active volcano, a "dead man slung on a pole" (from an article on cannibals, though we are not told this), babies with string round and round their necks, and naked black women with wire round and round theirs. "Their breasts were horrifying." The word "geography" has shifted to its adjectival form in the *National Geographic*. Geography, as the epigraph says, may well be the study of the earth's surface, but the *National Geographic* also studies what inhabits the earth's surface and sees it from a national perspective, that of the United States. Volcanoes are of wide and impersonal interest. The photographs of human cannibalism, strange bodily decorations, and sagging breasts are different. They show *them* versus *us*, show "the other." As for horrifying a young child, I still remember carefully calculating what pages of the *National Geographic* I must not look at again, age eight or so. I lifted only the corner and sped past whatever scene it was of human cruelty.

The second paragraph opens abruptly:

Suddenly, from inside,
came an *oh!* of pain
— Aunt Consuelo's voice —
not very loud or long.

The child's first reaction is impatience — "I knew she was / a foolish, timid woman" — until the cry somehow becomes her own: "it was *me:* / my voice, in my mouth."[5] There is no sympathy but a sudden inrush of empathy and involuntary imitation. I would argue that this scene of recognition marks a nascent poet. It is impossible to write many kinds of poetry without a sense of empathy — not necessarily sympathy but an imaginative ability to be someone or something else, to willingly suspend disbelief for the moment. The double shock is compounded by a sense of "falling, falling," as the child becomes faint in the heat of the waiting room.

In the child's faintness, some sensations are heightened while others fade, and the whole sense of inside and outside starts to spiral out of control. She talks to herself quite sternly: "three days / and you'll be seven years old." Young people of any age do that (the seven-year-old Alice of *Alice in Wonderland,* for example, though she is a very different child). But the phantasmagoria this child experiences coalesce in a powerful feeling akin to a mystical experience.

But I felt: you are an *I,*
you are an *Elizabeth,*
you are one of *them.*
Why should you be one, too?

The revelation is so complete and so startling that the child knows "that nothing stranger / had ever happened, that nothing / stranger could ever happen."[6]

At the end, "I was back in it," and the poem circles back to the beginning, suggesting a neatly encapsulated incident. But it is a different child who is "back in it" again. It is a child who has shocked herself with instinctive empathy and mimicry, who has felt in her bones revulsion against the oddity of some human beings and the cruelty of others (including the background cruelty of World War I), who has recognized that she herself is inevitably one of this species, and who also dislikes the fact. Part of all this is growing up. But the intensity of her empathy and her strong innate sense of individuality suggest, I think, that this poem is also a portrait of the artist as a young girl.[7]

"Crusoe in England" was titled "Crusoe at Home" when Bishop first began it in 1964 (LOA 913). The questions of home and travel that are so central to *Questions of Travel* reappear here too. It is a topographic poem, in which geography can even become a nightmare, as Crusoe dreams he has to live on countless islands "for ages, / registering their flora, / their fauna, their geography." Like "In the Waiting Room," it is written in verse paragraphs of varied length and is mostly unrhymed (though with some occasional striking end rhymes, repetitions, etc.). A single line stands by itself: "And then one day they came and took us off." The overall effect is of an interior monologue or else an interview with some unidentified auditor. It is the longest poem in *Geography III* at 182 lines, compared with 120 for "In the Waiting Room." *Robinson Crusoe* is a favorite children's book in a much-simplified form, and the little girl in Worcester, Massachusetts, could well have read it. Crusoe sounds as if he might even be addressing her as he starts his poem.

A new volcano has erupted,
the papers say. . . .

. . . .

Well, I had fifty-two
miserable, small volcanoes I could climb.

This is in answer to, "[I] carefully / studied the photographs: / the inside of a volcano, / black, and full of ashes," from "In the Waiting Room." As "First Lessons in Geography" asks, *"In what direction is the Volcano?"*

Bishop gives Crusoe an expressive vocabulary, a middle style favoring the exclamatory mood, sometimes hyperbolic to match the landscape that looks hyperbolic to a northerner. He can be accurate in surprising ways. His volcanoes are out of scale, and their paragraph ends with out-of-scale "overlapping rollers / — a glittering hexagon of rollers / closing and closing in, but never quite." "Hexagon" is an example of Bishop's surprising diction, yet not so surprising, for Crusoe is a sailor, accustomed to watching lines and reading geometrical shapes on his instruments. The word is precise, if stylized, as anyone who has been upended by a powerful breaker knows. Bishop's "cloud-dump" of an island is an invented compound, appropriate to Crusoe's voice. He personifies the many waterspouts with heads and feet, before they metamorphose into "Glass chimneys, flexible, attenuated, / sacerdotal beings of glass . . . / Beautiful, yes, but not much company." "Glass chimneys" recall kerosene lamps, though these are very different. And "attenuated, sacerdotal"? Is this the diction of a Robinson Crusoe? In fact, the OED shows both words turning up in nineteenth-century military or naval accounts. (Has this Crusoe migrated into the nineteenth century, as his later quotation from Wordsworth suggests?)

The little girl's diction in "In the Waiting Room" is a child's and impressive as such but limited, as she knows. Bishop draws attention to her search for a word for her strange experience: "How — I didn't know any/word for it — how 'unlikely' . . .'" She also draws attention to Crusoe's search for a forgotten word, a frustrating search for a word that would have put the lie to Wordsworth, had he remembered it:

> Why didn't I know enough of something?
>
> .   .   .   .
>   I tried
> reciting to my iris-beds,
> "They flash upon that inward eye,
> which is the bliss . . ." The bliss of what?
> One of the first things that I did
> when I got back was look it up.

The word is of course "solitude." Crusoe himself comments on his use of words when he christens one volcano *"Mont d'Espoir"* (Mountain of Hope) or *"Mount Despair"*: "I'd time enough to play with names." So also, though without comment, he plays on the old saying "Charity begins at home" (see OED, s.v. "charity" 9.a, with one illustration from Sir Thomas Browne). "What's wrong with self-pity anyway?" he asks, before his engaging little mock syllogism: "'Pity should begin at home.' So the more/pity I felt, the more I felt at home." But he never feels at home. The word returns shortly:

> and so I made home-brew. I'd drink
> the awful, fizzy, stinging stuff
> that went straight to my head
> and play my home-made flute

(I think it had the weirdest scale on earth)
and, dizzy, whoop and dance among the goats.
Home-made, home-made! But aren't we all?

The little girl in the first poem tries to find language for a profound experience. Bishop finds a way for her Crusoe to present
profound questions in simple, familiar, and entirely accurate
language.

Bishop was interested in Crusoe's experience long before she
went to Brazil. Her notebook that starts on an island ("Cuttyhunk, July 1934," Vassar 72A.3) opens with reflections on islands
and with the goats that make their way into her poem thirty-
seven years later: "On an island you live all the time in this
Robinson Crusoe atmosphere; making this do for that, and con-
triving and inventing. . . . A poem should be made about making
things in a pinch — & how it looks and when the emergency is
over. . . . It joins us to children pretending to . . . do complicated
things in a simple way. . . . The goats are so tame they allow you
to hold their pointed chins in the palm of your hand and look
into their beautiful yellow eyes" (1). Goats are present in Defoe's
Crusoe but not the noisy gulls whose sounds plus the goat sounds
haunt Bishop's Crusoe even in England ("*Baa, baa, baa* and
shriek, shriek, shriek"). The observation about children is quite
right. In another setting, both the little girl and Crusoe could
be playing at inventing things in a pinch. At the end of "Crusoe
in England," Crusoe notes that Friday died of measles. Nothing
is made of this, but it's worth remembering that measles is a
passing childhood disease for most children like the little girl
of "In the Waiting Room." It was a fatal disease for many na-
tives on first contact with outsiders.

May Swenson caught the tone of "Crusoe in England" when it first appeared: "I saw your *Crusoe in England*. . . . Wonderful, and sad, and absurd, and true. The one of a kind, explorer, marooned, mate-less — who chose uniqueness, invented his survival equipment and lived on [*sic*] his own world — only to find in the end that he's no *exception* to the common fate of all those others who never ventured . . . A great and remarkable poem, on all its levels — there are at least three levels that I see" (2 Dec. 1971, Swenson-Bishop letters; second ellipsis in original). Bishop replied, "You so beautifully get the point (I've been re-reading H. James' letters, for my seminar — as you might guess) of the *Crusoe* poem that I want to write you a note to thank you" (5 Dec. 1971, Swenson-Bishop letters). "Survival equipment": "a poem should be made" about this, Bishop thought at age twenty-three, although she had in mind making do with things "in a pinch," a poem about ingenuity. Over thirty years later, "survival equipment" was seriously needed for any continuing meaningful life. Poetry at last, and as so often, provided it, and Bishop recorded the means: "First Lessons in Geography," "In the Waiting Room," "Crusoe in England."

It bears repeating that these two opening poems are poems and not diaries or confessions, all the more because I opened this chapter with biographical background. "In the Waiting Room" works with an experience from Bishop's childhood, but the experience may be more usual than we think. Bishop did a rough translation in Portuguese for a friend, who told her that it gave her gooseflesh on her arms because this (the strange experience) happened to her as a child when she looked in a mirror. "Others have told me the same thing — 5 years old, brushing his teeth, etc." (Bishop to Frank Bidart, 27 July 1971, L 545). Crusoe is not Bishop in disguise. Rather, her experience in returning to the Boston area heightened her sense of what a Crusoe character might endure, coming home, including memories of someone cherished and now dead. Whatever part of herself was like some kind of Crusoe character, there were many other parts, including the poet who wrote this poem.

Tone

I want to pause briefly over the word "tone," the word for what Swenson caught in "Crusoe in England." This is a term I've used regularly without stopping to examine it: for example, the changes of tone in "The Map" and "At the Fishhouses," the tone of authority in "The Monument," the tone of "The Shampoo," and so on. "Tone" is a curious literary term. It cannot be measured quantitatively like the standard number of lines in a sonnet. It cannot be classified according to evidence like genres. It's true that a tone can be called "ironic" or "satiric" and that irony and satire are modes of writing. But it is not a modal term either, for the adjective "tonal" by itself tells us nothing at all. All sorts of adjectives are judged suitable to modify the noun "tone." Reviewers can use it casually, even carelessly, to cover a multitude of sins.

Yet listen to Robert Lowell, trying to catch the tone of Elizabeth Bishop's poem "Brazil, January 1, 1502": "Your poem is one of your most beautiful, I think — wonderful description, the jungle turning into a picture, then into history and the jungle again, with a practical, absurd, sad, amused and frightened tone for the Christians" (4 Jan. 1960, LEBRL 307). Or listen to Bishop herself, responding to the tone of May Swenson's *Another An-*

imal: "I find the tone so admirable: cheerful, brave, energetic, 'open,' etc. — and such a relief after the attempts at infinite knowledge, wisdom, experience, and oh-the-weariness-of-it-all of so many contemporary poets" (14 Nov. 1954, Swenson-Bishop letters). Richard Howard in 1974 called "In the Waiting Room" and Herbert's "Love Unknown" "triumphs of tonality" ("Comment," 208). Seamus Heaney has written some of the best commentary we have on "At the Fishhouses," including this sentence on its ending: "The lines are inhabited by certain profoundly true tones, which as Robert Frost put it, 'were before words were, living in the cave of the mouth.'"[8]

That is why tone is so difficult. For Eliot, it was one of the hardest challenges for a writer. "One can groan enough over the choice of a word, but there is something much more important to groan over first. . . . The words come easily enough, in comparison with the core of it — the *tone* — and nobody can help in the least with that."[9] Nowadays we hear the term "voice" more often, and James Merrill thought that "voice" is simply the democratic word for "tone." "'Tone' always sounds snobbish, but without a sense of it how one flounders!"[10] Merrill then goes on to discuss the art of speaking "naturally, with pleasure." It shows one's attitude to the reader, he comments, one's manners in the true sense of the word: "Manners are for me the touch of nature, an artifice in the very bloodstream. Someone who does not take them seriously is making a serious mistake. . . . And manners — whether good or bad — are entirely allied with tone or voice in poetry" ("An Interview with Donald Sheehan," 33).

Bishop learned to read tone early in her life. "All this I understood, like Beppo, by tone of voice rather than by words, but I listened and listened while pretending to play cards" ("The

Country Mouse," *CProse* 23). The occasion was an argument about Christian Science between her Worcester grandfather and a neighbor; Beppo was the dog.

Though Bishop knew well how to read tone as a child, judging tone in her own writing was another matter. She would develop an almost uncanny sense of tone in her mature writing, rather like a musician's sense. But her command of tone in her earlier work is not always sure. It is not that she herself has not thought through the tone of a given poem. It is that she expects a great deal of the reader, as for example in her 1937 short story "The Sea and Its Shore." Marianne Moore questioned the word "picturesque" in the closing sentence of the story, "It is an extremely picturesque scene, in some ways like a Rembrandt, but in many ways not" (quoted by Bishop in letter to Moore, 5 Jan. 1937, L 54; see LOA 581; *CProse* 180). The sentence echoes and expands an earlier one: "Every night he walked back and forth . . . — a picturesque sight, in some ways like a Rembrandt" (LOA 575; *CProse* 172). Bishop replied, "You say you feel it to be too 'automatic.' In a way, that was what I meant it to be — I was, I suppose, making fun of an automatic reaction to the scene I was describing and I wanted, as the only 'moral' to the story, to contradict, as quietly as possible, the automatic, banal thing that one might have said: 'How picturesque — He looks like a Rembrandt!' That is, the conclusion of the sentence, 'but in many ways not,' is really thought of as being spoken in a different tone of voice" (5 Jan. 1937, L 54). Note the quality of attention needed from the reader. Bishop, still in her midtwenties, expects too much of her readers here, I think.

Consider also a few of the early poems in *North & South*, such as "The Imaginary Iceberg" and markedly "The Colder the Air." There is a draft of this latter poem in Bishop's poetry notebook of "1935 (some 1934–36)" (Vassar 72A.1). In the margin, beside the last stanza, she has penciled, "pun on the word *spring* understood?" Well no, though it is distantly implied: a spring in a watch plus spring as a season. But the implication is closer to solving a cryptic crossword puzzle than to reading poetry. Expecting too much of a reader or expecting a reader to be something of a mind reader: these show a writer whose manners toward his or her readers are still imperfect. It is a question of deciding who the reader is and finding just the right way to speak. As with Bishop's gradual command of diction through a discipline of simplicity, so also with tone. She began to work at making her tone attain Herbert's "absolute naturalness of tone."[11]

She was thinking further about tone when she wrote "Roosters" and had to defend it against Moore (and Moore's intrusive mother): "I can't bring myself to sacrifice what (I think) is a very important 'violence' of tone — which I feel to be helped by what *you* must feel to be just a bad case of the *Threes* [the poem's triplet stanzas]. It makes me feel like a wonderful Klee picture I saw at his show the other day, *The Man of Confusion*" (17 Oct. 1940, L 96–97). When a poem's subject is violent, then manners toward the reader require a certain violence of tone. The way in which this is handled is a lesson in itself.

But in poem after poem of Bishop's mature work, she is fully in command of tone. She can alter the dominant tone like a musician. She can shift tones very quietly within a poem, like the slight altering of a repeating phrase in music. Or she can change tone *fortissimo*, like a change of key in music. Her short story "In the Village" was earlier titled "Clothes. Food. Animals," but she decided that was "a little chichi" — not quite the right tone (to Kit and Ilse Barker, 12 Oct. 1952, L 249).

In "Crusoe in England," the tone changes at the end. Crusoe, so expansive and hyperbolic, so full of details, turns suddenly reticent. Friday has appeared in his poem ("Friday was nice, and we were friends"), with a memory of regret that neither could propagate and a memory of Friday playing with the animals and of his "pretty body." The word "nice" itself is general and avoids emotion. Shortly after, rescue arrives, then a transition to present life, in which old objects from the island seem meaningless, then the closing two lines, abruptly:

> —And Friday, my dear Friday, died of measles
> seventeen years ago come March.

Bishop's Crusoe, unlike Defoe's, makes his attachment to Friday clear, and his grief. It is the reticence that tells, along with the endearment and the precision of the memory. How many of us remember the seventeenth anniversary of a death? James Merrill wanted more attention given to Friday. Bishop told him that she had originally written a lot more, and thought about restoring a few lines, but stuck by her decision (20 Apr. 1974, L 584). She was right. It was a superior instinct about tone. Crusoe's grief cannot but evoke Bishop's grief for Lota, dead just over four years when this poem was first published in the *New Yorker* in November 1971. It links this poem with the following short poem, "Night City."

Counterpoint: The Everyday and Its Underside

"Night City" is a poem of ten rhymed short-line quatrains *(abcb)* in contrast to the long verse paragraphs of the two earlier poems. "From the plane" says the epigraph, but the sight is not geographical, not points of light outlining a city plan at night. It is allegorical, it is Milton's Hell in modern form. It is general: no geographical name locates it, as the preceding poems are located. Intense fires burn like "the Lake with liquid fire" (*Paradise Lost* 1.229). There is "a pool of bitumen" like Milton's "black, bituminous gurge [surge, eddy] [that]/Boils out from under ground, the mouth of Hell" (ibid. 12.41–42). It might be any city attacked by modern weapons or urban unrest, although in "Night City," it is a tycoon who weeps that pool of bitumen, as if this were also an Orozco painting and so speaking to social justice.[12] The city burns tears, and

> The city burns guilt.
> —For guilt-disposal
> the central heat
> must be this intense.

We expect to hear "garbage-disposal," but this is a city different in kind. It is also a city of the mind. As for guilt, Bishop thought that she was "born guilty" or was "one of those born-guilty people" (Vassar 27.3; Vassar 27.5). In 1973, she replied to a confessional letter from Robert Lowell: "We all have irreparable and awful actions on our consciences — that's really all I can say now. I do, I know. I just try to live without blaming myself for them *every* day, at least — every *day*, I should say — the nights take care of guilt sufficiently" (22 July 1973, LEBRL 753). It is not only tycoons who bear a burden of guilt at night.

Still, the poem concludes,

> (Still, there are creatures,
> careful ones, overhead.
> They set down their feet, they walk
> Green, red; green, red.)

The airplanes are flashing their wing-end taillights regularly, one port (red), one starboard (green). They look strange to inhabitants below. Still, they offer ongoing life to the people in them, at least after the night is over.

Bishop's great poem "The Moose" follows, and it moves her book to ordinary everyday life. The two opening soliloquies are poems by solitaries trying to orient themselves. Both are related obliquely to Bishop's earlier poems. "The Moose" is quite different: mostly third person with some use of first person but in the plural; not an internal crisis but an external drama provided by nature; and especially not a sense of solitude but of community.[13] The poem is the third long poem, the center of the five long poems, and it grounds them. The two remaining long poems retain this sense of stability.

Some of the linguistic patterns of tension in the earlier poems settle into calm, normal everyday life in "The Moose." The taillights of "Night City" extend into "The Moose," in which "a red light," "a ship's port lantern," is glimpsed as the bus travels past a New Brunswick port (Moncton?). The lights in both poems remind us of two different ways of traveling and of the long-observed conventions of green for starboard, red for port. The word "creatures" also migrates from "Night City" to "The Moose": "'Sure are big creatures.'" "'Curious creatures,'/says our quiet driver,/rolling his *r*'s." The word now bears its common meaning in a poem that has changed back to the common, everyday world, a world that comes with its own recognitions, its own rare joys. Volcanoes or lava connect the book's epigraph and the first four poems. "In what direction is the Volcano?" asks the epigraph. Over the page to "In the Waiting Room" is one answer, where the *National Geographic* first shows "the inside of a volcano,/black, and full of ashes." Then comes a pic-

ture of a volcano "spilling over/in rivulets of fire." Over the page
again, and Crusoe's poem opens, "A new volcano has erupted."
Over the page yet again to "Night City," in which rivers "run,
molten," though they run "green and luminous/silicate." Finally
over the page to "The Moose," in which an utterly different tone
describes the setting sun on the red, damp soil of the Bay of
Fundy, a sun that "veins the flats'/ . . . rich mud/in burning
rivulets." It is a farewell to volcanoes and lava, and another return to everyday life.

"The Moose" is a late version of "From the Country to the
City," with a memory of the local bus in "Cape Breton." It moves
as if archetypally from the area of Bishop's childhood village
toward the city that she knew and where she finally settled,
Boston. This trip is not in a speeding car but in a bus stopping
at local places, casual, relaxed. We do not see highway lights at
night but sunset and then darkness. There are not two contrasting commedia dell'arte figures in a context of love but a
group of ordinary travelers ("A woman climbs in," "brisk, freckled,
elderly," surveying her fellow passengers "amicably"). The poem
is not built with interwoven terza rima lines but with six-line
rhymed stanzas in trimeters. This is not the tense childhood world
of Worcester, Massachusetts, nor the Boston of someone recently
returned from Brazil. We are back to the Nova Scotia world of
Bishop's earlier childhood poems.

"The Moose" is a topographic poem, like the loco-descriptive
poems of the eighteenth century that set the pattern. It is a
journey mapped geographically. (A *New Yorker* editor who
hadn't bothered looking at a map challenged the direction in
"a bus journeys west" and even challenged the name of the
well-known Tantramar marshes.) Its pace is steady, its tone
steady too.

The opening sentence is a virtual study of prepositions and conjunctions. It is a tour de force of no less than thirty-six lines. Just try parsing this sentence. (It would make a nice challenge for a grammar class.) It builds like a Latin sentence, with the main clause deferred until line 26 and the preceding lines all dependent phrases and clauses (from A, where B, where C . . . to line 26: "a bus journeys west"). Each of the six stanzas of this sentence opens with a preposition or a conjunction: "From," "where," "where," "on," "through," "down." The rest of the main clause follows in line 32. By contrast, the next stanza contains three short sentences. Of the remaining twenty-two stanzas, only three open with a preposition, none with a conjunction. Prepositions and conjunctions are virtually always in relation grammatically, that is, part of a sentence dependent on a main clause. They themselves map relations ("expressing a relation," "used to connect," OED, s.vv. "preposition" 1.a and "conjunction" 6.a). What better way to construct a poem on relations, with family relations at the core in memories of grandparents? The topography's various relations are mapped (tidal movements, height and depth of land and water, color, etc.). At the end, the relation of the moose to bus and driver and passengers takes over the poem — not just the relative size but the relations between humans and animal. As for the relation of all those phrases and clauses in the opening sentence, syntax and grammar hold them together, tracing the meandering bus journey on its course and also giving an overview, just like a map.

This is only one way in which Bishop made sure her poem was not too old-fashioned or faulted by simplicity. ("And maybe you'll find it entirely too 19th centuryish, anyway," she wrote to her editor at the *New Yorker*. "I gave the poem the subtitle of

Back to Boston, but . . . it makes things too clear — and simplicity
is the biggest fault of this poem, anyway, I'm afraid" [to Howard
Moss, 15 June and 7 July 1972, LEBNY 344, 346].) There are
other ways as well, for example, two momentary suggestions of
personification, one of the bay, one of the bus. The tides mean
that the bay may be "coming in" or may be "not at home." This
last phrase can slide by so quickly that we do not notice that it
usually applies to humans, not to tidal waters. So does "coming
in." The noun also picks up "home of the long tides" (l. 3), so that
an impersonal geographical metaphor is quickened into a literal
human home, as Bishop delicately intimates what this landscape
can mean. The bus itself is very briefly personified as an animal
when the sun's color is "brushing" its "dented flank."

   With dusk and night, the rhythm of the journey changes.
So far, the prolonged steady pace has been following what the
bus passengers see of the outside world. Darkness brings only
the occasional glimpse of the outside, and sound takes over.
Sentences correspondingly shorten; phrases burst on the scene
abruptly. Quiet reigns, then "Snores," and the familiar murmur
of quiet talk among mostly dozing passengers. The pace slows
further when the sounds change in a "dreamy divagation," a
journey into memory, prompted by the low conversations. And
there it all is, life, death, tribulations, and acceptance of it all by
the old and experienced who have gone before us. Among the
sounds is a small Nova Scotia phonic sound, not to be heard in
a Boston accent or I daresay elsewhere: "'Yes . . .'/A sharp, indrawn breath,/half groan, half acceptance,/that means 'Life's
like that./We know *it* (also death).'" (The Cape Breton writer
Alexander MacLeod kindly imitated it for me when I asked,
and it is very distinctive.) It all brings reassurance, or rather, in

the mind's own phrase, "Now, it's all right now/even to fall asleep." If we have not realized it before, we do now: that "The Moose" is a contrary poem to the first two poems, a poem of great strength and courage, not the courage of the short heroic action but the everyday courage of endurance and persistence, of finding sufficient.

The bus passengers are a community in little with none of the estrangement felt by the little girl in the waiting room. Memory and murmured late-night bus conversations merge sleepily to offer a safe home:

> Talking the way they talked
> in the old featherbed,
> peacefully, on and on,
> dim lamplight in the hall,
> down in the kitchen, the dog
> tucked in her shawl.

In a bed, in a hall, in a room, in a shawl, and earlier "in the night," "In the creakings and noises," "in the bus," "in childbirth," "in Eternity." Before that, there are other examples in other contexts, for example, fog "closing in" with its crystals "in the white hens' feathers,/in gray, glazed cabbages" (but "*on* the cabbage roses"). Space, condition, time, place, action: geography calls on them all.

An encounter with a moose is common enough on New Brunswick highways at night. In the Maritime provinces you can see highway signs warning of animals crossing at night that show not a deer but a moose. Collision with one can be fatal; they are enormous. But an encounter in which the moose behaves like a large dog and can be safely seen by safely sheltered passengers is rare. So is the strong word that describes their collective response, "joy"; it does not appear in any other of Bishop's collected poems. How does she know that "we feel/(we all feel)" this joy? All I can say is that such collective emotion happens, as it did on a whale-watching boat run by the Center for Coastal Studies in Provincetown. A whale swam under the boat, its long head stretching out on one side and its long body stretching far out on the other side. One leap and it would have capsized us. Complete silence fell. "These whales like to play," the biologist on board assured us, whereupon the whale swam off a bit, spouted, and then did a perfect dive, flukes upright. We certainly felt collective emotion — wonder, I'd have said, more than joy.

This is not a bull moose resembling Frost's buck in "The Most of It," nor does it come crashing.[14] It is a female, a cow moose, simply standing "in the middle of the road," having "come out of/the impenetrable wood." It sniffs at the hot engine, looks over the bus, "grand, otherworldly." "Curious creatures" is the driver's comment. There are two indications that Bishop wanted her readers to stay away from the moose as a portentous symbol. The first is a revision that she made before collecting the poem. In the *New Yorker* version, "the sun sets/facing a Red Sea," but in *Geography III*, it is "a red sea." She did indeed have in mind the Red Sea of Exodus, famous for parting to allow the fleeing Israelites under Moses to escape, then drowning the Pharaoh's chariots. "I liked the Red Sea with a capital, two capitals," she wrote to her editor. Otherwise, it "is just descriptive — and it isn't the sea anyway — it's the Bay of Fundy *looking like* the Red Sea (which it does, that is, if the Red Sea is RED). 'Led them with unmoistened foot/through the Red Sea waters . . .' (I'm afraid you aren't apt to be familiar with one of my favorite hymns!)" (to Howard Moss, 7 July 1972, LEBNY 346–347; the

hymn is "Come, ye faithful, raise the strain . . ."). Why this allusion? For one thing, it brings a sense of the miraculous to this
famed natural tidal phenomenon. Possibly it was indulging a
childhood memory. What else would a child raised by Baptist
grandparents think when she was told the story of Pharaoh's
chariots and the Red Sea? Later, Bishop apparently thought it a
distraction or possibly misleading for this poem.

The second indication remains in the poem: "impenetrable
wood," "in the middle of the road." Look again at the opening
lines of Dante's *Inferno:* "Nel mezzo del cammin di notra
vita / miritrovai per una selva oscura." In the middle of the road
of this life, / I found myself in an impenetrable wood. (*Oscura*
means "dark, obscure, mysterious," while *selva selvaggia* in line
6 describes the wood as "wild, savage.") Three menacing wild
animals then threaten Dante in his dream vision. Instead, here,
just as passengers are drifting into sleep and dreams, a female
moose stands still, sniffing the bus as though it were another
nonthreatening animal. The poem quietly reminds us of another journey (and is Bishop reminding herself of being lost on
life's way for a while?). Here, the context is entirely natural and
it is benign, a blessing of sorts.

In the fifth poem, "12 O'Clock News" a small reconnais-
sance group marches over Bishop's working desk much as the
Lilliputians marched over Gulliver's body. This is a prose poem
with an utterly different tone from "The Moose." Like "Night
City," it makes a contrast with the narrative poem of everyday
life that precedes it. Bishop now alternates longer narrative
poems of everyday life with shorter poems from a different world,
whether interior or exterior or some mixing of the two — not
that the everyday poems are mundane. On the contrary, they
include spots of time that are quite extraordinary. The whole

process is also retrospective. The lava and volcanoes, for example, take us back. Similarly, the alternating poems take us back to poems of everyday life, reminding us of undercurrents there. While the connecting strands of "in" and "volcanoes" and red lights and "creatures" weave a loose texture, the basic rhythm is the one that matters: the alternation of everyday wide-awake poems with poems of a world gone strange or hostile or loveless, poems that are the reverse side of the everyday poems. The same contrast informs the three earlier poems that Bishop insisted on keeping together: "A Summer's Dream," "At the Fishhouses," and "Cape Breton." *Geography III* might be called a tapestry, where we see the right side and the underside in alternating views.

"12 O'Clock News" resembles "Night City" in its change of perspective. In fact, most of the poems in *Geography III* have to do with scale in one sense or another. The science of geography depends fundamentally on scale, of course. In the two opening poems, the scale of things is uncomfortable. In the waiting room, "the knees and inert 'pairs of hands,' [are] seen backlit from a seven-year-old's low perspective," as James Longenbach puts it.[15] Crusoe finds his strange island landscape grossly out of proportion: "I had fifty-two / miserable, small volcanoes," "I had / become a giant." And the moose itself dwarfs our familiar human scale, making an encounter with it a thing of wonder.

Like "Crusoe in England," "12 O'Clock News" explores a strange and here a hostile territory. Victoria Harrison reads it as a war poem, and so it clearly is ("our opponents"), though Bishop denied having a specific war in mind.[16] ("[It] was begun years earlier. . . . It had nothing to do with Viet Nam or any particular war when I first wrote it, it was just fantasy. That's the way things catch up with you.")[17] The enemy is seen as a primitive superstitious people, observed through the lens of anthropological geography. In one way, the poem is funny; in its misapprehension of reality, it is not.

Diction that looks self-evident and is not also continues, "glacis," for example, in this poem. How many readers know without checking that "glacis" means a "bank sloping down from fort, on which attackers are exposed to defenders' missiles" *(Concise Oxford Dictionary)*? The form, a prose poem, is new for Bishop, though not as an exercise. In 1948, she acquired a book on Henri Michaud: "but so far it seems like little bits of prose-poems, not very serious. . . . Maybe these make me particularly mad because I used to amuse myself by writing things rather like them — & then I don't think I even saved them" (31 Dec. 1948, LEBRL 73).

The sixth poem and the fourth long poem is titled simply "Poem." It retains the sense of stability established by "The Moose," focusing on one incident and using the first-person singular. "Poem" is a generic title, not "Sestina" or "Anaphora," not even "A Poem." It sounds like a definition of "poem," a definition by example — not of "poetry" but of what a single poem is. It opens by establishing the scale and the colors of what turns out to be a painting: "About the size of an old-style dollar bill, / American or Canadian," that is, roughly thirteen by six inches. The colors are "mostly the same whites, gray greens, and steel grays." But unlike the dollar in its day, it "has never earned any money in its life." As it turns out, the painter was a great-uncle, family, and "an R.A." (a member of the British Royal Academy), which means some of his paintings did earn money, if not this little sketch. But Bishop defers telling us this. What might another poet say after the funny remark about never earning money, despite a resemblance to a dollar bill that was genuine currency when it was painted? Hardly what follows here: "Useless and free," the painting has been a family memento or rather "relic." *Free?* The combination of these two adjectives points toward profound questions of the uses of art and of art in relation to freedom. They implicitly ask whether (or when) either question can be discussed without the other.[18]

The poem is disarmingly casual in tone at first. It returns us to Bishop's beloved province: "It must be Nova Scotia" — "must be" because, for one thing, houses are painted in "that awful shade of brown." Details, tiny as they are in this small painting, begin to emerge, for this is an ekphrastic poem. After the brown paint come white houses, a "gray-blue wisp" that is possibly a church steeple, then "some tiny cows." Bishop has built toward the next move so that it comes smoothly: "tiny cows, / two brush-strokes each, but confidently cows." She will continue this back-and-forth between paint and what it represents, just as someone in an art gallery may come close to a painting to look at how it is done, then back away to an optimum viewing distance. The white-and-yellow iris comes "fresh-squiggled from the tube." Steel-gray storm clouds "were the artist's specialty." And then comes the fun that Bishop enjoys (as do I) in her mature poems: "A speck-like bird is flying to the left. / Or is it a flyspeck looking like a bird?"

Suddenly a scene of recognition erupts into this poem, a scene of recognition named as such — not of a person but of a place: "Heavens, I recognize the place, I know it!" What follows continues remarks on the painter's medium and method ("titanium white, one dab," "filaments of brush-hairs"). But now the speaker is identifying the details, the farmer's barn, the Presbyterian church steeple (it "must be"), Miss Gillespie's house (probably). Only now does the poem insert the circumstances of inheriting this painting, using a dramatic family voice, and ending "he was quite famous, an R.A."

What follows makes this into one of the great ekphrastic poems and one of Bishop's most beautiful. Though the speaker did not know her great-uncle, both knew this place and memorized it. "And it's still loved, / or its memory is." The change of tone is palpable, along with clarity about getting the language right, not inflating it or letting a stereotyped word like "vision" take over. Much better to use a plain vocabulary. The parenthesis is a virtual instruction to the reader.

> Our visions coincided — "visions" is
> too serious a word — our looks, two looks:
> art "copying from life" and life itself,
> life and the memory of it so compressed
> they've turned into each other. Which is which?

Small, even cramped and dim as this painting is, it is alive. Its detail shows

> — the little that we get for free,
> the little of our earthly trust. Not much.
> About the size of our abidance
> along with theirs: the munching cows,
> the iris, crisp and shivering, the water
> still standing from spring freshets,
> the yet-to-be-dismantled elms, the geese.

The word "free" has reappeared in a way reminiscent of Thoreau. Landscape is ours when we look at it and possess it in a different way from owning it in law. The memory of it is free too. As for our "earthly trust," a typical earlier use of the phrase is seen in an old hymn, in which it signifies "pleasure, vanity, and pride" in contrast to "celestial gain" ("I looked upon the righteous man"). Bishop's earthly trust is none of these.

At the end, we look through painting to actual scene, realized in the sense of art making something real, Paul Cézanne's verb for the process, *réaliser*. The adjectives are sensuous, cows "munching," iris "crisp" like something edible and "shivering" like a creature. The compound adjective in the last line is so compact that it can make a reader smile. It gives so much pleasure that readers commonly ignore the slight oddity of the past participle. "Dismantled"? First, it needs a footnote to explain that Dutch elm disease spread to eastern Canada during World War II and by 1989 had wiped out 75 percent of some seventy-seven million elms in North America as of 1930 (*New York Times*, 5 Dec. 1989). We take down, chop down, saw down trees, though diseased trees are handled more carefully. We usually dismantle something constructed, a ship, a fortification. The verb can signify "take to pieces, destroy, raze," and that makes sense here. Yet to dismantle trees makes them also sound like parts of a stage set. It is time to close the curtain on this scene, the verb also says, on the reality this scene brought alive, remembering that it is always available again in some degree.

Bishop chose to place just after this poem her villanelle of love and loss, "One Art," then her final long poem, "The End of March," a poem swept clear of memory.

"One Art," in contrast to "Poem," is about loss without compensation. It has an ambiguous title, then an arresting one-sentence first line that is part of the villanelle's refrain: "The art of losing isn't hard to master." The third line completes the refrain with the rhyme word "disaster." Is this one art among many or not? And losing versus what? Winning? Keeping? Losing objects? People? The poem is one of Bishop's best known, and it is finely executed, though its polish holds off a reader, even as it holds a possible disaster at arm's length.

It is a poem based on scale, starting with an everyday loss that is simply a nuisance (keys), then one that is usual but regretted, "the hour badly spent" (second stanza), then some losses of memory (third stanza), loss of a small and two large cherished objects (fourth stanza), and in a sudden jump loss of whole swatches of territory. What could be greater? "Losing you." As with Crusoe's reticence, so it is with the reticence here at the end, as the speaker summons the necessary strength to deal with this possible loss, "though it make look like (*Write* it!) like disaster." As the little girl in "In the Waiting Room" talked sternly to herself, so the adult woman here talks to herself, steeling herself.

The poem grows out of an echo from Emily Dickinson about forgetting, memorable partly because of Dickinson's concept of an art of forgetting:

> Knows how to forget!
> But could It teach it?
> Easiest of Arts, they say,
> When one learn how
> (Dickinson, poem no. 391)

> The art of losing isn't hard to master.
> (Bishop, "One Art")

Dickinson is one of the great writers about loss and about memory, as is Bishop.[19]

Geography in the four long North American poems includes the seasons: a February winter in "In the Waiting Room," summer flowers and vegetables in "The Moose," a remembered spring with iris "crisp and shivering" in "Poem," and now "The End of March," when the weather is unpredictable. February matters in the first poem of *Geography III,* and March in the second, where it is the last word. It has now returned. The short poems make no mention of the seasons, though a bird's note at dawn is less likely in a cold winter ("Five Flights Up"). At the end of March, April has nearly arrived with its "shores soote" (sweet showers) as in Chaucer's famous opening line to the prologue to the *Canterbury Tales.* The opening section of "The End of March," a prologue of sorts, is point by point the contrary of Chaucer's April: no sweet showers of rain but "steely mist," no Zephyrus or mild west wind with a sweet breath but a "rackety, icy, offshore wind," no small birds making melody but "seabirds in ones or twos." In April, "then longen folk to go on pilgrimages." Not here. Or is this wrong? After all, the third section begins, "I wanted to get as far as my proto-dream-house" — hardly a pilgrimage but a walk with a goal in view.

The weather is not propitious. "It was cold and windy, scarcely the day / to take a walk on that long beach." "Everything was withdrawn as far as possible, / indrawn." Nature seems to have withdrawn any favors, drawn in any breath let alone an inspiring breeze, even retracted her claws. The ocean seems "shrunken," an observation that Bishop retrieved or remembered from an early notebook of 1934. ("From the top of the cliff the sea looked settled down and shrunken" [Vassar 72.A, 4].) The wind disrupts the V of Canada geese on high and blows back the rollers in "steely mist." The walk begins along the beach with the second section and returns along the beach in the fourth section to end the poem. Both sections are twelve lines long, unrhymed, of irregular length, with much varied stress.

The tone that increasingly takes over until it names itself in the last line is "play." It grows despite the weather. Facing it, though it "numbed our faces on one side" and "froze [them] on the other side" on the return journey, especially facing it with a companion or two, offers chances for play. It begins in the outward journey, where the water was "the color of mutton-fat jade" — a pragmatic test for the reader. (Have you ever looked at the color of meat fats? Do you cook at all? What do you make of a description of nature like this?) The water *was* that color, she told Jerome Mazzaro, who thought he had found some literary echo (27 Apr. 1978, L 621). Dog prints have been enlarged by watery sand so that they look the size of lion prints. March is apparently going out like a lion, not a lamb. The beach, far from being littered with the detritus of Eliot's tour de force at the start of "The Dry Salvages," holds only one piece of flotsam, an oddity: "wet white string" very different from the "wet white string" supporting sweet-pea vines in "The Moose." There are endless lengths of it from tide line to water. A "white snarl, man-size . . . / rising on every wave, a sodden ghost / . . . sodden, giving up the ghost." "A kite string? — But no kite." Dog prints as lion prints. The string man as some embodied spirit of place, perhaps haunting it? Fancy plays with both.

The poem moves in toward the goal of the dream house in a section over twice as long as any of the three others. "I wanted to get as far as my proto-dream house, / my crypto-dream house." The compounds are worth savoring, especially because of Bishop's play, not only in their variation but also with tone. How do we read them? "Proto-" is familiar enough, but "crypto-" lives in my head as pejorative ("crypto-Jesuit," "crypto-Fascist"), although strictly it means only "secret"; the prefix "crypt-" in science simply means "hidden." The two terms play with this dream house too, in a touch of humor, much broadened in what follows. For the house is "shingled green, / a sort of an artichoke of a house, but greener / (boiled with bicarbonate of soda?)" — again, a cook's experience; that's what you do to retain the green color of some vegetables. Now, it is an outright joke — a metaphor, the house as an artichoke, hardly a real estate agent's term. It is impossible to be solemn about this dream house. All this gives a reader pause. But there is Bishop anticipating such a reaction: "(Many things about this place are dubious.)" She changed that last word from "uncertain" in the *New Yorker* to the much-stronger "dubious," strengthening the tone to "fraught with doubt or uncertainty" (OED). She is perfectly aware that she is indulging a fantasy about her dream house, but a fantasy real in many ways, including its dream of retirement.

Her persona says,

> I'd like to retire there and do *nothing,*
> or nothing much, forever, in two bare rooms:
> look through binoculars, read boring books,
> old, long, long books, and write down useless notes.

Here is a test of tone. Some readers take the word "boring" literally, but why would an ideal retirement, full of other pleasures (binoculars, observing light and water, drinking *grog à l'américaine*), include deliberate boredom? Or, to put it another way, what reader has not been enthralled with some long book that would bore someone else to tears? Take Wallace Stevens. In 1946, he found a book written in "pure Pennsylvania German, and, while it might bore anyone else to shreds it has kept me up night after night, wild with interest."[20] Regular readers have such books, including long ones they are saving for retirement. Bishop's notes are "useless" only because they are not designed for a practical purpose. Inveterate readers often make notes by habit. Critics who take "boring" literally are unlikely to savor that prefix "crypto-" or laugh at the zany humor of "boiled with bicarbonate of soda?"

Bishop had long dreamed of living in such a house. "And then I've always had a day-dream of being a lighthouse keeper, absolutely alone, with no one to interrupt my reading or just sitting — and although such dreams are sternly dismissed at about 16 or so, they always haunt one a bit, I suppose" (to Robert Lowell, 27 July 1960, L 388). In 1974, the year before this poem was published, she bought a condominium at Lewis Wharf on the Boston waterfront, where she could watch ships come and go through her binoculars. And from 1975 on, she regularly spent part of her summer on North Haven island in Maine, where she lived quietly and simply, and wrote and wrote.

On the return trip in "The End of March," play takes over, and the tone becomes happy as well as playful. The sun comes out, and its light turns the watery sand around scattered stones into prismatic colors. (Bishop worked over these lines, for example, changing "all of different colors" in the *New Yorker* version to "multi-colored," which is compact and forceful, shortens the line, and gives more emphasis.) The stones become gemstones, "set in their bezels of sand." Stones high enough "threw out long shadows." Here is another kind of play, play with shadows. When the sun goes in, there are no more shadows, as the stones "pulled them in again," drew them in, indrawn — claws, they must be. Bishop takes up her early metaphor in a virtuoso display, where the stones "could have been teasing the lion sun," who, as lion, has his own claws. The sun, however, is now behind them — the same sun who walked this beach "the last low tide," making those paw prints, "who perhaps had batted a kite out of the sky to play with."

Octavio Paz wrote an homage to Joseph Cornell, an homage that is also an ekphrasis, "Objects & Apparitions." It is the only translation Bishop ever included in one of her collections. She privately thought it was "not one of his best, but he did it by request" (to Ashley Brown, 11 June 1974, L 586). Why include it? It weights the end of *Geography III* toward art, several arts, in fact. It has an oblique relation to the other ekphrastic poem in *Geography III*, "Poem." It is not, this time, a great-niece and her unknown great-uncle united through a small painted sketch of a mutually loved scene. Here, two fellow artists in words are looking at the work of a mutually admired master artist of collages, using objects, paint, and more for his constructions. Bishop loved Cornell's work. Paz was a friend. The three-way conjunction comes happily toward the end of *Geography III*, focusing on art before the final poem.

The poem opens with "Hexahedrons of wood and glass, / scarcely bigger than a shoebox." Yet these small boxes can hold "night and all its lights." The opening word recalls Crusoe's hexagon waves and suggests that we think about Crusoe's objects and apparitions in comparison and, further, that we think of objects and apparitions throughout the collection, that we think of perspective too, of unity versus randomness, of odd connections. The world's odds and ends, refuse sometimes, are gathered here, where "things hurry away from their names" — an odd thought, and yet a poet's job is to keep us from automatically assigning easy words to objects, let alone people and situations. Think what Lewis Carroll did with things and their names in the Alice books. "Joseph Cornell," the poem ends,

"inside your boxes / my words become visible for a moment."
This is yet another use of the preposition "in": "inside" the magic
of Cornell's art.

Bishop's final poem, "Five Flights Up," grew out of some
temporary dejection: "Thanks for being so patient with my ridiculous gloom last night. Here is a wretched copy of the short sad
poem I mentioned ['Five Flights Up']. . . . It began with a
dream — a few of the first lines — about Alice's apartment" (to
Loren MacIver, 1 Jan. 1974, L 582–583). It was published a year
before "The End of March" and over two years before "One
Art," but it is what Bishop chose to end her collection. It is relatively short: four stanzas, from five to nine lines, with varying
stresses and feet.

"Five Flights Up" is a predawn-to-dawn poem, set in autumn,
with two creatures whose creaturely life once again steadies the
speaker: an "unknown bird . . . on his usual branch" and the
"little dog next door." The bird never sings in the poem, but it
"inquires / once or twice, quavering," while the dog "barks in
his sleep / inquiringly, just once." This is how someone who cannot
sleep hears these sounds from the natural world. Whatever the
inquiries, they are "answered directly, simply, / by day itself."

The oddest word in the whole poem is "ponderous" in line 1
of the second stanza: "Enormous morning, ponderous, meticulous" — enormous, yes, as light gradually suffuses the entire sky.
But when has a morning ever been ponderous? The dominant
meanings are altogether wrong: "heavy, weighty, . . . clumsy,
unwieldy" (OED 1.a). Only "slow-moving" works from this category. Bishop adds "meticulous," as "gray light" streaks every
branch and twig, making an optical illusion of another tree, a
ghost tree, with "glassy veins." And there it is, one answer to

"ponderous," an answer that matters in the memorable ending, a pun on "light": "light" as noun and "light" as adjective in the sense of weight.

Dog and bird carry on their creaturely life, the dog rebuked by its owner, "You ought to be ashamed!" For answer, the dog "bounces cheerfully" and plays "in circles in the fallen leaves," with "no sense of shame." ("Shame" is rhymed with "again" and produces the ghost rhyme of "game," just right for the dog.) The speaker ponders, marvels, and ends the poem:

> — Yesterday brought to today so lightly!
> (A yesterday I find almost impossible to lift.)

It is not "I found" but "I find," as the weight of yesterday continues. Bishop also weights this final line metrically: to my ear, it has six stresses.

As ending to Bishop's collection, this poem's closing lines have puzzled some critics. It is too easy to read into them what Bishop is at pains not to put there, the specific cause of the weight. She does not say despair or guilt or even shame. She remains reticent. I have noted the counterpoint at the core of *Geography III*, long poems of everyday life alternating with poems of a haunted interior life (guilt, war images, reflection on loss). This poem brings the two kinds of life together, restoring an everyday world with growing daylight but retaining a nearly unbearable, unnamed burden. Unlike "Anaphora," day does not arrive with Blakean exuberance. But it does arrive. If any emotion prevails at the end, it is endurance, together with a pleasure in nature's creatures. In Coleridge's *Ancient Mariner*, it is all-important for mental well-being to be able to lose oneself in another's life, including animal life. So it is here.

And what has this poem to do with geography? It is five floors up but otherwise unlocated. Yet it centers on the largest geographical phenomenon of all, the whole on which everything else depends: the earth's rotation around the sun and the sun's regular return to all regions of the earth. Geography, being a human science, would disappear if sunrise stopped.

CHAPTER NINE

Late Poems

Bishop worked steadily after *Geography III* as time permitted but had approved for publication only four poems before her death: "Santarém," "North Haven," "Pink Dog," and "Sonnet." They are quite different one from another, and they are all masterly. The first two make use of allusion, and I want to pause over this term before looking in detail at them.

Though many critics are interested in how Bishop works with memory in her poems, they are chiefly interested in memory as recollection of events. How does she translate memories of her childhood and earlier life into art? But Bishop also had a preternatural memory for words. They too were part of her memory, and her verbal memory cannot be divorced from her memory of events. One art that grows from verbal memory is the art of allusion.

Bishop liked experimenting with allusion's effects from the start. It is more marked in *North & South* than in *A Cold Spring*, returns somewhat in *Questions of Travel*, and continues through *Geography III* and the four late poems. Five of the first nine poems in *North & South*, all published when she was in her twenties, make use of allusion, but in surprisingly different ways. The allusion to T. S. Eliot's essay on Hamlet in "The Map" is so quiet that we might call it an echo. This is to follow John Hollander's very useful scale of volume in *The Figure of Echo:* quotation, allusion proper, and echo.[1] A quotation is marked as such by italics, by author or title, and so on. I would define allusion as what a likely reader would likely hear in a given time and place. Allusion can fade into echo, as time passes and a given work is no longer widely known. Allusion also fades into echo depending on the loudness of the repeated words. Do they say, "You know where I come from" (allusion), or do they whisper, "Am I perhaps familiar?" (echo). Hollander usefully suggests a scale of echo itself, from a strong allusive echo to a faint, faint echo, where we may be hearing things.

> And faint, faint, faint
> (or are you hearing things), the sandpipers'
>   heart-broken cries.
>   ("Twelfth Morning; or What You Will")

A powerful use of allusion can call up a whole other world in a most economical way. E. M. Forster, for example, titled his novel *A Passage to India,* calling up Whitman's "Passage to India." For each fresh use of allusion, we can work out the likenesses and differences. "My own thought about allusions is that if they work, they're gravy," says Mary Jo Salter.[2]

It is the third poem in *North & South,* "Casabianca," that shows such a remarkable and self-confident use of quotation, as we have seen. Tennyson's "The Lady of Shalott" is the point of departure for "The Gentleman of Shalott." In "Wading at Well-fleet," Bishop varies her technique, using a phrase in quotation marks that is not hard to find. "A case of knives," from George Herbert's "Affliction" (IV), confirms the personal tension suffusing this shoreline poem. "My thoughts are all a case of knives, / Wounding my heart / With scattered smart" (second stanza). The poem opens, "Broken in pieces all asunder," and the metaphor informs Bishop's ending ("the wheels / give way; they will not bear the weight"). She uses the same technique in "From the

Country to the City," in which Aphra Behn's unidentified phrase in quotation marks, "fantastic triumph," places the poem in a certain historic time and adds to the Harlequin-Pierrot drama. Later, a common Shakespearean stage direction in "Little Exercise" (1946) reminds a reader about genre and metaphors and perhaps at a distance about a war just ended. All these uses of allusion bring a weight of context to bear. At this stage, Bishop sidesteps historic uses of allusion, those words or phrases rebounding through poetic history, like "darkling" in Milton, Keats, and Hardy.

In Bishop's earlier poems, she prefers quotation to allusion or echo. Seven poems in *North & South* have quotations, variously deployed, while three have echoes or allusive echoes. Quoted phrases are central in "Roosters" and important in "Wading at Wellfleet," though both poems can be read to a degree without much knowledge of the actual quotations. In "The Unbeliever," the quotation from Bunyan gives Bishop her fine central metaphor and implicitly extends the context. Otherwise, she has three quiet echoes, possibly allusive, and two references, one to a fairy tale, "Hansel and Gretel" (in "Sleeping Standing Up"), and one indirectly to biblical matters (in "A Miracle for Breakfast"). In sum, there are ten uses of allusion (quotation, allusion proper, echo) in thirty poems, with a strong preference for quotation.

In the sixteen poems of *A Cold Spring*, there are two quotations, one a historical marker, the other familiar. "Over 2,000 Illustrations and a Complete Concordance," recalling travel in Mexico, remembers a jukebox that "went on playing 'Ay, Jalisco!'" (Bishop traveled with Marjorie Stevens in Mexico for eight months in 1942.) The quotation is a historical marker.[3] The second, in "At the Fishhouses," is amusing and precise: Luther's famous hymn in the Hedge translation, "A Mighty Fortress Is Our God." "The Prodigal" uses biblical reference to a well-known parable. In "Letter to N.Y.," Bishop echoes a proverbial saying about sowing wild oats, a type of allusion that brings no particular context to bear, just a general one. The possible echo of a popular song in "Insomnia" works in a similar way: "wrap up care in a cobweb" ("Wrap up your troubles in your old kit bag, and smile, smile, smile"). Bishop does little work with allusion in *A Cold Spring*.

In *Questions of Travel*, the quotation from Pascal is prominent in the title poem, while "Squatter's Children" makes use of a one-word biblical echo. Can a single word work this way? Only if it is distinctive, I think, as this one is. "Sandpiper" refers obliquely to Blake's well-known line "To see a world in a grain of sand," the opening line of *Auguries of Innocence*. "Poor bird, he is obsessed!" writes Bishop, "a student of Blake" — an allusion at one remove and smiling a little, surely. As noted already, "First Death in Nova Scotia" alludes to the popular Canadian song "The Maple Leaf Forever" and echoes language that the child has absorbed, while "Visits to St. Elizabeths" is built on the nursery rhyme "The House That Jack Built."

The most interesting use of allusion in *Questions of Travel* is in "Twelfth Morning; or What You Will," playing back against *Twelfth Night; or What You Will*. Repeating Shakespeare's subtitle indicates that Bishop wants to make sure this allusion is heard — not the ribaldry and sense of Saturnalia in *Twelfth Night*, nor the solemnity and weariness of Eliot's "Journey of the Magi," but a sense of joyful celebration for this Feast of the Three Kings. The three kings bring gifts of gold, frankincense, and myrrh, each one symbolic. Balthazar is traditionally the third king, here in the modern world as a young black boy, carrying on his head a "four-gallon can," "flashing" in the light. It contains the boy's gift: not myrrh but ordinary, everyday water, a gift essential for life.

In *Geography III*, Bishop specifically draws attention to the art of allusion in Crusoe's "'They flash upon that inward eye, / which is the bliss . . .' The bliss of what?" "Night City" allusively echoes Milton, while "The Moose" has a quiet allusive echo of Dante. Dante, Milton, Wordsworth: Bishop is moving toward well-known allusions, and she will continue this trend in two of the late poems, "Santarém" and "North Haven."

Milton's great pastoral elegy *Lycidas* is the fountainhead for elegy in English-language poetry and the best starting point for Bishop's "North Haven," which is placed in the mainstream of elegy. *Lycidas* gathers in classical and Christian traditions of mourning. It starts with the topic of returning, which lies at the center of all elegy: "Yet once more, O ye Laurels, and once more / Ye Myrtles brown, with Ivy never sere, / I come to pluck your Berries harsh and crude" — returning, or *repeat, repeat, repeat,*" as Bishop's sparrows sing.[4] That is part of the burden of elegy, the knowledge and feeling of what returns and what does not. The natural world also figures prominently in the elegy, where its patterns of return can both console and burden the mourner and where it is sometimes reproached.

The poem has three movements. First is an opening stanza in italics, separated from the rest like a prologue and setting the scene on the island of North Haven, Maine. The speaker is a persona of Bishop herself, with her far-sighted gaze. This is the place, the prologue implies, in which to utter this elegy. "The first stanza I wanted to give a feeling of an intensely quiet meditation" (to Frank Bidart, 9 July 1978, L 624). Three stanzas then focus on the island itself, including one flower stanza and one bird stanza. Then come the closing two stanzas, which move to Lowell himself.

In the second stanza comes returning, both in memory and in the natural world. The pretense that the earth might move after this death is not a seismic thought but a dreamy one. "The islands haven't shifted since last summer, / even if I like to pretend they have." Then comes the flower stanza, following the tradition of strewing the hearse with floral tributes, as in *Lycidas:* "Primrose," "Crow-Toe, and pale Jessamine," "Pink," "Pansy," "Violet," "Musk-rose," "Woodbine," Cowslips," "Daffadillies" (ll. 142–150). Bishop has placed the flowers earlier in her poem than Milton and adapted them from Shakespeare ("Daisies pied," "paint the meadows with delight," from the spring song at the end of *Love's Labour's Lost*). Archaic diction and capitalized flower names signal the presence of allusion: "Buttercups, Red Clover, Purple Vetch, / Hawkweed still burning, Daisies pied, Eyebright."

To the flower catalogue, Bishop adds a bird stanza with goldfinches and the white-throated sparrow. Milton does not include birds as part of the ritual of mourning in *Lycidas,* but Whitman, one of Milton's descendants, does in his memorable "When Lilacs Last in the Dooryard Bloom'd," deliberately choosing a North American bird, the thrush.

"The flowers & bird parts are actually the best," Bishop commented (to Bidart, 9 July 1978, L 624).

> The Goldfinches are back, or others like them,
> and the White-throated Sparrow's five-note song,
> pleading and pleading, brings tears to the eyes.
> Nature repeats herself, or almost does:
> *repeat, repeat, repeat; revise, revise, revise.*

And here, just past the midpoint, Bishop quietly and succinctly revises a tradition of elegy. The ancient "Lament for Bion" is a long tribute to a master poet:

> Ay me! when the mallows and the fresh green parsley and the springing crumpled anise perish in the garden, they live yet again and grow another year; but we men that are so tall and strong and wise, soon as ever we be dead, unhearing there in a hole of earth sleep we both sound and long.[5]

But as any gardener knows, mallows and parsley and anise don't live yet again, not the selfsame plants. Only the roots remain, except for annuals where nothing at all stays except for the seed. We usually let this go as an understandable trope, if we bother with it at all. But Bishop shows a constant faithfulness to the creaturely world in all her work. Here she revises the ancient lament three times, altering the complex genre of elegy, repeating it, yes, and revising it too. "The Goldfinches are back, or others like them," "Nature repeats herself, or almost does." Parsley repeats itself, or almost does. This is how genres like elegy change over time: *repeat, repeat, repeat; revise, revise, revise.* This is also how allusions work: we both repeat and revise. Allusion as in "Daisies pied" repeats words but revises the context.

The white-throated sparrow's song, "pleading and pleading, brings tears to the eyes." A mourner finds voice in the song — a sweet and plaintive minor third, often a harbinger of returning spring — and hears it pleading for the return of a lost friend. What is the sparrow itself pleading for? Most immediately, this is a mating song — thus the logic of the fifth stanza:

> Years ago, you told me it was here
> (in 1932?) you first "discovered *girls*"
> and learned to sail, and learned to kiss.

Both spring birdsong and Lowell's discovery of *"girls"* have to do with a world of generation, a world hard to avoid in elegy. Bishop touches on this side of Lowell's life obliquely, with the tact of true friendship. Her small scheme embodies this world too. Children *"repeat, repeat, repeat; revise, revise, revise"* their parents and grandparents — repeat, obviously, but also, and happily, revise. Nobody wants a clone for a child.

With this fifth stanza, the tone and focus change. Now come personal memories connected with this island and a personal reflection. James Merrill saw how the white-throated-sparrow stanza anticipates the ending. Lowell had compared Bishop's patience to an inchworm. Bishop also finds something in nature "whereby his [Lowell's] lifelong recyclings of earlier work come to seem not so much tortured as instinctive, part of a serene Arcadian world."[6] For the white-throated sparrow does repeat and can revise its song. Bishop's scheme mimes a six-note song, not a "five-note song," and the actual birdsong does vary in length. There is also "enough flexibility within the pattern for regional and individual variation."[7]

At the end, the white-throated sparrow's song breaks in two over the semicolon, and we see its full elegiac force. As long as bird or man is alive, the song can be changed. Once dead, song and words can only repeat in our heads, never again to be revised by the originator. No more can he himself change:

> You can't derange, or re-arrange,
> your poems again. (But the Sparrows can their song.)
> The words won't change again. Sad friend, you cannot
>   change.

The whole nub of grief and solace in elegy is caught by Bishop's simple scheme. Grief lies in the word "repeat," cut off from any revising from the dead. Yet solace also lies in the word "repeat," as elegy turns away from a nadir of grief to some form of continuing life, whether in a younger generation or in lasting work or in some continuing tradition.

Merrill saw how both these "brilliant, complex, and often self-destructive people late in life chose to depict one another as bent, like those fragile totem creatures, unambiguously upon survival. . . . What remained constant in the poets was their inability not to reach out for words. . . . Their feelings, too, of mutual protectiveness. . . . Seeing each other's best."[8]

Santarém is the name of a town on the Amazon, the town where the Tapajós and the Amazon, "two great rivers," converge. I have argued elsewhere that Bishop's poem "Santarém" is suffused with allusions to the golden streets of the New Jerusalem in the last book of the Christian Bible, the Book of Revelation or the Apocalypse. Looking at the poem this way, we can see the town becoming an iconographical painting, touching on the repeated white raiment (Rev. 4:4, 7:9, 19:8), the marriage, and even the fire and brimstone in Revelation. As in Revelation, we have come outside ordinary time to a timeless place, at least until the tour ship's whistle blows and the passengers return on board.[9]

Here I want only to add a few remarks about Bishop's opening lines and about her biblical knowledge.

Santarém seems a kind of earthly paradise, a watery *locus amoenus*. It is one of those places where you want to stay forever, as we say, or more accurately, "That golden evening I really wanted to go no farther; / more than anything else I wanted to stay awhile." A caveat precedes, for this is a memory poem: "Of course I may be remembering it all wrong / after, after — how many years?" In the port, everything looks "bright, cheerful, casual" not "awful but cheerful," as in an earlier port, but altogether

cheerful. The speaker not only liked the place. In a phrase reminiscent of Wallace Stevens, she "liked the idea of the place." A
second caveat follows, for the two rivers appropriately recall the
Garden of Eden until the speaker recalls that there were four
rivers, not two, and more important, "they'd diverged."

> Here only two
> and coming together. Even if one were tempted
> to literary interpretations
> such as: life/death, right/wrong, male/female
> — such notions would have resolved, dissolved, straight off
> in that watery, dazzling dialectic.

Again, Bishop is presenting significant questions simply and
precisely, here with a touch of colloquial language ("straight off").
Thesis and antithesis resolved in synthesis? Apparently. Even
more, the notion of thesis and antithesis would have dissolved
beforehand. The word "notion" rather than "idea" is a fine touch.

And that final word, "dialectic"? It all depends on context,
as Bishop would know. This context appears to be the older of
two dominant meanings: "a synonym of *logic* as applied to formal
rhetorical reasoning," one of the three essential advanced subjects for centuries in medieval and early Renaissance education
(grammar, rhetoric, dialectic or logic).[10] But the more modern
meaning is not absent, especially in the phrase "literary interpretations": "the art of critical examination into the truth of an
opinion" (OED, s.v. "dialectic," sub. 1.a). Bishop, I think, is having
fun and demonstrating that for all her simple diction, she too
can match literary scholars — all the more because of her adjectives, "watery, dazzling." What are the adjectives we commonly
use of dialectic? Razor-sharp, keen, impeccable. Our stereotyped
adjectives elevate the status of the noun they modify. How could

dialectic possibly be watery? Bishop forestalls any obvious pejorative use by adding "dazzling" — not solid dialectic but watery,
not a "hard" science, as we say, without reflecting that "hard" is
simply a metaphor.

This poem is further removed from Brazil in time than is
"Crusoe in England," and it brings back one of Bishop's hap-
piest moments there.[11] It stays away from the social questions and personal matters that inform virtually all of her Brazil
poems. Not that she ignores them. Those southern slaveholder
immigrants introduced *"oars"* and "no one / on all the Amazon's
four thousand miles / does anything but paddle" — a detail that
suddenly stretches out the Amazon in our mind's eye. The Catholic nuns sailing to the interior are sketched with no judgment
about their purposes. Judgment would introduce "right/wrong"
again.

Does it seem far-fetched that Bishop would allusively echo a
biblical passage and then offer further iconographical suggestions? Not at all. Bishop, like most of her generation, was familiar with the Christian Bible in the classic King James Version
of 1611 — familiar, that is, with its stories, structure, rhythms,
and a number of texts. Though she was not religious, she knew
and loved many hymns. "After an hour of W. [William Carlos
Williams]," she once wrote, "I really want to go off and read
[A. E.] Houseman [*sic*], or a hymn by [William] Cowper. — I'm
full of hymns, by the way — after church-going in Nova Scotia,
boarding-school, singing in the college choir — and I often catch
echoes of them in my own poems" (to Anne Stevenson, 8 Jan.
1964, LOA 862). As for biblical matters beyond those already
mentioned, a Vassar notebook of 1934–1935 (Vassar 72A.1) has a
passage about afflictions that bears on the quotation in "Wading
at Wellfleet" from Herbert's "Affliction." Bishop adds several

quotations from Job: "I am a brother to dragons, and a companion to owls" (Job 30:29); "My harp also is turned to mourning, and my organ into the voice of them that weep" (Job 30:31). In 1943, she wrote that she had "been reading Job on and off for ten years and always trying to 'do something' with it — from a story to an opera libretto" (to Marianne Moore, 15 July 1943, L 113).

"Pink Dog" is a very different Brazil poem, an allegory and a social protest poem in one. If "Santarém" catches the idyllic sense of Bishop's Brazil, "Pink Dog" joins poems like "Squatter's Children" and "The Armadillo" as indirect protest. It was begun in 1963 under the title "Goodbye to Rio" (LOA 919). (Bishop by 1963 was living in the Rio apartment and doubtless longing to be back in the hills above Rio.) The dog is pink because it has lost its coat to disease, scabies, not rabies, for there is no sign of madness. Nonetheless it is in danger from ignorant and fearful passersby. After all, beggars who are "idiots, paralytics, parasites" are now being tossed into tidal rivers to drown. The solution is to don a Carnival costume and dance, dance:

wear a fantasia.*

Tonight you simply can't afford to be a-
n eyesore. But no one will ever see a

dog in máscara this time of year.

A footnote translates "fantasia" as "Carnival costume." Bishop's play with enjambment carries on from "Arrival at Santos," but here it is in the transgressive spirit of Carnaval. For the walk over the end of the line, the root meaning of enjambment, divides a two-letter word. Bishop needs an *a* rhyme for her *aaa* tercet, and here is an "a" — well, an "an" anyway. The walk becomes the blink of an eye, a brief possibility of a word starting with a consonant, a sudden adaptation of sound, an end word that is an eyesore of a kind, a disguise of sorts. Come, join me in Carnival, Bishop suggests to the reader, and dance along, remembering all the while murderous attacks on "idiots, paralytics, parasites," "anyone who begs, / drugged, drunk, or sober." The play with Miss Breen is all of a piece with "Arrival at Santos." This poem's tone is very mixed, appropriately for a poem of mixed genres.

"I have a rather ghastly Carnival poem that will be in the *New Yorker* at Carnival time," Bishop wrote to Ashley Brown. "It may turn out to be one of a group about Brazil." Then, a bit later, she writes, "Well, I meant my Carnival poem was 'ghastly' as to subject matter — not such a bad poem! — I have two or three more equally 'ghastly' I feel I must publish some time" (8 Jan. and 1 Mar. 1979, L 629, 632).

"Sonnet" radically revises a form in a bravura display of mastery of the short line. The wonder of it is how much substance Bishop can incorporate in a poem of two sentences and forty words. It was the last poem that she approved for publication and appeared posthumously in October 1979. The title "Sonnet" takes its place with all those titles using genres or forms or schemes: "Anaphora," "Letter to N.Y.," "Sestina," "Poem." It links Bishop's last poem with her first, "The Map," in which two stanzas work with a sonnet octave, and it draws attention to her adaptation of the sonnet form all through her work. This sonnet is a tour de force, using Bishop's command of the short line to write fourteen two-beat lines. Octave and sestet are reversed. Each consists of one sentence that opens with a single word and a dash: "Caught —"; "Freed —" The poem plays with "mercury" (quicksilver) running free from "the broken thermometer." "The empty mirror" follows. Mirrors used to be manufactured by applying an amalgam of quicksilver and tin, before the dangers of mercury poisoning were understood (OED, s.v. "quicksilver," vb.). An empty mirror reflects nothing. Bishop leaves it to us to decide if it reflects no creature or nothing whatever. Its narrow bevel, however, is intact so that in the sun it casts a prism of rainbow colors, a "rainbow bird."[12]

Under "Caught," the poem gathers up all Bishop's uses of "divided" and "undivided," her uses of the compass needle, and the wobbling of the compass needle between true north and magnetic north. Under "Freed," the octave gathers up all the mirror poems through her work. The rainbow bird like the quicksilver is freed, "flying wherever/it feels like, gay!" The terminal word, "gay," with an exclamation mark is freed here to bear both its meanings.

The four distinct late poems remain deeply satisfying, not only in themselves but also in the way each one gathers in Bishop's earlier work and extends it.

Conclusion

Bishop died quite suddenly and unexpectedly of a cerebral aneurysm on October 6, 1979, age sixty-eight. She was preparing to go out for dinner and had been occupied with her usual tasks throughout the day. She wrote and posted a letter about footnotes to poems, for example (to John Frederick Nims, L 638). Her shocked friends and colleagues arranged for a memorial service at Harvard on October 21 and contributed in varied and moving ways. The service appropriately included six hymns, including the one in "At the Fishhouses," Luther's "A Mighty Fortress Is Our God." Harvard's Poetry Room has now made available online a recording of the service itself (http://hcl /harvard.edu/poetryroom/listeningbooth/poets/Bishop.cfm).

Our first and abiding reaction is likely to be the pity of this comparatively early death, coming when Bishop was writing steadily, each poem a small masterpiece. The service at Harvard took this for granted and did not dwell on it. In Alice Methfessel's opening tribute, she read from one of Bishop's favorite authors, Sydney Smith, who in 1820 wrote a letter on ways to combat melancholia or low spirits — the "only sensible advice she [Bishop] had ever heard." Among the prescriptions are "Take short views of life," "Be as busy as you can," "Live as well as you dare," "Make no secret of your low spirits to your friends," "Compare your lot with that of others," "Be as much as you can in the open air without fatigue," "Don't expect too much of life, a sorry business at the best." Bishop wrote in 1962 that she couldn't think of "any more cheering reading, really [than Smith's letters]," and she would "go through them regularly two or three times a year — even if he is so anti-poetic" (to Robert Lowell, 8 Oct. 1962, LEBRL 420). It was a fine reminder of the very practical side of Bishop, who knew life on a farm as a child, who loved to cook, who was a good sailor, and who put all these things into her poems. It was also an indirect reminder of what she struggled with intermittently throughout her life. It was especially a reminder of Bishop's courage as a survivor.

Robert Fitzgerald spoke of Bishop's "long perspectives" and how within them she "pinpointed actual things." "The world to her was our experience of it, and what we experienced were particulars." He added that these particulars "very often amused her." His illustration was Bishop's amused phone call about a wild-eyed man rushing into a gift shop where she was on Christmas Eve, demanding, "Have you got any of those goddamned tags?" She "loved the oddities and beauties among things seen and heard." One of the oddities was the incident that ends "Santarém." The speaker, returning to her ship with an exquisitely shaped wasps' nest, a gift, a talisman from this idyllic place, meets a fellow passenger, Mr. Swan. He is Dutch, a retiring CEO, and "really a very nice old man, / who wanted to see the Amazon before he died." He asks, "What's that ugly thing?" and there the poem ends. When a literary critic became overingenious, Bishop corrected him: " 'Santarém' *happened*, just like that, a real evening & a real place, and a real Mr. Swan who said that — it is not a composite at all" (to Jerome Mazzaro, 27 Apr. 1978, L 621). As for ending her poem with the incident, Bishop has already written an appropriate ending at the start of "Santarém," with reflections on dialectics and dualism. This ending, bringing us back to earth abruptly, seems to say like the grandparents in "The Moose," "Life's like that." Fitzgerald concluded that when these particulars, including oddities and beauties, became part of a poem, they were "subject to a serene order."

Robert Giroux testified to Bishop's interest in all aspects of production, not only typography but also bindings and dust jackets. Anne Hussey read "Twelfth Night; or What You Will," commenting that it was "almost like reading a painting." Helen Vendler read Herbert's "Love Unknown." Among those who were listed by Penelope Laurans as attending were two young poets, J. D. McClatchy and Gjertrud Schnackenberg.[1]

Of the poems read at Bishop's memorial, only one was not from her last two collections and late poems, and it was un-scheduled. John Ashbery, who was to read "Manners," came late (as the recording makes clear) and read "A Miracle for Break-fast," which he chose for personal reasons. Otherwise the selected poems were "Manners" (read by Robert Fitzgerald), "Twelfth Morning; or What You Will," "The Moose," "Objects & Appa-ritions" (read in Spanish by Octavio Paz and then in English), and "Sonnet." There is good reason for these choices, as I hope this study has made clear. For Bishop really came into her own with the poems of *Questions of Travel,* as these choices tacitly acknowledge. The sense of constraint in some of her earlier work vanishes, her poetic voice becomes more confident, her generic repertoire increases, and a growing sense of freedom is evident.

In the thirty poems of *North & South,* no form of the word "free" appears at all. By contrast it comes to the fore in *A Cold Spring,* notably in the 1947 poem "At the Fishhouses," where the sea is "icily free," "utterly free." The imagined flame of the Nativity scene in "Over 2,000 Illustrations and a Complete Concordance" is "freely fed on straw." In "Faustina, or Rock Roses" also from 1947, possible "freedom" is contrasted with a possible "worst . . . unimaginable nightmare." Birds are twice associated with freedom: "thousands of light song-sparrow songs floating upward / freely, dispassionately, through the mist" in "Cape Breton" and the release of love "freeing, I think, about a million birds" in "Rain towards Morning" (part 2, "Four Poems"). Five of sixteen poems written from 1947 to 1951 are considering what it is to be free, including the apparent freedom of the natural world and its song.

From this point on, there are only two examples in Bishop's collected poems, one in *Questions of Travel* and one in *Geography III*. Both are striking in their implications and both come with a sense of authority. It is as if Bishop had thought through questions of freedom and was now ready to translate her conclusions into action. Her own best field of action was writing poetry. (In practical and personal terms, she also had a new freedom to write, thanks to the security Lota gave her in Brazil for over ten years.) The example from *Questions of Travel* is in the title poem (1956) where the concluding stanza begins: "*Continent, city, country, society: / the choice is never wide and never free.*" In "Poem" (1972) from *Geography III*, the small painting is "useless and free," a weighted phrase that is really only completed toward the end in the memorable line "the little that we get for free." The effect is of a writer summing up in words of wisdom. In "North Haven" (1978), the first stanza plays with the fancy that islands in the bay can move around, "free within the blue frontiers of bay."

Then comes the posthumous poem "Sonnet" (1979). Bishop cast a wide net over the years: matters of freedom occur in the context of nature (sea, birds), otherworldly scenes (the Nativity), and art. They are also important in the context of human constraint ("Faustina"), love ("Rain towards Morning"), and choice ("Questions of Travel"). In its fourteen short lines, "Sonnet" touches on most of these contexts, an astonishing breadth of intimation.

As she developed in her art, Bishop's growing sense of freedom included her sense of play. It came naturally to her, given her innate sense of humor, though it must have needed releasing because it is more apparent in her mature poetry. There is plenty of wit in the earlier work, but it is play that breaks out in "Arrival at Santos" and "Miss Breen's // skirt!" — Miss Breen, who comes from "Glens Fall // s, New York. There. We are settled." The technical bravado is sheer fun in itself and also doing something more. It is offering us mimesis in both senses, description plus miming. I think it is the first instance of Bishop conversing with her readers, telling us indirectly how to read her poems. What else is the double high-wire act with Miss Breen doing than pointing to the way enjambment works? A boat hook catches a skirt in that airy space between stanzas. We can visualize it flying over, before it's released. Similarly we can visualize the falls as they cascade into the following stanza. I called this mischievous, and so it is; but it also says to the reader, "Now you see what can be done with enjambment, so you might pay some attention in the future. Now you see how to mime action in a poem." Some twenty-five years later, Bishop offers a similar display of dark Carnival high jinks in "Pink Dog."

The fence in "Twelfth Morning; or What You Will" is doing something similar with an added effect:

The fence . . .
          comes hopefully
across the lots; thinks better of it, turns
a sort of corner . . .
(final ellipsis in original)

A personified fence walks the lines this time, but then we do commonly say, "The fence comes . . ." It "turns / a sort of corner," and there the reader is, turning the end of the line to the next one, turning a corner of sorts. The fence, being "three-strand, barbed-wire" is then described as "three dotted lines," thereby also drawing attention to the closing ellipsis. So it is that we also come to pay attention to ellipses in Bishop's work, and she is fond of them. We also learn to pay attention to the look of poems on the page.

Those repeated uses of "in" at the start of *Geography III* also converse with the reader, saying, "Have you thought about prepositions? They're worth watching, unimportant though they may seem." In "Crusoe in England," allusion calls attention to the workings of memory that make it possible ("The bliss of what?") and thereby to the way it functions. I have used the verb "converse" more than "teach," because I do not think Bishop had a strong didactic bent. In her letters, she converses with friends, and these examples are as much conversation as teaching.

In diction too, where this study began, there is an overt invitation to watch Bishop at her desk, when second thoughts are incorporated in a poem: "Our visions coincided — 'visions' is / too serious a word" ("Poem"). The enjambment makes us pause for just a moment: "'visions' is" — what? Bishop's play with diction at the beginning of "Santarém" is sheer fun and serious as well ("Even if one were tempted / to literary interpretations / such as: life/death" etc.). Bishop is playing with critics a little, as I think she is playing with them in "Crusoe in England." Consider her use of scale, so prominent in *Geography III*, as noted. Critics quite often observe it, sometimes adding portentous remarks. Crusoe prepares us for scale, since his landscape is weirdly out of proportion. And after all, his home-made flute plays "the weirdest scale on earth" — which I read as a deliberate pun. As so often, Bishop is out in front of her critics, waiting ahead as Whitman was and is.

In Fitzgerald's phrase about the messy particulars of experience being subject to a "serene order" in Bishop's poems, the word "order" subsumes a good deal. It means all the discipline that governs the shaping of a good poem, the ordering of diction, rhythm, all the subjects treated here. Latin *serenus,* "clear, bright, serene," is the root of the English adjective and is just right. It is not that the subject or the emotions evoked are serene but that these are ordered, shaped, made bearable (if they are difficult), enhanced (if they are happy). Fitzgerald is not denying the Bishop who read Sydney Smith to combat low spirits. He is saying that in her art, this was how she was.

Something else is evident in the memorial tributes to Bishop: her gift for friendship and her great generosity of spirit. Vendler remarked on her kindness to younger writers. As Richard Wilbur said, in a tribute for the American Academy of Arts and Letters, "She attended to her art, but she also attended to other people and to the things of every day."[2] I think of it in relation to the poems too. Bishop's mature poems breathe a generous spirit, much as George Herbert's do. Her desire was to remain "new, tender, quick," in her responses, like Herbert's chastened and revived heart at the end of "Love Unknown." She kept in mind not only the ideal of being "new, tender, quick" but also the process of chastening, and chastening for herself, not just for others. The counterpoint of long, everyday narrative poems and shorter chastening poems in *Geography III* embodies this pattern.

Bishop had a "lifelong sense of dislocation," as Wilbur put it, which meant that her mapping instinct and acute sense of place remained throughout her life ("Elizabeth Bishop," 263). They are evident in *Geography III* and the late poem "Santarém." It also meant that she cherished the idea of home, "wherever that may be." A number of her last fourteen poems claim the world as home fully, if never permanently: the joy felt at large in "The Moose," the sense of "our abidance, / the little that we get for free" in "Poem," the golden evening in "Santarém," the freedom in "Sonnet." "The End of March" claims its world more than any other seashore poem. Despite cold and wind and a shrunken ocean, the lion trope comes to life as a lion-sun who played with a gigantic kite. The poem ends, "to play with," the tone is joyful, the action all part of our abidance, and the reclaiming of a sea-shore world by the play of poetry is complete. Though it was an accident that "Sonnet" was Bishop's last published poem, it seems fitting that it contrasts "Caught," then "Freed." The sense of freedom seems to me to increase yet further with these last fourteen poems — a sense of personal freedom, yes, and as always an awareness of the need of political and social freedom, as in "Pink Dog" and "12 O'Clock News." But most of all, the freedom that comes with mastery of an art, a hard-won freedom.

Notes

INTRODUCTION

1 See Chapter 4, "Diction on the Move."

2 Robert Lowell, "For Elizabeth Bishop 4," in *History* (New York: Farrar, Straus and Giroux, 1973), 198.

3 The total is complicated by poems that Bishop collected and then cut from later editions. Only a handful were published and not collected.

4 Jay Macpherson, *Welcoming Disaster,* in *Poems Twice Told* (Toronto: Oxford University Press, 1981).

5 The first version reads, "I believe I have been strongly feminist since the age of six, however, I also believe art is art, and no matter how great a part these ineluctable facts play in its creation, the ages, races and sexes should not be segregated." Then she revised it ("I didn't say it right the first time"). To Ms. Joan Keefe, 8 June 1977, NYPL: FSG, Box 547.

6 David Kalstone, *Becoming a Poet: Elizabeth Bishop, with Marianne Moore and Robert Lowell,* ed. Robert Hemenway (Ann Arbor: University of Michigan Press, 1989), 220.

7 Herbert Marks, "Elizabeth Bishop's Art of Memory," *Literary Imagination* 7 (2005): 197.

8 Elizabeth Bishop, in "Influences," ed. Henri Cole, *American Poetry Review* 14, no. 1 (1985): 15.

9 Randall Jarrell, in his 1955 *Harper's* survey of poetry, collected in his *Third Book of Criticism* (New York: Farrar, Straus and Giroux, 1969).

10 For an excellent account of Bishop's wide knowledge of, and use of, visual art, see Peggy Samuels, *Deep Skin: Elizabeth Bishop and Visual Art* (Ithaca, NY: Cornell University Press, 2010).

11 Quoted in Craig Watson, "'The Mystery of the World': On the Criticism of Fairfield Porter," *Yale Review* 100, no. 4 (2012): 73.

12 "Elizabeth Bishop," in *Poets at Work: The Paris Review Interviews,* ed. George Plimpton (New York: Penguin, 1989), 376.

13 Edward Hirsch quotes Malebranche in his fine book *How to Read a Poem and Fall in Love with Poetry* (New York: Harcourt, 1999), 1: "Attentiveness is the natural prayer of the soul."

14 Jerry Brotton, *A History of the World in Twelve Maps* (New York: Penguin, 2014), 265.

15 E. H. Gombrich, *Art and Illusion: A Study in the Psychology of Pictorial Representation*, Bollingen Series 35 (Princeton, NJ: Princeton University Press, 1960).

16 Randall Jarrell, review of *North & South*, in *Poetry and the Age* (New York: Farrar, Straus and Giroux, 1953), 235.

I. LAND, WATER, FIRE, AIR

1 See the standard handbook by Charles F. Chapman, *Piloting, Seamanship, and Small Boat Handling* (New York: Motor Boating, 1922).

2 Victoria Harrison, *Elizabeth Bishop's Poetics of Intimacy* (Cambridge: Cambridge University Press, 1993), 268.

3 In letters of 1946 and 1951, for example, Bishop mentions Sable Island as the place where Hutchinson's ship sank; Sable Island is known as "the graveyard of the Atlantic." To Marianne Moore, 29 Aug. 1946, L 139; also to Robert Lowell, 11 July 1951, L 221. Later, she corrected this to Cape Sable, the southernmost tip of Nova Scotia. "My great-grandfather & his ship & all hands went down in a famous storm off Cape Sable — not the Island, the cape." To Philip Booth, 5 Feb. 1973, Vassar 25.1. Sandra Barry pointed out to me that oral memory is at work here.

4 Gary Fountain and Peter Brazeau, *Remembering Elizabeth Bishop: An Oral Biography* (Amherst: University of Massachusetts Press, 1994), 30.

5 "Travel Diary to Newfoundland," 1932, MS and TS, Vassar 77.1, TS, 2.

6 Fountain and Brazeau, *Remembering Elizabeth Bishop*, 44. Robert Fitzgerald is said to have remembered Bishop saying to him that she would have been a sailor if she had been born a boy (ibid., 1).

7 The compass rose inlaid in the ground floor of the main Vassar Library, the Frederick Ferris Thompson Library (1903), was covered by carpeting about 1998. It was a blue-and-gray mosaic, about four feet in diameter. I owe these details to Dean Rogers's memory. To date,

the Vassar historian does not know whether it was part of the original floor.

8   A letter to Marianne Moore on 25 Jan. 1935 (L 29–30) comments on Moore's introduction to Bishop's poems in *Trial Balances;* presumably Moore had a copy of "The Map" by then.

9   Quoted in Craig Watson, "'The Mystery of the Word': On the Criticism of Fairfield Porter," *Yale Review* 100, no. 4 (2012): 73.

10 Helen Vendler, "Elizabeth Bishop," in *The Music of What Happens: Poems, Poets, Critics* (Cambridge, MA: Harvard University Press, 1988), 298. Vendler was one of Bishop's earliest and most appreciative critics.

11 T. S. Eliot, "Hamlet" (1932), in *Selected Essays,* 3rd ed. (London: Faber and Faber, 1951), 145. Bishop's use of "Tradition and the Individual Talent" in her student essay "Dimensions for a Novel" (1934, LOA 671–680) demonstrates how clearly she read his criticism; see Bonnie Costello, "Elizabeth Bishop's Impersonal Personal," *American Literary History* 15 (2003): 342.

12 See Isaiah 40:12, 15: "Who hath measured the waters in the hollow of his hand . . . behold, he taketh up the isles as a very little thing." On the *deus artifex,* see Ernst Robert Curtius, *European Literature and the Latin Middle Ages,* trans. Willard R. Trask, Bollingen Series (Princeton, NJ: Princeton University Press, 1953), 544–546.

13 The quotations are from Milton, *Comus,* l. 21; the hymn "O Worship the King" by Sir Robert Grant (1779–1838); Arnold, "Dover Beach"; Melville, *Moby-Dick,* the last sentence of the last chapter before the epilogue; Stevens, "The Idea of Order at Key West," *Alcestis* 1 (Oct. 1934).

14 T. S. Eliot, "The Dry Salvages," l. 30, by another poet who was also a sailor.

15 "Elizabeth Bishop — swan boat or/Amazon steamer? Neither: a Dream Boat." James Merrill, "Her Craft," in Schwartz and Estess 241.

16 Certain diction, said Dante, is smooth rather than shaggy *(De vulgari eloquentia).* Hamlet directs the players, "in the very torrent, tempest, and, as I may say, whirlwind of your passion, you must acquire and beget a temperance that may give it smoothness" (3.2.6–8).

17 D. W. Prowse, *A History of Newfoundland from the English, Colonial and Foreign Records* (1895), facsimile of the first edition (Belleville,

ON: Mika Studio, 1972), 607. Bishop found this book very interesting and bought a copy when in Newfoundland in 1932.

18   That is why Bishop speaks of the English government's help in the
Depression. "The Government Fisheries are here. Newfoundland
pays half, and England pays half" (Vassar 77.1, TS, 3).

19   *The Canadian Encyclopedia*, s.v. "Labrador" (by James H. Marsh, revised
3/4/15), www.thecanadianencyclopedia.ca. Labrador was transferred
by statute to Québec in 1774, then reannexed to Newfoundland in
1809. The 1927 decision in favor of Newfoundland was made by the
British Judicial Committee of the Privy Council.

20   The line elicits some astonishing remarks by literary critics about history and historians, as if they had never read any good history or
given a moment's thought to the art and discipline of writing history
or as if they had never observed that Bishop is talking here about "historians," not about "history" as the march of events. John Ashbery is
naturally an exception; see his "Second Presentation of Elizabeth
Bishop," *World Literature Today* 51 (1977): 8–11.

21   Interview with Alexandra Johnson, in *Conversations with Elizabeth
Bishop*, ed. George Monteiro (Jackson: University Press of Missis-
sippi, 1996), 101.

22   David Kalstone, *Becoming a Poet: Elizabeth Bishop with Marianne
Moore and Robert Lowell* (New York: Farrar, Straus and Giroux, 1989),
220.

23   EAP 155, just before "A mother made of dress-goods . . ."; for the
various drafts, see EAP 346–347.

24   Mark Ford hears in lines 4 to 8 of "The Map" a contrast, the "maternal
land" leaning down and lifting a garment quite unperturbed. Mark
Ford, "Elizabeth Bishop at the Water's Edge," *Essays in Criticism* 53
(2003): 245. Jonathan Ellis notes the connection of "yard-goods" with
memories of Bishop's mother. Jonathan Ellis, *Art and Memory in the
Work of Elizabeth Bishop* (Aldershot, UK: Ashgate, 2006), 66.

25   "Recorded Observations, under 'Cuttyhunk, July 1934,'" Vassar 72A.3.
According to Robert Seaver's sister, who stresses her brother's deep
attachment and her own expectation of an engagement, Bishop told
him before leaving for Paris in July 1935 that she would never marry

anyone. Fountain and Brazeau, *Remembering Elizabeth Bishop*, 44–47, 64, 67–68.

26 See interview with Frank Bidart in Fountain and Brazeau, *Remembering Elizabeth Bishop*, 70.

27 Victoria Glendinning, *Edith Sitwell: A Unicorn among Lions* (London: Weidenfeld and Nicolson, 1981), 29.

28 Rex Stout, *Please Pass the Guilt* (New York: Viking, 1973), 114.

29 Richard D. Beard, "Introducing Elizabeth Bishop," *Times Literary Supplement*, 25 Mar. 2011. See also the fragment, c. 1937, on prose as land transportation, music as sea transportation, and poetry as air transportation (EAP 31). In "Efforts of Affection: A Memoir of Marianne Moore," Bishop changes her image "from air to water" to evoke Moore's presence (LOA 484, c. 1969). The elements matter in a number of poems.

30 The story later provided the hinge between the two sections of her 1965 collection *Questions of Travel*, titled "Brazil" and "Elsewhere." Happily the 2008 Library of America edition reprinted the story as in 1965.

31 William H. Pritchard, "Bishop's Time," *Hudson Review* 61 (2008): 321–334. (I would confine this tendency to the earlier poems.)

2. ELIZABETH BISHOP'S ORDINARY DICTION — YES, *BUT* . . .

Epigraph: From "Writing poetry is an unnatural act . . . ," late 1950s–early 1960s, LOA 702–706.

1 Cf. Donald Davie, *Purity of Diction in English Verse* (1952; repr., Manchester, UK: Carcanet, 2006), chap. 5, "The Classicism of Charles Wesley."

2 As Davie and others have observed, the *religious* effect of poorly written hymns may be considerable and is not to be scorned per se (ibid.).

3 To Robert Lowell, 27 July 1960 (LEBRL 334). But, she added, "as Lota says, it's still better than the lower cliché."

4 David Kalstone, *Becoming a Poet: Elizabeth Bishop with Marianne Moore and Robert Lowell* (New York: Farrar, Straus and Giroux, 1989), 99 (quoting Moore).

5 To Ilse and Kit Barker, 22 Jan. 1979, Barker letters. But in a letter of 26 Dec. 1975 to James Merrill, Bishop says, "I . . . shall have to wait

until I get to my big OED in Boston for some of them [words re: plants]" (Vassar 33.4). Is "my big OED" the Shorter Oxford?

6   *Dictionary of Newfoundland English*, 2nd ed., ed. G. M. Story, W. J. Kirwin, and J. D. A. Widdowson (Toronto: University of Toronto Press, 1990), s.v. "pinnacle," defs. 1 and 2, which cites the *National Geographic* for July 1929 (108): "The captain sends men overboard to cut pinnacle ice." See also s.v. "ice-pinnacle."

7   NYPL: FSG, Box 31, File 1970–80, General Correspondence (2 of 2).

8   NYPL: FSG, Box 31, File 1967–76: *Complete Poems*.

9   Francis Sparshott, *The Theory of the Arts* (Princeton, NJ: Princeton University Press, 1982), 540n51.

10 The first date given in the OED is 1922 in a United States scientific study, where the word is in quotation marks. The 1931 *American Tramp and Underworld Slang* listed it, Auden used it as a noun in 1932, and the *Listener* said in 1937 that "queer" in the sense of "homosexual" was a usage imported from the United States.

11 NYPL: FSG, Author Files, file 546.12.

12 Jay Macpherson, "Isis," in *The Boatman* (Toronto: Oxford University Press, 1957).

13 Vassar notebook 72A.3 copies some of the mnemonics on p. 17. The quotation from "The Sea and Its Shore," which is not identified in the LOA edition (578), begins, "The habit of perusing periodical works" and is drawn from chapter 3 of *Biographia Literaria*.

14 10 Feb. 1954, Swenson-Bishop letters. See also Bishop to Swenson, 25 Jan. 1954, ibid.

3. ON THE MOVE

1   See letters of 1 Nov. 1937, 22 Mar. 1938, 26 Feb. 1939, and 13 Mar. 1939 in the New Directions Publishing Corp. Records, bMS Am 2077 189, Houghton Library, Harvard University, Cambridge, MA.

2   For a detailed account of when and where many of the poems were written, as recalled in 1963, see Bishop's letter to Anne Stevenson, 20 Mar. 1963, LOA 843–844; for publication details, see MacMahon.

3   Bishop to Michael di Capra, 5 Feb. 1969, NYPL: FSG, Box 31, file 1967–76.

4   It is tempting to cast Bishop herself as Pierrot or rather Pierrot as a part of her. When May Swenson quoted from *The Selected Writings of the Ingenious Aphra Behn*, Bishop replied, "I have that book on Aphra Behn, too — and I also have the Sackville-West biography. . . . She was the 1st woman to earn her living by writing, you know, so we should all look up to her very much — maybe she was the last, too?" 16 Mar. 1954, Swenson-Bishop letters.

5   Robert Lowell, "From an Interview" (1961), Schwartz and Estess 197. Kafka's *Metamorphosis* was published in 1915. Bishop greatly admired him; she read *The Castle* "long before" writing her 1938 "In Prison." To Robert Lowell, 31 Jan. 1949, LEBRL 85. See also letter to Anne Stevenson, 8 Jan. 1964, LOA 864, on Kafka's humor.

6   For Bishop's 1956 review of an edition of Laforgue's "The Manipulation of Mirrors," see LOA 693–698. Her knowledge and admiration are clear.

7   Ashley Brown, "An Interview with Elizabeth Bishop," Schwartz and Estess 297.

8   Oscar Wilde, *Letters and Essays*, vol. 3, *Oscar Wilde* (London: Folio, 1993), 130.

9   A reader for Harvard University Press mentioned "three sheets to the wind" as apropos: yes, indeed.

10 The LOA edition of the poem glosses the epigraph by quoting from *The Life and Death of Mr. Badman* but erroneously attributes it to *Pilgrim's Progress* (LOA 933).

11 EAP 263. See also her letter to Anne Stevenson, 18 Mar. 1963, LOA 842.

12 David Bromwich, *Skeptical Music* (Chicago: University of Chicago Press, 2001), 117–120. Bonnie Costello has some very helpful remarks on surrealism, frottage and "The Monument" in her *Elizabeth Bishop: Questions of Memory* (Cambridge, MA: Harvard University Press, 1991), 26–28, 218–223. See also Zachariah Pickard's chapter "Surrealism," in *Elizabeth Bishop's Poetics of Description* (Montreal: McGill-Queen's University Press, 2009), 38–57.

13 Samuel Hynes, *The Auden Generation: Literature and Politics in the 1930s* (1972; repr., Princeton, NJ: Princeton University Press, 1976), 193.

14   Eleanor Cook, *Against Coercion: Games Poets Play* (Stanford, CA: Stanford University Press, 1998), 44–50.

15   For Bishop, "one French literature course, 16th–18th centuries, and maybe something in Art" (to Frani Blough, 20 Oct. 1935, L 37). In the winter, she underwent surgery for mastoid, at the time a dangerous condition (to Marianne Moore, 4 Feb. 1936, L 38–39).

16   Wallace Stevens, postcard, 1909, in Holly Stevens, *Souvenirs and Prophecies: The Young Wallace Stevens* (New York: Knopf, 1977), 246.

17   In French, an accent on a capital letter is optional, and Bishop has chosen to omit it here, as I have for the sake of consistency. "Etoile" and "Étoile" are equally correct.

18   *Fodor's Around Paris with Kids,* 3rd ed. (New York: Random House, 2008), 67.

19   John Lehmann, *The Whispering Gallery,* quoted in Samuel Hynes, *The Auden Generation* (New York: Random House 2011), 176.

20   20 Nov. 1935, NYPL: Berg, Muriel Rukeyser Papers.

21   31 Aug. 1936, ibid. See Marit J. MacArthur's excellent background article "'In a Room': Elizabeth Bishop in Europe, 1935–1937," *Texas Studies in Literature and Language* 50 (2008): 408–442. See also Linda R. Anderson, "A Window into Europe," chapter 2 in *Elizabeth Bishop: Lines of Connection* (Edinburgh: Edinburgh University Press, 2013), especially the opening on Bishop's voyage across the Atlantic in 1935.

22   William Maxwell, *So Long, See You Tomorrow* (1979), in *Later Novels and Stories* (New York: Library of America, 2008), 515.

23   In 1934, Bishop contributed a short piece on a neighbor to the *New Yorker's* "Talk of the Town" (10 Nov. 1934, 15). The next item, "War Birds," was an account of "the pigeon branch of the U.S. Signal Corps" and two carrier pigeons with "citations from the War Department for heroic work in France." The more famous was Cher Ami: he "flew forty kilometers in the Argonne in October, 1918, with one leg shot off and a hole in its breast, carrying a message from Major Whitney's Lost Battalion, which was being shelled by its own artillery."

24   W. H. Auden, "Petition," *Collected Shorter Poems* 1930–1944 (London: Faber and Faber, 1950), 120.

25 Chandler S. Robbins, Bertel Bruun, and Herbert S. Zim, *Birds of North America: A Guide to Field Identification* (New York: Golden Press, 1966), 268.

26 For the way that "tiers and tiers of immaculate reflections" evokes Dante's *Paradiso,* see my *Against Coercion,* 178–179.

27 The Latin word for an inhabitant of what is now French territory, Gaul, was *Gallus,* while the Latin for "cock" is *gallus.* The pun makes the *coq gaulois* an obvious symbol.

28 David Kalstone, *Becoming a Poet: Elizabeth Bishop with Marianne Moore and Robert Lowell* (New York: Farrar, Straus and Giroux, 1989), 82.

29 Jessica Weare, "Anaphora," in *Princeton Encyclopedia of Poetry and Poetics,* 4th ed., ed. Roland Greene (Princeton, NJ: Princeton University Press, 2012).

30 Emily Dickinson, "A Guest in this stupendous place," no. 304; "The Infinite a sudden Guest," no. 1344, in *The Poems of Emily Dickinson,* ed. R. W. Franklin (Cambridge, MA: Harvard University Press, 1999).

4. DICTION ON THE MOVE

1 Alan Ansen, *The Table Talk of W. H. Auden,* ed. Nicholas Jenkins (New York: Sea Cliff, 1989), 50–51 (23 Apr. 1947); emphasis added.

2 W. H. Auden, introduction to *Nineteenth-Century British Minor Poets,* ed. W. H. Auden (New York: Dell, 1966), 23.

3 W. H. Auden, "An Appreciation of the Lyric Verse of Walter de la Mare," in *Prose,* vol. 4, ed. Edward Mendelson (Princeton, NJ: Princeton University Press, 2010), 8. Bishop reviewed the new edition of this 1923 book in 1958 (LOA 698–701).

4 Ashley Brown, "An Interview with Elizabeth Bishop" (c. 1965), Schwartz and Estess 292.

5 Elise Partridge, "A Dipody in a Billabong: Studying Prosody with Robert Fitzgerald," *Literary Imagination* 13 (2011): 278–282.

6 Elizabeth Bishop, in "Influences," ed. Henri Cole, *American Poetry Review* 14, no. 1 (1985): 13.

7 "Editor & Author: Jonathan Galassi and Gjertrud Schnackenberg," Work in Progress (FSG), Jan. 2001, http://www.fsgworkinprogress.com/2011/01.

8   Robert Pinsky, "The Idiom of a Self: Elizabeth Bishop and Wordsworth" (1980), Schwartz and Estess 49.

9   "There is an essay to be written on de la Mare's metrical fingering, in particular, his use of the spondee." Auden, "Appreciation," 35. Auden surmised that he learned much of his metrical skill, including the use of the spondee, from Christina Rossetti. There are hardly any essays on de la Mare listed in T. V. F. Brogan's indispensable annotated bibliography, *English Versification, 1570–1980* (Baltimore: Johns Hopkins University Press, 1981), but one by Robert M. Pierson observes that in de la Mare's eerie poem "The Listeners," the even lines are much stricter metrically than the odd lines, while the passages on the Traveller are wilder metrically. Brogan, *English Versification,* E846.

10   See Gerard Manley Hopkins to Robert Bridges on "Spelt from Sybil's Leaves" and how to read it: "This sonnet shd. be almost sung: it is most carefully timed in *tempo rubato.*" In *Poems and Prose of Gerard Manley Hopkins,* ed. W. H. Gardner (Harmondsworth, UK: Penguin, 1953), 238–239n39.

11   Marianne Moore, "A Modest Expert: *North & South,*" Schwartz and Estess 178. Jonathan Ellis also notes Bishop's frequent use of ellipses, which he calls "silences." Jonathan Ellis, *Art and Memory in the Work of Elizabeth Bishop* (Aldershot, UK: Ashgate, 2006), 50.

12   Eleanor Cook, *Against Coercion: Games Poets Play* (Stanford CA: Stanford University Press, 1998), 227.

13   Mary McCarthy, "Books of the Year: Some Personal Choices," *Observer,* 10 Dec. 1966: "Surely she is a poet of Terror" (Lionel Trilling's phrase about Robert Frost). Anthony Hecht, *Melodies Unheard: Essays on the Mysteries of Poetry* (Baltimore: Johns Hopkins University Press, 2003), 159.

14   *The New Princeton Encyclopedia of Poetry and Poetics* (Princeton, NJ: Princeton University Press, 1993), s.v. "Terza Rima."

15   James Merrill, "An Interview with Ashley Brown," in *Recitative: Prose by James Merrill,* ed. J. D. McClatchy (San Francisco: North Point, 1986), 46.

16   James Merrill, "An Interview with J. D. McClatchy," in McClatchy, ed., *Recitative,* 79.

17 Anne Ferry, "The Anthologizing of Elizabeth Bishop," *Raritan* 19 (2000): 40.
18 Penelope Laurans, "'Old Correspondences': Prosodic Transformations in Elizabeth Bishop," Schwartz and Estess 93.
19 Quoted in John Hollander, "Donne and the Limits of Lyric," in *Vision and Resonance: Two Senses of Poetic Form,* 2nd ed. (New Haven, CT: Yale University Press, 1985), 45.
20 "Rattletrap rhythm" (to Marianne Moore, 17 Oct. 1940, L 96). Moore and her mother had smoothed the draft poem into a bland mixture.
21 W. K. Wimsatt, "One Relation of Rhyme to Reason," in *The Verbal Icon: Studies in the Meaning of Poetry* (New York: Farrar, Straus and Giroux, 1954), 152–166.
22 To Donald E. Stanford, 21 Jan. 1934, L 16, where she quotes from Browne, so that she read at least some of the six volumes in Sir Thomas Browne, *Works,* ed. Geoffrey Keynes (London: Faber and Gwyer, 1928–1931).
23 John Hollander, *Melodious Guile: Fictive Pattern in Poetic Language* (New Haven, CT: Yale University Press, 1988), 6; see further the entire essay, "Turnings and Fashionings," 1–17.
24 For a contemporary example, see Rosanna Warren's ekphrastic war poem "Mud" from her *Departure* (New York: Norton, 2003): "It's not as simple as rhyming 'mud' and 'blood'/as Owen did and does . . . / Or feces and 'fecit' which is/a kind of rhyme as in/'Walker fecit,' which he/did and does through/mud." The reference is to the painter John Walker (*fecit* is Latin "did"), who turned rhyming words into other figures, figures of men dead in battle in his series of paintings on World War I.

5. RHYTHMS OF *A COLD SPRING*

Epigraph: From Robert Frost to Sidney Cox, 2 Feb. 1915, in *Selected Letters of Robert Frost,* ed. Lawrance Thompson (New York: Holt, Rinehart, Winston, 1964), 151.
1 See MacMahon 10–16 for details.
2 *The Complete Poems 1927–1979* shows only sixteen poems. See LOA edition for the first edition of *A Cold Spring* with eighteen poems, including "Arrival at Santos" and "The Mountain."

3   George Orwell, *An Age Like This, 1920–1940*, vol. 1 of *The Collected Essays, Journalism and Letters*, ed. Sonia Orwell and Ian Angus (New York: Harcourt, Brace and World, 1968), 441, 443.

4   James Merrill, "An Interview with Fred Bornhauser," in *Recitative: Prose by James Merrill*, ed. J. D. McClatchy (San Francisco: North Point, 1986), 60.

5   Robert Frost to John T. Bartlett, 4 July 1913, in *Robert Frost: Collected Poems, Prose & Plays* (New York: Library of America, 1995), 664, and see entire letter.

6   David Bromwich, "Elizabeth Bishop's Dream-Houses," *Raritan* 4 (1984): 91. He mentions the optative mood, as well as "the discreteness of its sentences" (93, 91).

7   From Bishop's jacket blurb for Robert Lowell's *Life Studies* (New York: Farrar, Straus and Cudahy, 1959). The Bulmer family Bible is held by Acadia University, and the opening pages may be viewed online at http://openarchive.acadiau.ca; I am indebted to Sandra Barry for this information. See the illustration that reproduces the crowded title page, where "Embellished with over 2000 Fine Scripture Illustrations" appears, as does "A CAREFULLY ABRIDGED EDITION OF Dr. Wm. Smith's Complete Dictionary of the Bible."

8   In a draft of the poem, Bishop wrote "silent sight," which gives a very different effect. See David Kalstone, *Becoming a Poet: Elizabeth Bishop, with Marianne Moore and Robert Lowell*, ed. Robert Hemenway (Ann Arbor: University of Michigan Press, 1989), 130. The pun in Eliot refers to the infant Christ as the Word incarnate.

9   John Ashbery, "Second Presentation of Elizabeth Bishop," *World Literature Today* 51, no. 1 (1977): 11.

10 W. H. Auden, "An Appreciation of the Lyric Verse of Walter de la Mare," in *Prose*, vol. 4, ed. Edward Mendelson (Princeton, NJ: Princeton University Press, 2010), 7.

11 Miles explains this in her still-useful *Eras and Modes in English Poetry*, 2nd ed. (Berkeley: University of California Press, 1964), chap. 1.

12 Bonnie Costello, "Elizabeth Bishop's Impersonal Personal," *American Literary History* 152 (2003): 334–366.

13 Elizabeth Bishop to May Swenson, 3 Mar. 1964, in "Elizabeth Bishop — May Swenson Correspondence," ed. Richard Howard, *Paris Review* 36 (1994): 5.

14 Brett Millier quotes the OED on "shall" and "will" in her *Elizabeth Bishop: Life and the Memory of It* (Berkeley: University of California Press, 1993), 242.

15 T. S. Eliot, "Professional, or . . . ," *Egoist*, April 1918, 61.

16 "Would you consider spacing the 4 poems of the 'Love Poems' on separate pages?" To Paul Brooks, 10 Sept. 1953, MacMahon 14.

17 David Wagoner, "Poem about Breath," *Poetry*, August 1981, 249.

18 Seamus Heaney, "The Government of the Tongue," in *The Government of the Tongue* (London: Faber and Faber, 1988), 105–106.

6. KINDS OF TRAVEL, KINDS OF HOME, KINDS OF POEM

1 William Pritchard, "Bishop's Time," *Hudson Review* 61 (2008): 330.

2 John Hollander "'Sense Variously Drawn Out': On English Enjambment," *Vision and Resonance: Two Senses of Poetic Form*, 2nd ed. (New Haven, CT: Yale University Press, 1985), 112.

3 Pascal is not new in Bishop's work. He provided the epigraph for the first publication of "A Miracle for Breakfast" in the July 1937 issue of *Poetry* (see Chapter 3). "I am reading [Pascal's] *Pensées* for the first time and I find them so full of magnet-sentences that accumulate strayed objects around them. . . . Or it may be just the correspondence of the book to the scenery — the French *clarity* and the mathematics fit so well with the few repeated natural objects and the wonderful transparent sea" (to Marianne Moore, from Key West, 4 Jan. 1937, L 55).

4 See Fowler, *Kinds of Literature*, 112.

5 Ernst Robert Curtius, *European Literature and the Latin Middle Ages* (1948), trans. from German by Willard R. Trask (Princeton, NJ: Princeton University Press, 1953), 192; see "The Pleasance," ibid., 195–200, for highly interesting developments of this topos in late Latin and medieval poetry. Bishop's classical training meant that she was familiar with the main examples in Curtius.

6 For ghost rhymes, see "Ghost Rhymes and How They Work," in my *Against Coercion: Games Poets Play* (Stanford, CA: Stanford University Press, 1998), 223–234.

7 The poem was later dedicated to Robert Lowell, after he wrote "Skunk Hour"; Bishop's poem, he testified, had suggested a whole new way of writing: "a way of breaking through the shell of my old manner. Her rhythms, idioms, images, and stanza structures seemed to

belong to a later century. 'Skunk Hour' is modeled on Miss Bishop's 'The Armadillo.'" Robert Lowell, "On 'Skunk Hour'" (1962), in *Robert Lowell: Collected Prose,* ed. Robert Giroux (New York: Farrar, Straus and Giroux, 1987), 227.

8   James Merrill, "An Interview with Ashley Brown," *Recitative: Prose by James Merrill,* ed. J. D. McClatchy (San Francisco: North Point, 1986), 46.

9   Northrop Frye, "Charms and Riddles," in *Spiritus Mundi: Essays on Literature, Myth, and Society* (Bloomington: Indiana University Press, 1976), 123–147.

10   Chinua Achebe, "The Education of a British-Protected Child" (1993), in *The Education of a British-Protected Child: Essays* (London: Bond Street Books, 2009), 15.

11   *Adoration of the Magi,* a painting from the Museo Grão Vasco, Viseu, painted c. 1501/1502 and attributed to Vasco Fernandes (Portuguese, c. 1475–1541/1542) shows one of the three kings as native. Tupinamba culture existed along the coast of Brazil, where a Portuguese fishing fleet landed in 1500.

12   Elizabeth Bishop, in "Influences," ed. Henri Cole, *American Poetry Review* 14, no. 1 (1985): 15.

13   George Monteiro, *Elizabeth Bishop in Brazil and After* (Jefferson, NC: McFarland, 2012), 63.

14   To Bishop, 22 Mar. 1965, NYPL: FSG, Box 32, File 1960, Poems (1).

15   MS note on "Sunday, 4 a.m.," NYPL: Berg, Randall Jarrell Papers, Bishop poems.

16   See the entry for the sanderling at the Cornell Laboratory of Ornithology's All about Birds website, http://www.allaboutbirds.org /guide/sanderling/id. Frank Graham Jr. recognized Bishop's sanderling in "A-Birding from a Beach Chair" (in the Florida panhandle), *Audubon Magazine,* 30 Nov. 2008.

17   For detailed background, see Stephen Cushman's excellent chapter "Elizabeth Bishop's Winding Path," in *Fictions of Form in American Poetry* (Princeton, NJ: Princeton University Press, 1993), 112–148.

18   Anthony Trollope, *North America,* 2 vols. (Philadelphia: Lippincott, 1863), vol. 2, chapter 1, 12. Subsequent page references are in the text.

19 Margaret Dickie, *Stein, Bishop, and Rich: Lyrics of Love, War, and Peace* (Chapel Hill: University of North Carolina Press, 1997), 114.

20 Bishop mentions her mixed feelings about Pound in letters to Isabella Gardner (May Day 1957, L 338) and to the Barkers: "I thought of going to see him again when I was in Washington but couldn't bear to somehow. Well, I think I've expressed my mixed emotions about him in the poem" (6 Jan. 1958, Barker letters). In 1973, she refused to participate in a "Pound 'Requiem' affair" (L 576). Some critics commenting on her "mixed emotions" seem unaware of Pound's vicious wartime broadcasts in Italy on behalf of the Fascists, including his vicious anti-Semitism. See *"Ezra Pound Speaking": Radio Speeches of World War II*, ed. Leonard W. Doob (Westport, CT: Greenwood, 1978). Who among those who admired his earlier poetry did not have mixed emotions? Bishop's use of the Jew in the ward obviously alludes to Pound's anti-Semitism.

21 Charles Darwin, *Voyage of the Beagle* (1839), ed. Janet Browne and Michael Neve (London: Penguin, 1989), chaps. 1, 23.

22 To Polly Hanson, 10 Apr. 1960, Vassar 32.4: "I am in love with it, that's all. It is like the very beginning of the world, — simplified pure, vast."

23 Ernst Robert Curtius, *European Literature and the Latin Middle Ages*, trans. Willard R. Trask (1948; repr., Princeton, NJ: Princeton University Press, 1953), 545.

24 There are "tiers and tiers of immaculate reflections" in "Seascape," in which the scene is like "a cartoon by Raphael for a tapestry for a Pope." "Song for the Rainy Season" has "warm breath,/maculate, cherished" — "maculate" having been revived by Eliot in "Sweeney among the Nightingales," as noted.

25 Quoted by Aristotle in his Poetics (XVI.4) from a play by Sophocles, now lost.

26 Arthur Golding, *Metamorphosis, Translated into English Metre* (London: William Seres, 1567, online through Chadwyck-Healy, English Poetry Full-Text Database) 6.850–853.

27 Charles Darwin, entry of 4–7 Sept. 1833, *Charles Darwin's Beagle Diary*, ed. R. D. Keynes (Cambridge: Cambridge University Press, 1988), 180; Bishop probably read Nora Barlow's 1933 edition. See also Francesco Rognoni, "Reading Darwin: On Elizabeth Bishop's Marked Copies of *The*

Voyage of the Beagle and *The Autobiography of Charles Darwin*," in *Jarrell, Bishop, Lowell & Co: Middle-Generation Poets in Context,* ed. Suzanne Ferguson (Knoxville: University of Tennessee Press, 2003), 239–248.

28 Robert Pinsky, "Poetry and American Memory," *Atlantic* 284 (Oct. 1999).

29 Elizabeth Bishop, "Reminiscences of Great Village," Vassar 54.13, quoted in Jonathan Ellis, *Art and Memory in the Work of Elizabeth Bishop* (Aldershot, UK: Ashgate, 2006), 86.

30 Alice Munro, "Princess Ida," in *Lives of Girls and Women* (Toronto: McGraw-Hill Ryerson, 1971).

31 I am indebted to Sandra Barry for this information (letter to the author, 17 Feb. 2012). See also Barry's *Elizabeth Bishop: An Archival Guide to Her Life in Nova Scotia* (Huntsport, NS: Elizabeth Bishop Society of Nova Scotia, 1996), 40.

32 Francis Kilvert, *Kilvert's Diary, 1870–1879,* ed. William Plomer (1940; repr., London: Jonathan Cape, 1964), 341 (24 Dec. 1878); Bishop was reading *Kilvert's Diary* in October 1950 (to Loren MacIver, L 207, mistitled *"Journal"*) ("lovely" bedside reading, "a little like Hopkins's Journals only more everyday").

33 Bishop commented on the flowers to James Merrill: "it was quite true — she had sort of framed him in lilies of the valley — *her* favorite flower — although where she got them in Nova Scotia in the winter I don't know — probably someone had raised them at home." 12 May 1972, L 566–567.

34 Incidentally, the Maple Leaf flag became Canada's official flag only on February 14, 1965, after sometimes-heated debates. Lowell commented on it: "I drove through New Brunswick and Nova Scotia on a short salmon fishing trip, to see everywhere the pale Maple Leaf Flag. . . . Embittered anglophiles still fly the Union Jack" (28 Oct. 1965, LEBRL 591). The "Maple Leaf" reference in Bishop's 1962 poem has nothing to do with the flag.

35 Elizabeth Bishop, "The Country Mouse," in *CProse* 24.

7. BRIEF INTERLUDE ON GENRE

1 The heroine's name, Mark Ford argues, is code for a lesbian ("penguin," via French slang *gouine* with "pen"). Mark Ford, "Elizabeth Bishop's Aviary," *London Review of Books* 29 (29 Nov. 2007): 20.

2   On prose poems, see Chapter 8. In 1955, she told May Swenson, "One of my ambitions is a PANTOUM" (4 Nov. 1955, Swenson-Bishop letters).

3   Steven Jay Gould, "Three Facets of Evolution," in *Science, Mind, and Cosmos*, ed. William H. Calvin et al. (London: Phoenix, 1996), 12.

4   Alastair Fowler, *Kinds of Literature: An Introduction to the Theory of Modes and Genres* (Cambridge, MA: Harvard University Press, 1982).

5   See also my extended discussion in "Questions of Riddle and Genre," in *Enigmas and Riddles in Literature* (Cambridge: Cambridge University Press, 2006), 110–138.

6   John Frow, *Genre* (London: Routledge, 2006).

7   John Frow, "'Reproducibles, Rubrics, and Everything You Need': Genre Theory Today," *PMLA (Publications of the Modern Language Association)* 122 (2007): 1626–1634.

8   It was anticipated in Fowler's list of fifteen traits commonly found in genre: "Every kind has its range of appropriate *style*." Fowler, *Kinds of Literature*, 70–72.

9   See John Hollander's indispensable *Rhyme's Reason: A Guide to English Verse*, 3rd ed. (New Haven, CT: Yale University Press, 2000), 40–41.

10 Letter to Jeff Balch, 11 Feb. 2003, in Anthony Hecht, *The Selected Letters of Anthony Hecht*, ed. Jonathan F. S. Post (Baltimore: Johns Hopkins University Press, 2013), 336–337.

11 Bishop noted that "A Miracle for Breakfast" is in a more correct meter for a sestina (pentameter) and mentions Auden's "fine traditional one — 'Paysage Moralisé.'" To May Swenson, 4 Nov. 1955, Swenson-Bishop letters.

12 Stephen Burt, "Scenic or Topographical, Poetry," in *A Companion to Poetic Genre*, ed. Erik Martiny (Hoboken, NJ: Wiley, 2012), 598–613.

13 Northrop Frye, "Charms and Riddles," in *Spiritus Mundi: Essays on Literature, Myth, and Society* (Bloomington: Indiana University Press, 1976), 141.

14 Elizabeth Bishop, in "Influences," ed. Henri Cole, *American Poetry Review* 14, no. 1 (1985): 15.

8. *GEOGRAPHY III*

1   For Lota's full achievement, see Orde Morton, *Rio: The Story of the Marvelous City* (Victoria, BC: Friesen, 2015), 293–295.

2   The three items appearing in the *New Yorker* in 1968 and 1969 were all in the hands of the editors by mid-1967 (see letters in LEBNY 289–295); presumably this is true of the two items in the *New York Review of Books* and the *Harvard Advocate*. MacMahon C143–147.

3   For Bishop's move from Great Village to Worcester and then Boston as a child, see "Chronology," LOA 906.

4   Lee Edelman's "The Geography of Gender: Elizabeth Bishop's 'In the Waiting Room,'" *Contemporary Literature* 26 (1985): 179–196, one of the earliest studies, remains the place to start.

5   The incident ends Bishop's posthumously published 1961 story "The Country Mouse," in which the aunt is identified by her actual name, Aunt Florence (*CProse* 32–33). She was more than foolish. When Bishop won the Pulitzer Prize in 1956, she wrote, "my elderly Aunt Florence gave an interview to the Worcester newspaper, and with true family ambivalence announced that I would have made a great piano player . . . and that 'lots & lots of people don't like her poetry, of course,' and that she was my 'closest living relative,' thereby insulting two perfectly good live aunts on the other side of the family" (to Pearl Kazin, 21 May 1956, L 318; and see L 320).

6   Deborah Forbes connects the child's reaction with Keats's "negative capability." "Reading is shown to be a ground upon which involvement and detachment, recognition and strangeness can become unexpectedly interchangeable." Deborah Forbes, *Sincerity Shadow: Self-Consciousness in British Romantic and Mid-Twentieth-Century American Poetry* (Cambridge, MA: Harvard University Press, 2004), 161.

7   See Richard Howard's fine comparison of "In the Waiting Room" and Herbert's "Love Unknown," the poem Bishop chose to pair with hers in Howard's 1974 anthology, *Preferences*. Richard Howard, "Comment on 'In the Waiting Room' and Herbert's 'Love Unknown,'" Schwartz and Estess 208–209.

8   Seamus Heaney, *The Government of the Tongue* (London: Faber and Faber, 1988), 106. For the quotation from Frost, see his letter to Walter Prichard Eaton, 18 Sept. 1915 in *Selected Letters of Robert Frost*, ed. Lawrance Thompson (New York: Holt, Rinehart and Winston, 1964), 191.

9   T. S. Eliot, to Lytton Strachey, 1 June 1919, in *The Letters of T. S. Eliot*, vol. 1, *1898–1922*, ed. Valerie Eliot (London: Faber and Faber, 1988), 298–299.

10 James Merrill, "An Interview with Donald Sheehan," in *Recitative: Prose by James Merrill*, ed. J. D. McClatchy (San Francisco: North Point, 1986), 26.

11 Ashley Brown, "An Interview with Elizabeth Bishop," Schwartz and Estess 294.

12 Marit J. McArthur suggests this reading in her "One World? The Poetics of Passenger Flight and the Perception of the Global," *PMLA (Publications of the Modern Language Association)* 127 (2012): 264–282.

13 See Bonnie Costello, "The Plural of Us: Uses and Abuses of an Ambiguous Pronoun," *Jacket2*, 6 Jan. 2012, http://jacket2.org/article/plural-us.

14 See Helen Vendler, "The Numinous Moose," *London Review of Books*, 11 Mar. 1993.

15 James Longenbach, "Elizabeth Bishop's Social Conscience," *ELH* 62 (1995): 467–486.

16 Victoria Harrison, *Elizabeth Bishop's Poetics of Intimacy* (Cambridge: Cambridge University Press, 1993), 202–203.

17 George Starbuck, "'The Work!': A Conversation with Elizabeth Bishop," Schwartz and Estess 320.

18 To take only one example, it is common to observe that art is especially valued in a police state, because a police state likes to control art, to make it "useful." In a democracy, on the other hand, art may be uncontrolled, "free," but is often less valued.

19 Bishop quoted Dickinson as early as 1934: "we play with paste till qualified for pearl." No. 282, Franklin, in Bishop's notebook, Vassar 72A.3. See *The Poems of Emily Dickinson*, ed. R. W. Franklin (Cambridge MA: Belknap Press of Harvard University Press, 1999).

20 Letter to Henry Church, 21 Jan. 1946, in Wallace Stevens, in *Letters of Wallace Stevens*, ed. Holly Stevens (New York: Knopf, 1966), 521.

9. LATE POEMS

1 John Hollander, *The Figure of Echo: A Mode of Allusion in Milton and After* (Berkeley: University of California Press, 1981).

2 Robert Stewart, "Order and Disorder: An Interview with Mary Jo Salter," *Poetry Daily* (University of Missouri), 2006, http://poems.com/special_features/prose/essay_salter.php.

3 "Ay, Jalisco, no te rajes" means "Hey, Jalisco, don't be mad" or "Hey, Jalisco, don't back down," part of a song praising Guadalajara in the

state of Jalisco. Jalisco should not be jealous, for the entire state deserves praise for its beauty, its macho men, etc. It was sung in 1941 by a famous film star from the golden age of Mexican film, Jorge Negrete, and very popular. I am indebted to Janice Yalden for this information.

4   Bishop's 1969 "Thank-You Note" opens, "Mr. Berryman's songs and sonnets say:/'Gather ye berries harsh and crude while yet ye may'" (*Poems* 233).

5   "Lament for Bion," ll. 99–105, in *The Greek Bucolic Poets*, ed. and trans. J. M. Edmonds, Loeb Classical Library (Cambridge, MA: Harvard University Press, 1960), 453.

6   James Merrill, afterword to *Becoming a Poet: Elizabeth Bishop with Marianne Moore and Robert Lowell,* by David Kalstone (New York: Farrar, Straus and Giroux, 1989), 261.

7   Roger Pasquier, *Watching Birds: An Introduction to Ornithology* (Boston: Houghton Mifflin, 1977), 112. See also Christopher Leahy, *The Birdwatcher's Companion* (New York: Hill and Wang, 1982): "relatively subtle individual variations of the 'basic' song seem to be more the rule than the exception" (660–661).

8   Merrill, afterword to *Becoming a Poet,* 262. For Bishop's work with this genre in unpublished material, see Charles Berger's recent "Bishop's Buried Elegies," in *Elizabeth Bishop in the 21st Century: Reading the New Editions,* ed. Angus Cleghorn, Bethany Hicok, and Thomas Travasino (Charlottesville: University of Virginia Press, 2012), 41–53.

9   See my "Grammar and the King James Bible: The Case of Elizabeth Bishop," *Literary Imagination* 14 (2012): 55–60, which includes the argument that Bishop is likely responding sotto voce to T. S. Eliot's apocalyptic writing in *The Waste Land.* For a thoughtful reading of "Santarém" as engaging with the sublime, see Ross Leckie, "'That Watery, Dazzling Dialectic': Elizabeth Bishop's Sublime Brazil," in *Jarrell, Bishop, Lowell & Co.: Middle-Generation Poets in Context* (Knoxville: University of Tennessee Press, 2003), 186–198.

10   For an outline of the ways in which the meaning of these terms have changed, see my *Enigmas and Riddles in Literature* (Cambridge: Cambridge University Press, 2006).

11   "And Santarém — I'd like to go there for a rest cure or something — no pavements, just deep orange sand, beautiful houses and absolute si-

lence — walks along the waterfront, and two cafés — just the way a town should be laid out." To Lota, 28 Feb. 1960, from Belém, EAP 325.

12 An actual rainbow bird exists in Australia, the rainbow bee-eater, named for its colors.

CONCLUSION

1 Penelope Laurans, in her brief account of her recollections, "Memorial Service for Elizabeth Bishop," *Poetry* 135 (Jan. 1980), http://www .poetryfoundation.org/poetrymagazine/browse/135/4#!/20593718.

2 Richard Wilbur, "Elizabeth Bishop," Schwartz and Estess 266.

Acknowledgments

I am grateful to the Social Sciences and Humanities Research Council for a Research Grant that greatly assisted the gestation of this book. The book has grown over the years, in part thanks to valued conversations with friends and colleagues, including poets, notably Sandra Barry, Margaret Michèle Cook, Kenneth Gross, the late John Hollander, Heather Jackson, the late Jay Macpherson, Herbert Marks, Carolyn Masel, and Rosanna Warren. Rosanna Warren also gave generously of her wide knowledge and wisdom in reading the entire manuscript at an earlier stage. My able research assistant, Stewart Cole, saved me much time. My editor, John Kulka, has been exceptional from the start, and the two anonymous readers for Harvard University Press were very helpful. My family as always provided indispensable support, and the two dedicatees, delight.

Sections of the opening material on "The Map" in Chapter 1 are drawn from my "Elizabeth Bishop's Cartographic Imagination Once More: Rereading 'The Map,'" in *Something Understood: Poems and Essays in Honor of Helen Vendler*, ed. Stephen Burt and Nick Halpern (Charlottesville: University of Virginia Press, 2009), pp. 207–226.

Elizabeth Bishop, published by Chatto & Windus. Reproduced by permission of The Random House Group Ltd.

Excerpts from unpublished letters written by Elizabeth Bishop to May Swenson, Kit and Ilse Barker, Muriel Rukeyser, Jean Garrigue, and Randall Jarrell. Copyright © 2016 by The Alice H. Methfessel Trust. Printed by permission of Farrar, Straus and Giroux, LLC on behalf of the Elizabeth Bishop estate.

Excerpts from unpublished journal entries (with drafts of poems "The Map," "First Death in Nova Scotia," "Crusoe in England," and "The Colder Air"); unpublished footnotes in letters to James Merrill and Polly Hanson; unpublished notebook entry about the poem "The End of March." Copyright © 2016 by The Alice H. Methfessel Trust. Printed by permission of Farrar, Straus and Giroux, LLC on behalf of the Elizabeth Bishop Estate.

Excerpts from unpublished letters written by Elizabeth Bishop to Joan Keefe and Robert Giroux and letters written by Robert Giroux to Elizabeth Bishop. Copyright © 2016 by Farrar, Straus and Giroux, LLC. Printed by permission of Farrar, Straus and Giroux, LLC.

I am also indebted to the following:

Vassar College Libraries, Archives and Special Collections, and in particular, Dean Rogers, for assistance with unpublished material written by Elizabeth Bishop and illustrations from the first editions of *North & South* and *Geography III*.

Princeton University Library: Kit and Ilse Barker Collection of Elizabeth Bishop (C0270); 1952–1984, Manuscripts Division, Department of Rare Books and Special Collections.

The New York Public Library: Farrar, Straus & Giroux, Inc. records, Manuscript and Archives Division, Astor, Lenox, and

Tilden Foundation; Randall Jarrell Papers and Muriel Rukeyser Papers, Henry W. and Albert A. Berg Collection of English and American Literature.

Carole Berglie, Literary Estate of May Swenson; May Swenson Papers, Modern Literature Collection, Manuscripts Special Collections, Olin Library, Washington University in St. Louis.

Illustration Credits

Title-page. *North & South*. Boston: Houghton Mifflin Company, 1946. Archives and Special Collections Library, Vassar College. *14*

Canadiens Francais. Montreal: Consolidated Lithographing & Mfg. Co. Limited, 1915. Image reproduced from Author's Collection. *84*

Title-page. *New Devotional and Practical Pictorial Family Bible, Superfine Edition*. Philadelphia: Chicago: St. Louis: The National Publishing Co., 1870. Bulmer-Bowers-Hutchinson-Sutherland family fonds, 1997.002 i.v.i. 2009. Acadia University, Esther Clark Wright Archives and Special Collections, Vaughan Memorial Library. *122*

Edward Hopper. "Gas," 1940. Digital Image © The Museum of Modern Art/Licensed by SCALA/Art Resource, NY. *167*

Title-page. *Geography III*. New York: Farrar, Straus, and Giroux, 1976. Archives and Special Collections Library, Vassar College. *207*

Title-page. James Monteith, *First Lessons in Geography*. New York: Chicago: A. S. Barnes & Company, 1884. From the library of Elizabeth Bishop. AC95.B5414.Zz884m.tp. Houghton Library, Harvard University. *211*

Lesson VI. James Monteith, *First Lessons in Geography*. New York: Chicago: A. S. Barnes & Company, 1884. From the library of Elizabeth Bishop. AC95.B5414.Zz884m.p12. Houghton Library, Harvard University. *212*

Lesson X and map. James Monteith, *First Lessons in Geography.* New York: Chicago: A. S. Barnes & Company, 1884. From the library of Elizabeth Bishop. AC95.B5414.Zz884m.p16. Houghton Library, Harvard University. *213*

Index to Bishop's Poems, Stories, and Essays

General Index

Achebe, Chinua, 159
Aesop, 164
Alpers, Svetlana, 7
Amiel, Henri-Frédéric, 58, 60
Ammons, A. R., 87
Anderson, Linda R., 280n21
Anne of Green Gables (Lucy Maud
  Montgomery), 165
Aristophanes, 195
Aristotle, 3, 6, 28
Arnold, Matthew, 157
Ashbery, John, 123–124, 265, 276n20
Atwood, Margaret, 194
Auden, W. H., 49–50, 91–92, 94,
  124, 133, 145, 289n11
Augustine, St., 58, 60

Bach, Johann Sebastian, 85
Barry, Sandra, 284n7, 288n31
Baudelaire, Charles, 50–51, 117
Baumann, Anny, 151
Beard, Richard D., 277n29
Behn, Aphra, 62–63
Beowulf, 133, 138
Berger, Charles, 292n8
Berryman, John, 292n4
Bible, biblical, 83–86, 88, 121–123,
  148, 162, 257–260
Bidart, Frank, 277n26
Blake, William, 89, 170, 252
Boyd, Mark Alexander, 29–30
Breughel, Pieter, 168–169
Brogan, T. V. F., 282n9
Bromwich, David, 70–71, 120

Brotton, Jerry, 7
Browne, Sir Thomas, 108, 283n22
Browning, Robert, 107, 110
Bunyan, John, 68–69
Burns, Robert, 158, 195
Burt, Stephen, 198

Campion, Thomas, 37, 39
Caplan, David, 197
Carson, Anne, 194
Cézanne, Paul, 239
Chapman, Charles F., 274n1
Chaucer, Geoffrey, 241
Clough, Arthur Hugh, 91
Cohen, Leonard, 77
Coleridge, Samuel Taylor, 39, 53–54,
  103, 247
Cook, Eleanor, 52, 285n6, 289n5,
  292n10
Cornell, Joseph, 245–246
Costello, Bonnie, 125, 275n11, 279n12
Cowper, William, 259
Crane, Louise, 71, 75, 77–78
Crashaw, Richard, 105
Curtius, Ernst Robert, 275n12, 285n5
Cushman, Stephen, 286n17

Dante, (Alighieri), 234, 275n16,
  281n26
Darwin, Charles, 6, 179–180, 185–186
Davie, Donald, 51
Defoe, Daniel, 209, 220, 226
Dewey, John, 164
Dickie, Margaret, 174

305

Salter, Mary Jo, 250
Samuels, Peggy, 273n10
Scarlatti, Domenico, 104–105
Schnackenberg, Gjertrud, 93, 265
Schönberg, Arnold, 65
sentences, 112, 119–127, 132, 139, 158, 230–231, 261
Shakespeare, William, 35, 69, 160, 181, 251, 252, 254
Sitwell, Edith, 30
Smith, Sydney, 192, 263–264
Stanford, Donald, 47–48
Stevens, Marjorie Carr, 78, 257
Stevens, Wallace, 41, 71, 80, 89, 115, 183, 243, 258
Stout, Rex, 30
Summers, Joseph, 48
Swenson, May, 54, 126, 167–168, 200, 221, 222–223, 279n4

Tennyson, Alfred, 39, 110, 119, 129, 152; "The Lady of Shalott," 100–101, 159, 200–201
Theocritus, 196
Thomas, Dylan, 186
Thoreau, Henry, 238

Trollope, Anthony, 8, 143, 171–176, 199
Twain, Mark, 30

Vendler, Helen, 19, 291n14, 265, 269
Verlaine, Paul, 65
Vermeer, Jan, 5, 16
Vuillard, Edouard, 5

Wagley, Charles, 158
Wagoner, David, 132–133
war, 71–75, 82–87, 112–113, 158, 171–176, 214, 235
Warren, Rosanna, 283n24
White, Katherine, 145
Whitman, Walt, 88, 115, 117, 250, 254
Wilbur, Richard, 269–270
Wilde, Oscar, 68
Williams, William Carlos, 82, 172, 259
Wimsatt, W. K., 106
Woolf, Virginia, 62
Wordsworth, William, 53, 58–61, 74, 112, 136–137, 219

Yalden, Janice, 291–292n3
Yeats, William Butler, 67–68